TEACHING FOR MUSICAL UNDERSTANDING

TEACHING FOR MUSICAL UNDERSTANDING

Jackie Wiggins

Oakland University

Boston   Burr Ridge, IL   Dubuque, IA   Madison, WI   New York
San Francisco   St. Louis   Bangkok   Bogotá   Caracas   Kuala Lumpur
Lisbon   London   Madrid   Mexico City   Milan   Montreal   New Delhi
Santiago   Seoul   Singapore   Sydney   Taipei   Toronto

McGraw-Hill Higher Education

A Division of The McGraw-Hill Companies

TEACHING FOR MUSICAL UNDERSTANDING

Published by McGraw-Hill, an imprint of The McGraw-Hill Companies, Inc., 1221 Avenue of the Americas, New York, NY 10020. Copyright © 2001, by The McGraw-Hill Companies, Inc. All rights reserved. No part of this publication may be reproduced or distributed in any form or by any means, or stored in a database or retrieval system, without the prior written consent of The McGraw-Hill Companies, Inc., including, but not limited to, in any network or other electronic storage or transmission, or broadcast for distance learning. Some ancillaries, including electronic and print components, may not be available to customers outside the United States.

This book is printed on acid-free paper.

4 5 6 7 8 9 0   BKM/BKM   0 9 8 7

ISBN-13: 978-0-07-230783-2
ISBN-10: 0-07-230783-8

Editorial director: *Phillip A. Butcher*
Senior sponsoring editor: *Christopher Freitag*
Developmental editor: *JoElaine Retzler*
Marketing manager: *David S. Patterson*
Project manager: *Rebecca Nordbrock*
Production supervisor: *Gina Hangos*
Designer: *Kiera Cunningham/Artemio Ortiz*
Supplement coordinator: *Jason Greve*
Media technology producer: *Kimberly Stark*
Cover design: *Kiera Cunningham;* Cover illustration: *Stock Illustration Source*
Interior design: *Kristyn Kalnes*
Associate photo research coordinator: *Judy Kausal*
Chapter openers: *1: Elizabeth Crews/Stock Boston; 2: Stone/Dan Bosler; 3: Gloria Honig; 4: Elizabeth Crews/The Image Works; 5: Photograph by Gloria Honig, courtesy of MENC—The National Association for Music Education; 6: Elizabeth Crews/The Image Works; 7: Lori Cleland; 8: Mark Regan; 9: Gale Zucker/Stock Boston; 10: Jonathan Nourok/PhotoEdit*
Compositor: *A-R Editions, Inc.*
Typeface: *10/12 Times Roman*

Library of Congress Cataloging-in-Publication Data

Wiggins, Jackie.
    Teaching for musical understanding / Jackie Wiggins.
        p. cm.
    Includes bibliographical references and index.
    ISBN 0-07-230783-8 (softcover : alk. paper)
    1. Music—Instruction and study.   I. Title.

MT1.W54 2001
780'.71—dc21   00-033925

www.mhhe.com

Dedication

For my mother and in memory of my father.

For my husband, Bob, whose patience, support, and expertise helped make this project a reality.

LISTENING EXAMPLES

Track 1:   Mid-sixteenth-century Renaissance dance, "Saltarello Giorgio"

Track 2:   Modest Musorgsky, "Ballet of the Unhatched Chicks" from *Pictures at an Exhibition*

Track 3:   Children's game song, "Lo Peter," Ghana

Track 4:   Bewa Song, "Kpaa ma," Ghana

Track 5:   Jacques Ibert, "Parade" from *Divertissement*

Track 6:   Arne Norheim, "The Hunting of the Snark" (excerpt)

Track 7:   Cyril Scott, Pastoral Reel for Cello and Piano

Track 8:   Dimitri Kabalevsky, "March" from *The Comedians*

Track 9:   Native American flute music, "Uncle Sam," South Dakota

Track 10: Anonymous villancico from *Cancionero de Upsala*, 1556,"Ríu, Ríu, Chíu"

Track 11: Chinese luogu (percussion ensemble), "Huagu Ge: Flower Drum Song"

Track 12: Edvard Grieg,"In the Hall of the Mountain King" from *Peer Gynt Suite No. 1*

Track 13: Igor Stravinsky, Finale from the *Firebird Suite*

Track 14: Peter Ilyich Tchaikovsky, "Trepak" (Russian Dance) from *The Nutcracker*

Track 15: Georges Bizet, "Farandole" from *L'arlésienne Suite No. 2*

Track 16: Robert Johnson, "The Satyr's Dance"

CONTENTS

Chapter 3
Teaching Music through Problem Solving 48

PART 2
Planning for Teaching and Learning 61

Chapter 4
Designing Musical Problems 62

Chapter 5
A Closer Look at Creative Problems 84

PART 3
Lesson and Unit Plans 113

Chapter 6
Designing Entry-Level Musical Problems 114

Chapter 7
Designing Middle-Level Musical Problems 161

Chapter 8
Designing Complex Musical Problems 199

PART 4
Your Classroom and Beyond 247

Chapter 9
An Interactive Music Classroom 248

Chapter 10

Making Connections to Other Ways of Understanding 270

(Coauthored by Robert A. Wiggins)

Chapter 11

Epilogue 292

PREFACE

Teaching music is both exciting and challenging. Whether you are a music teacher or learning to become one, you have probably chosen this path because of the powerful role music has played in your own life. You are probably quite eager to share what you know and understand about music with others. As you travel along the path of your own professional development toward this goal, it is important to understand that *what* you choose to teach and the *ways* in which you choose to teach it will make all the difference in your success with your students. Your capacity to be an effective music teacher is directly related to the extent of your own understanding of music and of the ways in which people learn music.

If you are a student, your personal understanding of music will be nurtured through other experiences in your professional education. However, learning to teach music will help you consider music from a slightly different point of view, which will also enhance your personal understanding of music. The main goal of a music methods course is to help a prospective teacher learn about the ways in which people come to understand music and to provide strategies for and ways of thinking about instruction that will empower that individual to be the best possible music teacher. Your experience with this book will serve as a starting point for this process.

Once you become a music teacher, your students' capacity for developing musical understanding is directly influenced by your own understanding of teaching processes and of music. *Teaching for Musical Understanding* is designed to promote your personal professional growth as a music teacher by providing opportunities for you to develop your own understanding of the ways in which people learn and the ways in which people learn music, in particular.

APPROACH

As cognition experts have learned more about the ways people learn, the notion of teaching for understanding has become a guiding force behind many visions of teaching. The principles behind teaching for understanding undergird innovative interactive approaches to teaching and have revolutionized the teaching of many subject areas other than music (e.g., Process Writing, Whole Language, Math Their Way, inquiry-based approaches to science, concept-based approaches to social studies, and so on). In this world of student-centered, project-oriented learning, music teaching has often remained teacher-directed and performance-oriented.

Teaching for understanding is a vision of teaching described in literature produced during the early 1990s, emanating from two extensive projects at the Harvard Graduate School of Education: the Teaching for Understanding Project and Project Zero. Howard Gardner suggests that what schools need to be about is "education for understanding." In his view, understanding means "a sufficient grasp of concepts, principles, or skills so that one can bring them to bear on new problems and situations, deciding in which ways one's present competencies can suffice and in which ways one may require new skills or knowledge" (1991, 18). In a discussion of how to put these ideas into practice, Gardner defines understanding as "the capacity to use current knowledge, concepts, and skills to illuminate new problems or unanticipated issues" (Gardner and Boix-Mansilla, 1994a, 200).

The principles behind the ways in which people learn hold true for all disciplines because our capacity to understand all disciplines resides in the same place, in our minds. If, as Gardner (1983) suggests, there are different ways of knowing and understanding the world, then there must be some commonality among the ways in which we come to understand the various ways of knowing. For example, if it is important for individuals to have opportunities to interact with subject matter on their own in order to "come to grips with it," then this must hold true for music as well. If students' ability to function within a particular discipline is dependent upon their capacity to understand the ways in which the discipline operates, then this also must hold true for music.

In *Teaching for Musical Understanding,* you will learn what contemporary learning theorists believe is important in the teaching/learning process and what this process looks like in a general music classroom. You will learn about the nature of understanding and the ways in which individuals construct understanding as a result of experience. You will explore the ways people develop understanding within a social context, and learn about the roles of the individual, of peers, and of the teacher within that context. Further, you will see what these ideas look like in music education practice through specific lesson plans, materials, and sample student work from actual music classrooms. This book describes an approach to music teaching that encourages students to think musically and think about music—in an interactive learning environment in which students perform music but also theorize about music, analyze music, and initiate original musical ideas.

As a teacher in the twenty-first century, you will need to have a broad vision of what music teaching is about in order to ensure that what you teach will be relevant to your students' lives. *Teaching for Musical Understanding* provides a basis for developing curricula that will always be relevant to students' lives because, while music may change and the ways people produce music may change, the ways in which people come to understand music will always remain the same. It is the human element that remains constant. The ideas set forth in this book are based on the ways in which humans understand music—all musics—even music that has not yet been invented.

"What teachers know and can do is one of the most important influences on what students learn," states the 1996 report of the National Commission on Teaching and America's Future (Darling-Hammond, 1998, 6). One of the report's authors and executive director of the commission, Linda Darling-Hammond, has written about the implications of the report for teacher education:

> We know that students learn best when new ideas are connected to what they already know and have experienced, when they are actively engaged in applying and testing their knowledge to real-world problems, when their learning is organized around clear goals with lots of practice in reaching them, and when they can use their own interests and strengths as springboards for learning.
>
> We also know that expert teachers use knowledge about children and their learning to fashion lessons that connect ideas to students' experiences. They create

a wide variety of learning opportunities that make subject matter come alive for young people who learn in very different ways. They know how to support students' continuing development and motivation to achieve, while creating incremental steps that help students progress toward more complicated ideas and performances. They can diagnose sources of problems in students' learning and identify strengths on which to build. These skills make the difference between teaching that creates learning and teaching that just marks time (Darling-Hammond, 1998, 7).

The approach to music teaching that forms the basis for *Teaching for Musical Understanding* is rooted in these same ideas. Knowing about the ways people learn and what teachers can do to help people learn is critical to the approach. The more teachers understand about teaching and learning processes, the more effective they can be. The ability to nurture understanding in others is dependent upon the teacher's understanding of the nature of learning. Understanding of learning theory and of its implications for practice are critical parts of the professional education of teachers.

Part of being a music teacher is knowing how to think like a teacher. You need to know how to figure out what your students already know and what they still need to learn. You need to understand what constitutes an effective learning situation and what motivates students to enter into a learning situation, willing to learn and excited about learning. You need to know how to design and carry out effective instruction and how to manage a classroom in ways that will maximize the potential for student learning. You need to know and understand all the roles that a teacher can play in effective teaching/learning situations. You need to know how to reflect on your own teaching to be able to assess the effectiveness of your own instructional planning and strategies with an eye toward your own professional growth.

AUDIENCE

This book was written for all music teachers. The principles set forth apply to any music teaching/learning situation. However, because the lesson ideas and vignettes were drawn from general music settings, the book has been designed as a text for a general music methods course. While an effort has been made to make the material easily accessible to preservice teachers, the ideas are far from basic, making the book valuable to practicing teachers as well.

CONTENT

This book addresses general issues about teaching for understanding and how these ideas apply to music teaching. It integrates theory and practice in a manner designed to promote reflective practice.

The book is deeply rooted in the author's extensive experience in the music classroom and work with preservice and in-service music teachers—strongly grounded in the research that has driven school reform. As such, it is interspersed with examples and vignettes from actual teaching and learning experiences. All of the lesson and unit plans in this book were developed for children in real general music classes and have been used in a variety of general music settings over many years. The vignettes throughout the text are transcriptions of actual interactions that took place during real music instruction in general music classrooms of the author, her colleagues, and students. None has been "manufactured" for the purpose of this book. The ideas shared here are grounded in actual music education practice.

In addition to the vignettes, there are places in the text where you will be asked to think about what you have read in terms of experiences from your own life. If you read the text carefully, you will realize that these vignettes and insets are critical to your understanding of the material presented. They provide opportunities for you to interact directly with the ideas—to set them into a context—to relate what you are reading to real-life experience. The more you are able to apply what you understand to real-life situations, the more the material presented here will make sense to you. In the best-case scenario, you will be able to take what you read here and apply it to actual teaching and learning experiences in music classrooms. If you are learning to be a teacher, carry these ideas into your practice teaching experiences. If you are a practicing teacher, you will come to understand this material in the context of what happens in your own classroom. If you are currently participating in classes as a student, think about how the ideas presented here connect to your own ways of learning and understanding. Are the ideas presented here important to you in your own learning?

ORGANIZATION

Part 1: Thinking about Teaching and Learning

- Chapter 1 describes the ways in which people formulate understanding.
- Chapter 2 applies these ideas to the ways in which people formulate musical understanding.
- Chapter 3 makes the transition to the teaching practice these ideas imply— students need to learn through problem solving.

Part 2: Planning for Teaching and Learning

- Chapter 4 suggests processes for planning instruction, based on the theory laid out in the first three chapters.
- Chapter 5 provides a closer look at planning composition and improvisation problems.

Part 3: Lesson and Unit Plans

- Chapter 6 discusses issues involved in designing instruction for inexperienced students of any age and provides sample lessons.
- Chapter 7 discusses issues involved in designing instruction for students of middle-level experience and provides sample lessons and units.
- Chapter 8 discusses issues involved in designing instruction for experienced students and provides sample lessons and units.

Part 4: Your Classroom and Beyond

- Chapter 9 provides more specific information about what an interactive music classroom is like and about how music teachers and learners function in this environment.
- Chapter 10, coauthored with Robert Wiggins, provides suggestions for extending these ideas beyond the music classroom to connect to what teachers in other subject areas teach.
- Chapter 11, the epilogue, challenges the reader to become a part of creating the future of music education.

SUPPLEMENTS

Available for purchase is a compact disc of listening examples used in the lesson plans. In addition, the text is supported by a website *(www.mhhe.com/wiggins)* that contains additional lesson plans and materials and provides a vehicle for interaction with the author, other readers, and music teachers.

ACKNOWLEDGMENTS

One of the premises of this book is that everything we know is directly related to our prior experience. My own understanding of teaching and learning processes has been directly influenced by my life experiences as a professional, including the influences of mentors, colleagues, and the students it has been my privilege to teach.

My mentors during my formative years as a teacher were Lawrence Eisman and the late David Walker, Queens College of the City University of New York. As a young teacher, I had opportunities to interact with many leaders in music education, including Bennett Reimer, Leonore Pogonowski, and Eunice Boardman. After 20 years in the classroom, graduate work at the University of Illinois with Eunice Boardman enabled me to better understand the paths I had taken as a teacher. I have benefited from interactions with so many mentors and colleagues through the years, including Eve Harwood and Liora Bresler, University of Illinois; Magne Espeland, College at Stord, Norway; technology expert Don Muro; Janet Barrett, University of Wisconsin at Whitewater; and my husband, Robert Wiggins, currently at Oakland University. For the material in Chapter 10, my husband and I are indebted to the teachers, principal, and students at Stadium Drive Elementary School of the Arts in Lake Orion, Michigan. For generously sharing their expertise in world musics, I am indebted to Bryan Burton, West Chester University, Pennsylvania, and Mark Stone, Oakland University.

I would like to thank the reviewers for their excellent comments:

J. Bryan Burton, *West Chester University*
Joi Freed-Garrod, *Simon Fraser University, British Columbia*
Eve E. Harwood, *University of Illinois at Urbana-Champaign*
Susan Kane, *Murray State University*
David G. Tovey, *The Ohio State University, Mansfield*

I would also like to thank the editors at McGraw-Hill for their careful attention to this project: Christopher Freitag, senior sponsoring editor, for believing in and understanding the nature of the project; JoElaine Retzler, developmental editor, for her expert advice and enthusiasm for the project; Judy Kausal, photo research coordinator; Rebecca Nordbrock, project manager; Kiera Cunningham, designer; and Gina Hangos, production supervisor.

Jackie Wiggins

TEACHING FOR MUSICAL UNDERSTANDING

PART 1
Thinking about Teaching and Learning

Part 1 is designed to help you understand current theories about the ways people learn and how your understanding of those theories will impact decisions you will make as a teacher. Chapter 1 is about how people learn. Chapter 2 is about how people learn music. Chapter 3 describes a vision of teaching music that is based on these theories of learning.

Chapter 1

TEACHING FOR UNDERSTANDING

Chapter 1 focuses on what cognition experts say about how people formulate under-standing of new ideas and how learning takes place in society, outside of school. It describes the role of the learner and the role of the teacher in the learning process. It also discusses what these ideas imply for classroom teaching in general.

Teaching music involves bring-ing together two closely related and intricately entwined areas of your knowledge, your personal development as a musician, and your understanding of teaching and learning processes. You have proba-bly already devoted a significant amount of time to developing your skills and abilities as a musician, but that is only one part of becoming a music teacher. How will you teach music in your own classroom? How will you teach your students to understand music and to make music? It is a natural impulse for music teachers to base such pedagogical decisions on their own music education experi-ences. Many music teachers teach their students in much the same way as they, them-selves, were taught. But is this enough? In recent years, educators have learned a great deal about the ways people learn, and what they have learned has the capacity to make a music classroom a better place for learning than it might have been in the past. What you will read in these pages is intended to help you design more effective music education than you may have experienced as a student.

As you will discover in this chapter, in order to learn, people need opportunities to construct their own understanding. They need to figure things out for themselves. In non-music classrooms, these ideas have been adapted to produce the curricular ideas that have driven the reform efforts of the last decades of the twentieth century. As a result of these efforts, many classrooms have become places where students' original ideas are valued along with those of the teachers—where students are encouraged to be independent thinkers and decision makers who initiate ideas, consider their own theories, and collaboratively discuss ideas. In science classes, students carry out hands-on experiments to learn the scientific concepts and principles behind them. In social studies classrooms, students work on projects with peers to develop understandings of the complex relationships among people and between people and their environment. In writing classes, students collaboratively brainstorm ideas and critique one another's work, learning to utilize writing as a means of personal expression. Many students learn to read through holistic, literature-based approaches and learn mathematics by developing their own theories as to how certain systems and processes operate. In visual art classrooms, students study the works of professional artists to develop understanding of the decisions and choices made by the artists, and then they work with peers or independently to make their own artistic decisions and create original work. Do the principles that underlie the hands-on, student-centered, interactive learning that takes place in nonmusic classrooms apply to musical learning as well? What would these approaches look like in a music classroom? How can music teachers capitalize on this new vision of teaching and learning?

To answer these questions, we first need to consider our own curricular goals. Many music teachers identify as their broad curricular goal the desire to enable their students to become musically literate. Musical literacy does not mean the ability to read standard notation, although that can certainly be one aspect. Musical literacy is the ability to understand a wide variety of music as it occurs within a broad range of contexts. It refers to one's ability to make meaning out of musical experiences and to use music as a means of personal expression. It means understanding the organization of music across time and place, the conventions and cultural characteristics of music, and its role in the lives of people. It means knowing enough about music to function with a certain amount of musical independence—and knowing enough about music to value it in one's life.

Like students in other subject areas, music students need to understand the ideas intrinsic to their discipline in order to know how to function within it. They need to work toward being able to apply their understanding to new situations without the help of the teacher. Students need opportunities to initiate original musical ideas and ideas about music. Music instruction should enable them to move toward a degree of autonomy in music. *Music instruction should empower students with musical understanding so that they can become musically proficient and, eventually, musically independent of their teachers.*

A CONSTRUCTIVIST VISION OF LEARNING

The theories underlying the innovative inquiry-based, concept-based approaches currently used to teach language arts, mathematics, science, and social studies are rooted in a postmodern vision of learning that characterizes learning as constructing understanding. In this cognitivist/constructivist view, it is the individual who must construct his or her own understanding in order to learn.[1] The theories of learning most closely associated with this vision are *schema theory* and *social constructivist theory.* Schema theory provides a framework for understanding how knowledge is constructed and utilized by the mind.

Social constructivist theory provides a framework for understanding how learning occurs in human society.

If people must formulate or construct their own understanding of their life experiences, in a sense, one cannot really teach anybody anything. People engage in experiences and, from those experiences, put ideas together and "figure things out for themselves." This is how we learn everything we know. Under this assumption, the role of the teacher is to make it possible for someone else to learn. Therefore, teaching involves developing experiences designed to enable participants to develop particular understandings through their participation. Further, if the experience is not meaningful to the individual, he or she will be unable to develop understanding from participation alone. The experience must make sense to the participant. If individuals cannot make sense out of a situation or experience, they cannot learn from it. (See Box 1.1.)

BOX 1.1   THINK ABOUT THIS . . .

Can you think of a time when you were involved in a situation so foreign to your experience that it made no sense to you? For example, have you ever taken a course or read a book dealing with something you know nothing about and found you had no frame of reference for understanding it?

In a cognitivist/constructivist perspective, learning is the development of conceptual understanding. The human mind is capable of holding and using the concepts we develop through experience. Throughout their lives, people act based on their conceptual understanding of their life experiences. Schema theory is an attempt to describe the ways in which we formulate and hold concepts in our minds, and the ways our conceptual understanding helps us know how to act.

HOW PEOPLE CONSTRUCT UNDERSTANDING: SCHEMA THEORY

In a postmodernist, cognitivist/constructivist viewpoint, a good analogy for understanding our mental processes is schema theory. A schema is an image that can help us better understand how we as humans hold concepts in our minds. Schemas or schemata, as they were called in some of the earlier writings, are mental structures or constructs that are interconnected, formulating networks of understanding (Anderson and Pearson, 1984). A schema for something we know consists of everything we know and understand about an idea—or all the concepts we hold about the idea. For example, a child's schema for "hamburger" might include the information presented in Figure 1.1.

FIGURE 1.1   **ONE POSSIBLE SCHEMA FOR "HAMBURGER"**

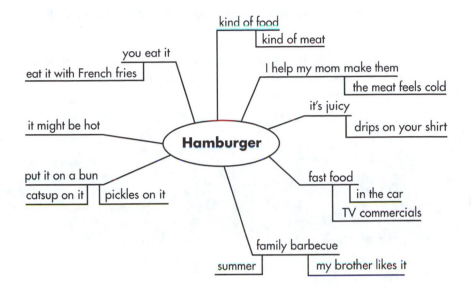

The "hamburger" schema could include many more descriptors, experiences, memories, relationships, connections, and extensions. Each of these ideas that the child associates with "hamburger" also belongs to many other schemas reflecting his or her life experience. For example, while "family barbecue" may be part of the child's schema for "hamburger," "hamburger" is also certainly a part of his or her schema for "family barbecue." Further, just as in word associations, "hamburger" may cause the child to think about "family barbecues," which may cause him or her to think of numerous other incidents and understandings related to "family" or "summer" or other aspects of his or her life experience. The schemas we hold in our minds are intricately interconnected. However, the patterns of construction and interconnection are different for each individual because no two people have had identical life experiences or perceive their life experiences the same way (see Box 1.2).

BOX 1.2 (ACTIVITY)

Construct and map out a schematic diagram for something in your own life. Try to think of everything you connect to the idea. See how far you can expand it and how many other places in your mind it can take you.

Schemas, then, are interactive networks of ideas. The source of these ideas is one's own life experience, including experience in formal learning situations such as the classroom. Schema theorists propose that we are born with the capacity to organize life experience.

The image they suggest is a series of networks that contain spaces called "slots." From the moment we are born, and even in the womb, we experience life through our five senses. As we perceive information through our senses, our minds organize it by finding appropriate slots for new information. When we engage in a new experience, we seek to understand it through our understandings of prior experience. We seek a slot that holds similar information and store the new information in association with the old. In other words, as we learn about new aspects of the world, we associate the new ideas we encounter with ideas we already know (see Box 1.3).

The Nature of Schemas

First, schemas have the capacity to *accept new information.* As a result of an experience, an individual may simply add one more new idea to a collection of ideas that already exists in his/her mind. Second, schemas *direct our actions.* They contain not only factual information but also procedural information. Therefore, schemas tell us how to act or react. Third, schemas have the capacity to *direct the plan* of how new learning and understanding will take place. The factual and procedural information we store in our networks of schemas can also tell us how to figure out something new. This is how we use what we already know and understand to learn something new.

While the schemas we hold in our minds share many common characteristics, not all schemas are the same. Some are far more complex than others. Our schema for making a peanut butter and jelly sandwich is certainly much simpler than our schema for dealing with other people during social interactions. In the one case, the number of variables is quite limited. In the other, it is infinite because no two people are exactly the same and each brings a different set of variables to a situation.

Further, some schemas are more structured and organized in our minds than others, partially because they reflect aspects of our life that are more or less ordered or predictable. For example, a study by Anderson (1978) suggests that remembering a random list of grocery items—and the order they appear on the list—is quite a difficult task. If you were familiar with the person who made the list and knew the layout of the store and the products he or she was apt to buy, the task might be easier. In this second case, you would possess a more highly structured and organized schema for that particular shopping trip. If someone were to describe to you what foods had been eaten in the various courses of a formal dinner and then ask you to recall the items in the order presented, it might be a much easier task. As members of our culture, we have a much more highly organized schema for the order of foods on a standard dinner menu than we do for the order in which foods are placed in a grocery store shopping cart.

How Schemas Frame Our World

When we encounter new information, we attempt to relate it to something we already know. We process new information through the network that has been created by our prior experiences and understandings. This concept is very important because it provides a basis for understanding multiple perspective. Multiple perspective means that no two people will view the same experience in exactly the same way. This is because no two people have identical life experiences. Since our network of schemas reflects life experience, each of us possesses a different network, arranged in a different way. One can say that our prior life experience and our interpretation of that experience frame our view of the world and, in many ways, determine how we will choose to act and react in new experiences. Multiple perspective is related to diversity issues because people bring to situations prior experience that is reflective of the culture in which they live.

It is also important to realize that differences in perspective do not only exist between people but also within people. Each of us is capable of viewing the world from a multitude of perspectives. As a result of our experiences in the world, we develop a collection of frames through which we formulate our understanding of our experiences in the world. Howard Gardner (1983) called these *Frames of Mind* and proposed a *theory of multiple intelligences* based on this view. His ideas have, in many ways, revolutionized educational thinking. Prior to his work, it was generally accepted that intelligence was a function of verbal and mathematical thinking. In contrast, Gardner suggests that there are multiple ways of knowing the world—that we can conceive of the world through the eyes of a painter or a mathematician or through the ears of a musician or a poet. He has made a strong case that all of us possess these various ways of understanding the world and that it is important to make it possible for students to explore all of these possibilities. In Gardner's view, musical thinking and spatial thinking are not "second class" to mathematical or verbal thinking. Gardner has done a tremendous service for arts education and for those of us whose preferred way of seeing the world is other than verbal or mathematical. His ideas enable all ways of thinking to be valued in the educational process and give credence to the notion of musical thinking as a unique way of knowing the world. People engage in musical thinking by thinking through musical schemas. (Musical schemas will be discussed in Chapter 2.)

How Schemas Change

When an existing schema is altered in some way, we say that learning has occurred. The alteration may be minimal, where new information is simply added to an existing schema in an appropriate slot. The alteration may also be more dramatic, causing a shifting in schema or in the relationship between the schema and others in the network. This represents a moment of conceptual change—of perceptual shifting—an "Aha!" moment. At such moments, schema theorists suggest there is an actual restructuring of the network of schemas in our minds (Vosniadou and Brewer, 1987).

As we live our lives and engage in a myriad of experiences, our understanding of our experiences is processed in this interactive and integrated fashion, and our networks of ideas become denser and more and more interrelated. In this way, sensory experiences are transformed into understanding. New experiences interact with and eventually become part of the network of schemas. As a result of this interaction between what is new and what has come before, a change in the individual's perspective or level of understanding occurs. Understanding, then, is the process of interaction between new and existing information, which is then transformed into new or altered schemas.

What Facilitates the Learning Process?

The closer the relationship between our existing network of schemas and new information, the more information is processed. This means that learning is more likely to take place when students possess a context for understanding new ideas. In other words, students can best learn new ideas when they can set them into a context with which they are already familiar and which they already understand. When teachers present ideas out of context, students will need to establish their own contexts in order to understand. If the teacher does not provide the context, there is always the danger that the student will access the wrong context and misunderstand. The more familiar we are with a context, the easier it is for us to understand new information. The closer the relationship between new information and something we already know, the easier it is for us to understand (see Box 1.4).

BOX 1.4   THINK ABOUT THIS . . .

If someone gives you directions to get to a place in your own community, it is relatively easy for you to find, because you have a rich understanding of the context in which the directions reside. When someone gives you directions to a place you have never seen, it is much more difficult for you to conceive of what they are talking about, because you do not really have a clear context. You probably require a more detailed explanation of the directions to the unfamiliar place, and maybe even a map. In your own community, "across from the gas station, just past the library" may be enough information to get you to your destination.

When we encounter new information, we instantaneously search through our network of schemas, seeking a slot that seems most appropriate to accommodate the information. For each individual, this network is slightly different because each of us has constructed our network of understanding from our own unique life experiences. Each of us perceives life experience through a lens or frame that reflects the sum of our prior experiences. Therefore, it is possible and quite commonplace for people engaged in the same experience to perceive it in radically different contexts. Read through the passage in Box 1.5. What do you think it is about?

BOX 1.5: EVERY SATURDAY NIGHT

Every Saturday night, four good friends got together. When Jerry, Mike, and Pat arrived, Karen was sitting in her living room writing some notes. She quickly gathered the cards and stood up to greet her friends at the door. They followed her into the living room, but, as usual, they couldn't agree on exactly what to play. Jerry eventually took a stand and set things up. Finally they began to play. Karen's recorder filled the room with soft and pleasant music. Early in the evening, Mike noticed Pat's hand and the many diamonds. As the night progressed, the tempo of the play increased. Finally, a lull in the activities occurred. Taking advantage of this, Jerry pondered the arrangement in front of him. Mike interrupted Jerry's reverie and said, "Let's hear the score." They listened carefully and commented on their performance. When the comments were all heard, exhausted but happy, Karen's friends went home.

As you may have guessed, this passage was written to be intentionally ambiguous. It was used as part of a study by Richard C. Anderson and his colleagues (Anderson et al., 1977) in their work in the development of schema theory. If you have read it as others have, you most likely decided that the passage is about a card game or perhaps the rehearsal of a recorder ensemble. In Anderson's experiment, a group that had more extensive musical background interpreted the passage as a recorder rehearsal while a group that represented a more generalized cross-section of the population identified it as a card game, most often a game of Bridge. Based on personal prior experience, each reader accessed what he or she believed to be an appropriate schema for interpreting the passage.

In order to facilitate the learning process, then, it is imperative for teachers to help students build a shared context for learning so they will all be "starting on the same page" as the lesson begins. Ausubel (1968) called this using "advanced organizers" and Hunter (1976) called it establishing an "anticipatory set" for a lesson. How you begin a lesson is critical to whether or not students will understand what you are teaching. It is important to take the time to be sure that all students have accessed an appropriate context for understanding what you are about to teach. Throughout a lesson, teachers must constantly assess student perspective, bearing in mind that *contextual understanding is crucial to conceptual understanding.*

What Inhibits the Learning Process?

If the learner has no related construct (schema) through which to interpret new information, he or she will either *reject* the information or attempt to relate it to some other construct, which can result in a *misconception*. In other words, if a learner does not have a context for understanding, he or she will either misunderstand or reject the new ideas.

Most teachers can readily supply examples of times when students have rejected information they have not understood. It can surface when a teacher attempts to review something she thought she had already taught and no one in the class seems to remember it. It can also surface in students' attitudes and reactions. Students who have no context for understanding what the teacher is teaching may eventually "turn off" and ignore what is happening in class or resort to disruptive outbursts.

Further, without specific contextual direction, people activate the schemas they think are appropriate in interpreting a new situation. Teachers must be aware, then, that misconceptions may occur as a result of the activation of alternate or inappropriate schemas (see Box 1.6).

BOX 1.6 (VIGNETTE): THE SAILBOAT

A young girl from an inner-city environment was working on a reading passage with a researcher. The passage was about an experience on a sailboat, including descriptions of ropes coiled on the deck and water spraying up over the side. When asked what the story was about, the girl replied that it was about a shopping mall. The researcher was quite astonished and questioned her further. The only prior experience the girl had had with the word "sail" was in the context of a "sale" at the mall. She proceeded to recount her own interpretations of each part of the story—equating the ropes to the stanchions outside the bank and the spraying water as coming from the fountain in the center of the mall. She had absolutely no idea that she had completely misinterpreted the passage. If this child had been taking a test of reading skill, she would probably have read the passage successfully but answered all of the questions incorrectly because she had mis-interpreted the context. A teacher might have concluded that she was not able to read, whereas in truth, she read the passage perfectly, but simply lacked the life experience to provide a context for understanding what she had read.[2]

These kinds of incidents occur in classrooms all the time without teachers necessarily being aware of their occurrence. During one of my own research studies, I inadvertently collected an example of student misconception. As part of an introductory discussion to a unit on jazz, fifth-grade students were constructing a web reflecting everything they already knew about the topic. One student, whose comments and participation in the lesson were being recorded for research purposes, contributed several strong suggestions for the web we were constructing. As the teacher, I remember thinking to myself that she seemed to have "a good handle on the situation." When I listened to the tape of her comments, I realized that she had not been talking about jazz music at all but rather was contributing her answers based on her experience in jazz dance classes (which has nothing to do with the musical style). As I listened to my interactions with the student during the class, I realized that because of my own frame I had interpreted her comments to be about music, although she was clearly talking about dance.

Sometimes, despite our best efforts as teachers, students still access inappropriate schemas for understanding. This is why it is so critical to build into the lessons we teach numerous venues for continual monitoring and assessment of student understanding.

Schema Theory: Implications for Teachers

Our network of schemas provides each of us with a kind of lens or frame through which we filter and process all of our life experiences. This lens or frame includes all of our personal experiences within the culture in which we live. We become enculturated into our families, communities, and societies through this process. It is the lens of our experience that helps us develop a sense of right and wrong, of appropriate and inappropriate behavior, of what is acceptable in society and what is not. It is through our lens that we learn about love and relationships, and anger, and fear, and hate. All that we do and all that we are, we perceive through the frame of our prior experience. We are, in essence, the sum of our prior experience.

Teachers need to be aware of this process. They need to understand that people construct their own understanding of new information by placing it in a context with which they are already familiar. Teachers need to be aware of the variety of perspectives different students bring to a given situation in order to know whether or not individuals are really "getting it." Part of what teachers need to do is to establish a common context for new ideas before introducing them.

The nature of this process also implies that it is easier for people to understand a "part" of something when it is learned in the context of a "whole." Understanding is holistic in that we can only understand things in relation to other things. Therefore, teachers need to be aware that they must present all material within holistic contexts. Language arts concepts should be taught within the context of literature. Musical concepts should be taught within the context of pieces of music.

The role of the teacher in this process is to establish a productive environment in which individuals can thrive and flourish and figure things out for themselves. This is not meant to imply that the teacher merely stands by and watches the student learn. Quite the contrary, the teacher takes on countless roles in the process, among them coach, guide, mentor, model, resource, cheerleader, facilitator, organizer, and referee. But it is important to hold an image of a classroom as one where students actively pursue their own learning and are responsible for their own learning, under the guidance of the teacher. (The role of the teacher will be discussed more thoroughly in Chapter 9.)

THE SOCIAL CONTEXT OF LEARNING: SOCIAL CONSTRUCTIVISM

While schema theory may help us to visualize the process of the construction of knowledge, it does not fully explain how individuals go about learning over the course of their lives. Schema theory is a theory of cognition but not a pedagogical theory. It explains how we formulate understandings and what that implies for teaching but does not describe the actual teaching process. Therefore, on its own, schema theory cannot fully inform education practice. Postmodernist learning theorists have looked to ideas first suggested by Vygotsky (1978) to best explain how an individual constructs networks of understanding—or learns—in life.

How Learning Takes Place in Society

Lev S. Vygotsky (1896–1934), a Russian psychologist, first proposed the theories that comprise social constructivism in the 1930s. His ideas were not known in the United States until translations of some of his works were published in the late 1970s (Vygotsky, 1978). Vygotsky believed that all human learning takes place in a social context—that is, between people. While this may not seem a startling viewpoint, very few theories of learning consider the role of other people in learning processes. Vygotsky's ideas were first brought to the attention of American educators through the work of contemporary cognition experts such as John Wertsch (1985) and Barbara Rogoff (Rogoff, 1990; Rogoff and Lave, 1984).

In Vygotsky's view, we construct our understanding of life experiences through interaction with others. Therefore, *all knowledge is socially constructed.* Social interaction is an essential ingredient of the learning process. It is through social interaction that more experienced members of society provide sources of information about cultural tools and practices for less experienced members of society. Everything we know, we have learned either through interactions with someone else or through applying skills we previously acquired from interacting with someone else.

Vygotsky explains this phenomenon by saying that everything we learn, we learn first on the *interpsychological* level and, later, on the *intrapsychological* level. When we operate on the *inter*psychological level, we learn through interacting with someone who is more knowledgeable about what we are trying to learn. Once we have developed some proficiency, we are more able to function independently, utilizing the tools we have learned and the understandings we have developed while working with the other person. Eventually, we are able to operate on the *intra*psychological level—able to internalize what we learned from the other person and operate independently.

Vygotsky refers to this other person as simply a "more knowledgeable other" because this person may be anyone in society—a parent, older sibling, teacher, or peer (even a younger peer) who has more expertise than does the learner. He refers to the learner as a "less knowledgeable other" because a learner can be of any age. Some literature refers to the two parties as "expert and novice" or "tutor and learner." What is important to realize here is that these labels are not age related but rather are experience related (as when a young child teaches an adult how to use a computer program). When two parties interact, teaching and learning occur as they work together and structure their communication such that the novice is brought into the expert's more mature understanding of the problem. The teaching and learning that takes place between these individuals may occur in a formalized setting (working with a teacher in school or with a parent to learn to tie your shoelaces) or may be an informal occurrence in everyday life (learning to eat with a fork by watching others at the table). The more life experiences we encounter, the more we are capable of operating on the intrapsychological level—that is, independently of others.

How Teaching Takes Place in Society

The Zone of Proximal Development

According to Vygotsky, although the child is capable of solving problems on his or her own, with the help of a more capable partner he or she can achieve a higher level of competence. When a less knowledgeable individual or novice engages in a new experience, he or she is highly dependent upon more knowledgeable others or experts. As the novice gains experience, he or she requires less and less assistance from experts. In fact, until the novice becomes an expert, it is most often the case that the novice can generally function on a higher level when *working together with* the expert than he or she would be able to function independently. In other words, with a teacher providing assistance and support, learners can accomplish more or work at a higher level of proficiency than they might have been able to manage on their own. If learners can function on a particular level of proficiency without the teacher and work on a higher level with the teacher's help, one might say that there is a gap between these two levels of competence. Vygotsky labeled this gap the *zone of proximal development.* Vygotsky (1978) describes the zone of proximal development as the region of sensitivity to social guidance where the child is not quite able to manage a problem independently but can work toward a solution when guided by an adult who structures and models the appropriate solution to the problem.

This is an important concept for teachers to understand, primarily because effective teaching actually takes place within this zone of proximal development. If a teacher works with a student on a level of proficiency and understanding that is *below* the zone of proximal development, that would mean the teacher is asking the student to practice or learn something he or she already knows and understands. It means the teacher may be offering support where it is no longer needed. If, on the other hand, a teacher works with a student on a level of proficiency and understanding that is *beyond* his or her capabilities within the zone of proximal development, it would mean the teacher is asking the student to work on a level the student is not yet able to manage. Teaching needs to take place somewhere between the level of proficiency a student can achieve on his or her own and the level at which he or she can be successful with teacher support.

This has tremendous implications for teaching—not the least of which is the importance of assessment. The teacher needs to know which aspects of the subject matter being learned the students already know and understand and which aspects are still too difficult and complex. Without this knowledge, how would the teacher know which aspects of the subject matter still need to be taught? One would also need to assume that, within any group, different individuals would be functioning on different levels within the continuum of understanding and proficiency. Therefore, different individuals would require different levels of support from experts. This is an important point in that it implies that a learning environment must be constructed such that it is possible for individuals to function on different levels simultaneously and that it is important for the teacher not to try to be the only expert working with the group. Establishing such a learning environment will be discussed more fully later in this chapter in the section dealing with cognitive apprenticeship.

Allowing others in the classroom to provide support through their own blossoming expertise will be dealt with in Chapter 9.

Scaffolding

To summarize a social constructivist viewpoint, then, we might say that children learn to become members of our society by learning from more knowledgeable members of society. We learn first by interacting with others in a social context and then by internalizing what we learn from others to the point that we are eventually able to function on our own. As we learn, we require support from more knowledgeable others. Children need opportunities to engage in problem solving with others (peers and teachers) and eventually on their own in order to develop the skills necessary to eventually achieve independence. What, then, is the nature of the role of the more knowledgeable others (teachers)? Exactly what is it that they need to do to facilitate someone else's learning?

The role of experts in providing support for novices in a learning environment has been characterized by Jerome Bruner and his colleagues as *scaffolding* (Wood, Bruner, and Ross, 1976). As a novice works side-by-side with an expert, the novice performs those portions of the task in which he or she is competent, and the expert fills in and provides support or scaffolding where necessary. Effective teaching includes providing scaffolding where it is needed and stepping back when it is not. Teachers and students determine where support is needed through their constant interaction as they work together to complete a given task. It is the responsibility of the teacher to sense when the scaffolding is not needed, and to gradually remove it until the student is functioning independently.[3] An example of scaffolding is helping students develop and identify appropriate strategies for solving a particular problem. Another example is singing or playing portions of melodic lines to provide support for groups of singers who are trying to sing a round or in two-part harmony.

A transcription of an actual instance of teacher-provided scaffolding during a compositional activity appears in Box 1.7. This is part of a transcript from an actual fifth-grade music class (Wiggins, 1992). After having studied and analyzed the form of a piece in ternary (ABA) form, ("Trepak" from Tchaikovsky's *The Nutcracker,* see Lesson in Figure 8.3, p. 210), a group of fifth-grade students was at work creating an original ternary piece.

BOX 1.7 (VIGNETTE)

Teacher: Is there anything I can do to help you finish?

Lynn: Well, yeah. I know my part in the beginning but Suzanne needs help with the A . . .

Kim: We need you to guide us along.

Lynn: Yeah. Guide us along.

Teacher (laughing): Guide you along? Well, do you want to play what you have so far? [Before offering any assistance, the teacher needs to determine what the difficulty is.]

Lynn: One, two, three, go.

[Lynn plays an introduction on the conga drum punctuated by Kim's cowbell at the end of each phrase. Then two other girls begin a melody on metallophones, but they begin playing while what seems to be the introduction is still being played.]

Teacher: Are they supposed to be playing already?

[The teacher makes a momentary evaluation of the situation, begins to identify the problem, but pauses before helping the children to find a solution.]

Lynn (to the metallophone players): You're not doing it right.

Teacher (trying to get a sense of the plan): Does Lynn go first?

Lynn: Yeah. Me and Kim start.

Teacher (to the metallophone players): Are you supposed to play *with* them though?

Lynn: No, it's Sheila's fault. She's not doing it right. We are supposed to play ours two times first.

Suzanne: No, you do it *three* times.

Lynn: O.K.

Teacher: Play it the way it's going to be.

[They play the introduction followed by the "A" theme.]

Lynn: And that's it. That's all we have.

[They did not need "guidance" after all, only reassurance that they were on the right track, and a better understanding of what still needed to be done.]

Teacher: Well, that's a beautiful "A" section! Sheila, you haven't played at all yet, right? Are you the "B?" [She nods.] O.K. Let her make up her part and then you just need your ending and you'll have the whole piece.

By the end of the class session, the students had successfully completed a piece in ABA form, with the A and B themes played on metallophones and the introduction and coda played on the conga and cowbell. They did not seek any further assistance from the teacher. They had needed a momentary bit of support from the teacher but, in general, had sufficient understanding of the problem to develop a viable solution on their own. (A transcript of the final version of this piece appears on pages 219–220 in Chapter 8.) This particular example is included to exemplify the kinds of interactions that can comprise a scaffolding situation. It is important to note that the teacher asked more questions than she provided solutions. The teacher needs to develop a keen awareness of the level of understanding of the students in the particular situation before helping out in the solution of problems. This kind of support is critical in moving students toward musical independence.

It is important to recognize that, in a classroom setting, students often provide scaffolding for one another, even when the teacher is not aware of the occurrence. Students often translate teacher-talk for peers or answer peers' questions during a class or group activity. Students often seek a peer's advice before bringing a question to the teacher. Part of providing scaffolding is helping students develop *metacognitive* skills (understanding how one learns, developing strategies for problem solving). Students can learn "how to learn" through working with the teacher, but also through working with peers. It is important to realize that peers often provide better models for one another than the teacher can provide, partially because peers share more of a common perspective developed from a stronger base of common prior experience.

The Nature of Mutual Understanding

In a social constructivist view, in order for learning to occur, there must be a common framework within which the teacher and learner operate. Shared or mutual understanding is critical to the teaching/learning process. A learner engages in a learning experience through what Rogoff calls *guided participation,* which she describes as learners and tutors working together in "the collaborative processes of (1) building bridges from children's present understanding and skills to reach new understanding and skills, and (2) arranging and structuring children's participation in activities," including shifts in responsibilities as learners move toward competence (1990, 8). Teachers and their students must operate within a level of shared understanding of the learning situation, including shared understanding of the problem to be solved, of possible solutions, and of how they will know they have succeeded.

Further, in order to learn, the learner must be directly involved in interacting with the subject matter, constructing his or her own understanding throughout the experience. It is not enough for the teacher to tell the student about the subject. Students must engage directly with subject matter in a hands-on fashion. The teacher must involve the learner in the solution of the problem rather than simply solving the problem and reporting the solution to the learner (Rogoff and Gardner, 1984).

It is also essential for the learner to understand what he or she is supposed to be learning—the goals of the learning experience. It is not enough for the teacher alone to possess this knowledge. If the learner is not fully cognizant of what it is he or she is supposed to be doing and learning, he or she cannot take responsibility for his or her own role in the process. Students need to understand the goals of a learning experience and how what they are learning relates to other things they know. The greater the extent of their understanding of the situation, the more they will be empowered as learners.[4]

From the other standpoint, it is equally important for the teacher to understand how the student conceives of the situation—what he or she brings to the situation, other experiences he or she has had with similar situations, and extenuating circumstances that might inhibit his or her learning. Both teachers and learners need to enter a learning situation understanding what is about to take place. Throughout the learning process, it is critical that both parties share an understanding of what is being learned and of how it is being learned. Monitoring progress is generally the responsibility of the teacher, but may be something of which the student is aware as well. The higher the level of mutual understanding among the parties involved, the more effective the teaching/learning situation will be.

Social Constructivism: Implications for Teachers

Based on what social constructivists say, it would seem that a healthy, productive learning environment needs to include opportunities for students to:

- Interact with and receive support from more knowledgeable others (both teacher and peers).
- Work independently.
- Deal with subject matter in ways that will enable them to construct their own understanding.
- Deal with subject matter within genuine contexts.
- Understand relationships between new ideas and their contexts.
- Understand what is to be learned and how they will know they have learned it.
- Engage in real-life, holistic problem-solving experiences.

This last point is one we have not yet considered. Think about learning environments as they exist both in and out of school settings. Outside of school, we learn by engaging in real-life, problem-solving situations. We tackle the problems of life with support and assistance from those around us until we gain proficiency in the skills and understandings we need to live our lives successfully. It would seem logical that we would want the school environment to approximate natural-life learning as closely as possible. One would expect that people would learn most successfully in ways that are natural to them.

Further, outside of school, individuals do not engage in series of "exercises" in order to learn. Life learning is not piecemeal. Children do not practice putting food on a fork repeatedly until they have mastered that skill and then move on to putting food into their mouths. Rather, they engage in the *whole* process of learning to feed themselves, from start to finish, seeking assistance when it is needed, but attempting to perform all aspects of the task throughout the process. Outside of a school environment, learning is *holistic* in nature. People participate in *whole* processes or experiences (dressing oneself, baking a cake, riding a bicycle) together with more experienced members of society. As they do, learners gradually take over the aspects of a task that they are able to do on their own while tutors continue to perform the parts that are still too difficult. Tutors provide a scaffold for the learner that is gradually withdrawn until the learner can stand on his or her own.

Considering the ways people learn outside of school, it would seem that school learning situations would be most productive if they were designed to enable students to engage in real-life, holistic problem-solving experiences (see Box 1.8).

BOX 1.8   THINK ABOUT THIS . . .

The relationship between a master carpenter and his or her apprentice may help you better understand the concept of mutual understanding. When the apprentice arrives for his first day of work framing a new house, one would not expect the carpenter to send him off to an area far from the house to hammer nails into two-by-fours until he had perfected that skill and then return for instructions for the next step. One would expect that the apprentice would work side-by-side with the carpenter—on the actual framing of the house. One would expect that the carpenter would inquire to find out which aspects of the job the apprentice already felt competent to do. One might expect, then, to find the apprentice working along with the carpenter, performing the tasks with which he is already familiar and competent, and seeking assistance with those that are new and more difficult. Over time, the two would develop a mutual understanding of the job and, within that understanding, the novice would develop his own expertise.[5]

COGNITIVE APPRENTICESHIP: APPRENTICESHIP IN THINKING

How, then, might one go about designing a learning environment that takes into account what we know about the ways knowledge is constructed by the individual (schema theory) within the context of social interaction with more knowledgeable others (social constructivism)? If we want to enable students to learn in classrooms in ways most like the ways they learn outside of school, what do our classrooms need to look like?

Rogoff (1990) describes a teaching/learning environment that takes into account understanding of the implications of schema theory and social constructivist theory as a *cognitive apprenticeship*. Gardner (1991) also advocates borrowing characteristics of apprenticeship learning to make school learning more like "life" learning. What, then, are the characteristics of a cognitive apprenticeship vision of teaching and learning?

- *Learners need to engage in real-life, problem-solving situations.*
  The more closely school learning approximates the ways people learn naturally, outside of school, the more powerful the learning situation will be.
- *Learning situations must be holistic in nature.*
  When students are asked to deal with fragments of information out of context, they have no frame of reference for understanding what the fragments represent. Learning situations must enable students to understand new ideas in the context in which they occur, which is how learning occurs in nonschool life.[6]
- *Learners need opportunities to interact directly with subject matter.*
  Students need to be actively engaged with subject matter throughout the learning experience. In music, this means engaging in genuine performing, creating, or listening experiences.
- *Learners need to take an active role in their own learning.*
  They need to function with a certain amount of autonomy and independence,

constructing their own understanding. This means that students must have opportunities to engage in genuine problem-solving situations within the various subject areas—utilizing the various ways of thinking (Gardner, 1983). They need opportunities to initiate original ideas, test and evaluate their ideas, revise their ideas, and share their ideas with peers and teacher.

• *Learners need opportunities to work on their own, with peers, and with teacher support, when needed.*
Therefore, it is important for teachers' organization for instruction to allow opportunities for interaction among students. This can include everything from student-student talk during large group instruction to small group, partner, and independent work formats.

• *Learners need to be cognizant of the goals of the learning situation and their own progress toward goals.*
Students need to be partners in their own learning, taking responsibility for their own learning. This can only be possible when the teacher shares with the students what they are trying to learn, how it will be learned, and how they will know when they have learned it. If teachers allow students to be partners in the assessment of their understanding, the task of finding out how much students know becomes much more straightforward.

If students need to be actively engaged, working independently, with peers, and with the teacher to solve holistic, real-life problems, this implies that the most productive learning situation is a collaborative problem-solving situation.

The concept of cognitive apprenticeship implies the kind of learning situation that exists between the carpenter and apprentice presented in Box 1.8 but takes this one step further by implying that teachers can work with students in an *apprenticeship-in-thinking* process. Teachers can teach students how to think by working side-by-side with them in problem-solving situations. Teachers can suggest strategies and propose alternatives. Helping students understand the thought processes necessary to solve a problem is what educators mean by *metacognition.*

One important characteristic of a classroom that operates as a cognitive apprenticeship is that not all students enter a real-life, problem-solving situation at the same place. It is important that the teacher construct learning experiences in ways that enable students with a wide range of levels of expertise to participate. Not all students "begin at the beginning." Not all learning is sequential, moving from simple to difficult. Sometimes, a student understands some of the more complex aspects of a situation before understanding the specifics (see Box 1.9).

BOX 1.9   THINK ABOUT THIS . . .

Can you remember things you learned as a child where you conceived of the whole before understanding the components?

For example:

- I remember being able to tie my shoelaces before I actually understood how a bow was made. I was able to manipulate the laces and produce a bow, but, to me, the process seemed like magic. I also remember eventually being able to slow the process down enough so that I was able to look at what my fingers were actually doing. Only then did I fully understand the path the laces traveled.

- Some children learn to read as preschoolers. However, they often know nothing about phonetic pronunciation or sentence structure or punctuation or even why some letters were capitalized and others not. They master the broad, overriding aspects of the reading process well enough to enable them to read the stories and understand their meaning, but they have no idea of the specifics involved.

Therefore, it is important to design instruction in ways that enable students to do the parts they already know how to do and learn more about the parts they have not yet mastered. This reflects the cognitivist/constructivist view of learning explained in this chapter—students use what they know to construct their own understanding of what they do not yet know.

This viewpoint represents a significant departure from a developmentalist view of learning, such as that espoused by Piaget and his followers. In a developmentalist view, teachers construct lessons based on what research (that seeks to identify "norms" in the population) indicates most children of a certain age should be able to do. Teachers who adopt this view are sometimes troubled by students on either extreme who do not fit the "norm."

Whereas a developmentalist may work from a vision of what a typical student of a certain age should be learning, a constructivist vision of learning offers a view that what is to be learned and how it should be learned are directly related to the learner's prior experience with the activity and prior knowledge of the subject matter. It implies that *a lesson needs to be designed so that individual students can participate at different levels of expertise within the same experience.* A lesson must contain a problem or set of problems that can be solved from a variety of perspectives and with varying levels of expertise. Designing such a lesson is not as difficult as it sounds because these are characteristics of real-life experiences in which individuals of differing levels of expertise and experience engage all the time. The viewpoint does not completely preclude a sensitivity to children's physical and developmental growth. It is still considered appropriate to be sensitive to the kinds of activities in which children of a particular age seem to prefer to engage. However, adopting this view enables a teacher to easily meet the needs of high-achieving and low-achieving students at the same time, within the same lesson.

Understanding teaching through real-life, problem-solving experiences makes main-streaming of special learners and highly gifted students less of a challenge for the teacher. In a well-designed learning experience, students should be able to participate from a wide variety of entry points along a continuum of competence. As they do, they are fully aware of where their expertise is located on that continuum, aware of what they need to do to become more competent, and aware of how they will know they have reached competency.

In a cognitivist/constructivist view of learning, teachers expect that individuals will bring to the learning situation a wide variety of prior experiences that may in some way influence their learning of the new material. Teachers can capitalize on what students already know by developing lessons that build on skills and knowledge gained during previous lessons. This is why curricular planning is so crucial. In this vision of teaching, teachers plan instruction such that all class members will be able to participate based on what they have learned before, although individuals will certainly participate with differing levels of expertise. The more prior experiences the students have in common, the greater their capacity to work together in new situations. By repeatedly engaging students in problem-solving situations with their peers, what develops in the classroom is a community of learners—a community in which each individual participates at his or her own level of expertise, and all individuals take responsibility for what happens within the community. The more experience the participants have working together, the higher the level of mutual understanding among community members.

In a cognitive apprenticeship setting, teachers work side-by-side with learners, participating in holistic experiences, allowing the learners to perform whatever tasks they are able to, but providing scaffolding where necessary. As students work with their teacher and peers in such a setting, each of them may be operating in a slightly different place along the continuum of understanding and proficiency, but the situation should be constructed so that all students will be able to participate at their own level. Further, if the teacher constructs the situation so that peers have ample opportunity to provide scaffolding for one another, the overall expertise of the group will blossom. In addition, in all cases, no matter what the level of participation of the individual, the group experience should be a complete experience and not an exercise in preparation for a "real" experience (Box 1.10).

BOX 1.10 (VIGNETTE): CHOCOLATE CHIP COOKIES

From the time my children were very young, we baked chocolate chip cookies together. One day, when my youngest was about 10 years old, she was baking cookies by herself. This was to be the first time she would be permitted to take the hot cookie sheet out of the oven without assistance.

As she waited for the first batch to finish baking, she mused: "Remember when we were just babies, and you let us help you bake cookies? We sat on stools by the kitchen counter, and you let us put the chips into measuring cups, one chip at a time. By the time you were finished measuring and beating the ingredients, we were ready to dump in the chips (at least the ones we hadn't eaten). We dumped them in, and you put everything together and into the oven. We thought we were really helping. Then, as we got bigger, you let us do more things—measure the dry ingredients, sift the flour, break the eggs. When we were pretty big, you let us use the mixer—first with your hand on it and then by ourselves. After a while, we were able to make the whole recipe, but you still had to do the hot cookie sheet and the oven so we wouldn't burn ourselves. But the whole time, we always thought we were baking cookies!"

It wasn't until years later that I realized what a marvelous description of the processes of apprenticeship learning this was. From the time they first counted out chocolate chips until the time they could function independently, the children thought they were participating in the whole process. We were all baking cookies. For many years, it did not matter to them how much or how little they did. They were still baking cookies—and eating the final product. It was not until the later years that they even strove to do the process independently. It was just something we all did together—we all had our roles, each as important as the next. The joy of engaging in the process was not diminished by the lesser participation required of them when they were younger and less experienced. The process was meaningful because it was a real-life, whole experience that we shared and because the cookies always tasted so good.

Learning under these circumstances is self-motivational. Children who have an understanding of where they are headed, and why, do not need to be "tricked" into learning by some new gimmick. Learning itself is exciting when an individual understands what and why he or she is learning.

The outcome of a cognitive apprenticeship is understanding—conceptual understanding and the ability to apply those concepts to a variety of situations. The ultimate outcome is independence of the learner.

ENDNOTES

1. For more information on the cognitive revolution that resulted in this postmodernist view, *see* Howard Gardner (1985), *The mind's new science,* New York. Basic Books.
2. This story was shared with the author by Richard C. Anderson.
3. What Bruner describes as "scaffolding" is similar to David Elliott's description of "fading" in *Music matters.* 1995, New York: Oxford.
4. This is a perspective I developed through work with Eunice Boardman.
5. This analogy comes from Steven Tozer, University of Illinois, Chicago.
6. Holistic teaching does not mean never getting to the details, however. It means that details are extracted from the whole, isolated for study, and then reset in context. The key issue is that the students need to be able to understand the relationship between the detail and the context in order to understand the detail. It is not enough for the teacher to have that knowledge; the students must have access to it as well. For example, a music teacher might extract a rhythm pattern from a song that the students have been singing and focus on very specific aspects of that rhythmic idea and how it is put together. The teacher then could reset the rhythm pattern into the song so that the students can see how it functions in the song.

SELECTED RESOURCES

Collins, A., J. S. Brown, and A. Holum. 1991. Cognitive apprenticeship: Making thinking visible. *American Educator* 15:6–11, 38–46.

Collins, A., J. S. Brown, and S. E. Newman. 1989. Cognitive apprenticeship: Teaching the craft of reading, writing, and mathematics. In *Knowing, learning, and instruction: Essays in honor of Robert Glaser,* ed., L. B. Resnick, 453–94. Hillsdale, N.J.: Lawrence Erlbaum Associates.

Educational Leadership 51(5 [February 1994]). Entire issue is devoted to "Teaching for Understanding."

Gardner, H. 1983. *Frames of mind.* New York: Basic Books.

Gardner, H. 1991. *The unschooled mind.* New York: Basic Books.

Gauvain, M., and B. Rogoff. 1989. Collaborative problem solving and children's planning skills. *Developmental Psychology* 25:139–51.

Palinscar, A. S. 1986. The role of dialogue in providing scaffolded instruction. *Educational Psychologist* 21(1 & 2):73–98.

Rogoff, B. 1990. *Apprenticeship in thinking: Cognitive development in social context.* New York: Oxford University Press.

Rogoff, B., and J. Lave, eds. 1984. *Everyday cognition: Its development in social context.* Cambridge: Harvard University Press.

Wertsch, J. V., ed. 1985. *Culture, communication and cognition: Vygotskian perspectives.* Cambridge: Cambridge University Press.

Chapter 2

TEACHING FOR MUSICAL UNDERSTANDING

In Chapter 2, you will learn how the theories discussed in Chapter 1 apply to musical learning. Understanding how students learn music will help you better understand how to teach music in your own classroom.

How do the ideas that comprise schema theory and social constructivist theory connect to music teaching and learning? First, if the goal of teaching is understanding, then the goal of music teaching must be musical understanding. This does not mean that music teachers do not want their students to know how to perform music, or listen to music, or create original music. It means that in order to know *how* to perform, create, or listen to music, one needs to understand the ways in which music works. One needs to develop conceptual understanding of musical ideas.

CONCEPTUAL UNDERSTANDING IN MUSIC

Musical Schemas

As you learned in the previous chapter, people formulate their understanding of everything in the world by filtering new information through schemas that have been developed through life experience. Schema theory has been embraced by music cognition experts (e.g., Dowling, 1984, 1988; Dowling and Harwood, 1986; Sloboda, 1985, 1988) because it seems to work so well for musical ideas. Musical ideas are not verbal ideas *about* music. Musical ideas are the ways we hold musical sounds in our minds. *Musical thinking is thinking in sound,* just as verbal thinking is thinking in words.

Schemas Held by Experts in Music

Musicians educated in music of the Western tradition hold in their minds schemas for (or conceptual understanding of) the sound of a minor third, a dominant-tonic resolution, a deceptive cadence,[1] sonata-allegro form, Baroque music, blues, popular song form. Musicians educated in the musics of other cultures hold different kinds of musical schemas, such as the organizational devices "raga" and "tala" in the music of India or the use of polyrhythms and other layered sounds in the music of Africa. Some musical schemas are quite complex, complete with information about conventions associated with a particular style or historical or cultural context. Some are very simple, like the sound of a particular interval or pitch or tone color. All are intricately interconnected, overlapping time and again, intertwined with schemas that reflect the physical motions necessary to produce particular sounds (with instruments or voice) and schemas that reflect social and cultural norms for particular musical styles. People who know non-Western musics often hold musical schemas that are intricately interwoven with other aspects of their culture and history, such as social function, narrative, or religious context.

Schemas Held by Novices in Music

Students also hold many schemas for musical ideas in their minds. Some are a result of experiences with music teachers. However, a large percentage of their schemas for musical ideas were constructed as a result of life experience within the music of their particular culture. Most American children come to school with a great deal of prior experience with music of the pop culture. They know a great deal about how pop songs are constructed, about music moving in duple meter, about music having a strong and obvious beat. In the world of their experience, most music is vocal music. That is, with the exception of themes and background music for movies and television, the music of their world is sung (or "rapped"). The music of their world is also most frequently paired with some sort of visual image. Most music of American students' experience is repetitive in nature without much development of thematic material. A large portion of their music is in a major key, and most of it has a rather traditional Western harmonic structure.

Many students from different parts of the world also hold some schemas for Western popular music—in addition to their knowledge of their own music—as a result of worldwide marketing of American popular music, television, and movies. However, for students from some areas of the world, Western music is quite foreign. For example, children raised in Iraq and Iran probably hold schemas for Arabic music almost exclusively because other musics are not often heard in these countries.

As a teacher, you will need to keep in mind that the development of musical understanding is deeply rooted in an individual's prior experience and cultural influences. You will need to be aware of and understand the knowledge base your students bring into your classroom, because it is through this filter of prior experience that they will formulate understandings of the ideas you are trying to teach them. What is sometimes perceived as closed-mindedness on the part of students is often a product of the limits of their experience in music. Older students in particular, who have had a great deal of experience with pop music culture, often balk at what music teachers try to teach. Teachers need to be sensitive to students' perspectives because the only way they can learn is to consider the ideas the teacher is presenting in terms of what they already know. You will need to start where students are and then gently expand their realm of experience with music of a wide variety of styles, genres, and cultural and historical settings.

Musical Concepts

What are musical concepts? There are certain characteristics of structure that are common to most anything we call music. The way we understand these structural characteristics could be called musical thinking[2] or musical ideas. One way to think about it is to say that the actual structural characteristics (or elements, such as melody, harmony, rhythm, etc.) are properties of the music itself, while it is in our conception of what we hear that our understanding of music resides. The ways we understand what we hear and produce are our musical ideas. From this perspective, we would say that music exists only in our conception of it because there is no other way we can possibly know it. This kind of thinking reflects a constructivist vision of knowledge, one that suggests that we can only know the world through our own perceptions of it. What is important here is that, because we hold in our minds a concept of, or schema for, music and all that it entails, we are able to identify and understand what music is.

How Are Musical Concepts Constructed?

One's concepts of music are constructed through experience with music. Music cognition experts (e.g., Hargreaves, Sloboda, Swanwick) recognize that the only ways of experiencing music are through *performing, listening,* and *creating.* These are the processes of music. These are an individual's means of interacting with music.

Performing can involve singing and/or playing instruments or other sound sources. Students can perform original music or music composed by someone else. People can listen to music being performed by others (including recordings), and listening is also an integral part of the processes of performing and creating. Creating can involve improvising, composing, or even arranging. When people improvise, they plan and execute musical ideas in "real time." When they compose, they plan musical ideas "ahead of time," before the time the performance actually takes place.

As individuals engage in the processes of performing, listening to, and creating original music, they make use of the conceptual understandings of music they already possess. However, participating in these processes also causes them to formulate *new* conceptual understandings of music. Each new experience has the potential to enrich prior understanding as people use what they already understand about music to expand upon their understanding of the new situation. It is essential for the individual to be engaged in genuine interaction with music in order for this to occur. It is not enough to just talk about music with students (or about how many children Bach had). In order for musical understanding to grow, an individual must interact directly with music through performing, listening, creating, or some combination of the three processes. As learners participate in these processes, their schemas of understanding of musical ideas become richer, denser, and more interconnected. They develop a rich network of musical schemas that hold factual, procedural, and contextual information that enable the individual to become more proficient at listening, performing, and creating.

Teaching Concepts, Not Labels

It is very important for music teachers to understand the difference between a musical concept or idea and the way musicians have decided to write those ideas down on paper. Our musical culture has developed quite a complex system of "labels" that represent the various things we understand about music. However, these labels are meaningless to people who do not understand the concept behind them. It is important for students to first experience and understand a concept before being expected to identify it with an appropriate label. For example, instead of teaching "time signature," teach the feeling of meter, how beats are organized into meter, and how rhythm operates within meter. Only when students fully understand the feel and sound of meter will time signature labels like $\frac{3}{4}$ have any meaning for them. Similarly, teach tonality and modality rather than "key signature." Students need to experience the concept of tonal center and the tension-and-release that defines tonal center within a work. They need to experience the various paths one can take when moving around a tonal center (major, minor, Dorian, whole tone, etc.) and the affective differences created by the use of the various modalities. Once students have the sound of a mode in their ears (formulate a schema for a particular mode), they need time to experiment with reproducing that sound from a variety of tonal centers. Only then will they have the background to understand what a key signature indicates or what the "key of G major" means.

Instead of teaching "quarter notes and eighth notes," teach that, in music, some sounds last longer than others. Instead of "lines and spaces," teach that music has melody, that melodic lines come in all sorts of shapes, that some sounds are higher than others, that some are lower, and that one way to write melody down uses a system of five lines. Students need to understand that there is a logic behind a notation system, a logic that is based on the way the music sounds (and not on "Every Good Boy Does Fine").

Of course, music teachers teach students to read and interpret music notation systems—but the systems will only make sense to students after they have established a strong base of prior experience with the concepts behind the ways in which we write down musical ideas. Without conceptual understanding, students are left to their own devices and may only be able to produce music through imitating the teacher or a peer or by making their best guess as to what they are supposed to be doing. Without conceptual understanding of the structural elements of music, a student cannot develop into an independent musician.

FINDING WAYS FOR STUDENTS TO EXPRESS MUSICAL UNDERSTANDING

Finding Out What Students Know

Students enter music classrooms with an enormous amount of knowledge about music—about what it is and about how it functions in their lives. As their teacher, you are then faced with the problem of finding out what students already know and deciding where to go from there. This problem is compounded by the fact that students generally know more about music than they are able to articulate. This is because they have some understanding of musical ideas but do not yet know appropriate terminology for labeling what they understand. Therefore, it is necessary for you to build into your lessons opportunities for students to express what they know about music through nonverbal means, such as gesture, movement, or graphic representation. Students also express their understanding using words other than those in standard musical terminology. A student who does not know the word *crescendo* may still be able to hear and identify the phenomenon and may say something like, "I hear the music getting louder and louder a little bit at a time." You need to keep in mind that conceptual understanding is more important than the ability to label that understanding. Much more important than the ability to *define* the term *crescendo* is the ability to *hear* a *crescendo* and to recognize that its presence plays a role in the effectiveness of the musical work and in the way a listener perceives the work. Once students understand a concept, it is easy to teach them an appropriate label.

Learning from What Students Do Naturally

When left to their own devices, how do novices express what they understand about music? Listening to children as they work with peers planning original compositions or listening to the ways they talk about music during discussions of listening experiences can teach us a great deal about the ways they communicate and describe musical ideas. Inexperienced listeners' descriptions of what they hear in a piece of music are often riddled with nonverbal sounds like "bum-bum-bum" or "dit-dah, dit-dah dot." Students trying to tell peers about their plans for a composition use similar means of communication. (A student talking to peers about a song they were writing: "We need a drum track. We need short-short-long, short-short-long, dum dum chhhh, dum dum chhhhh.") The nonverbal sounds are often a kind of rhythmic speech, almost scatting, or a sound that might indicate something about the tone color the students are trying to describe.

Students also utilize spontaneous singing as a means of communicating musical ideas to one another and to the teacher. It is quite common for students to vacillate between verbal speech and singing when they are trying to make a musical idea clear to someone else (see Box 2.1).

BOX 2.1 (VIGNETTE)

In the early stages of a composition project, a boy playing a gato drum asked one of his group members, "What should I play?" The group member replied in song:

Neh neh neh neh   neh neh   neh

In a different small group, a student suggested to her peers, "Who wants to start off? Barbara, you wanna go `Brinnnnnnng!'" (which is spoken while sliding upward in pitch).

Students also often use their hands and bodies to communicate what they are trying to say about the music they hear or are trying to create (see Box 2.2).

BOX 2.2 (VIGNETTE)

"This is what we're doing. I'm going first. This is our rhythm:

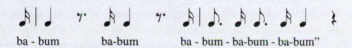

ba - bum   ba-bum   ba - bum - ba-bum - ba-bum"

(The rhythm syllables are spoken as she slides her hands past one another making a rubbing sound to emulate the sound of the cabasa, which would play that part in their piece.)

Although used less frequently than the other means of expression, students will sometimes ask for a pencil or piece of chalk to show someone a dimension of what they are trying to communicate about a sound they hear or have thought of. An example of this is provided in Box 2.3.

BOX 2.3 (VIGNETTE)

A student, engaged in predicting what the music might do as the class prepared to hear Grieg's "In the Hall of the Mountain King" (Figure 7.10, pp. 189–195), asked if he might draw his idea because he could not describe it. He went to the chalkboard and drew:

As he drew, he said: "It's going like this and then it gets really loud and then suddenly starts from here again."

If, when left to their own devices, students choose to utilize these various means of non-verbal communication of musical ideas, it would seem that teachers could also make use of these means of expression on a more formalized level. When designing lesson plans, it is important to think about including a variety of ways for students to express what they know. When carrying out lesson plans, it is important to be sensitive to the ways in which students express what they know. If you do not understand what a student is trying to say about a particular musical idea, you need to ask questions about the student's comment. A teacher needs to let students know that he or she feels that what they have to say is valuable. It is important to encourage students to utilize alternate ways of expressing what they are trying to communicate ("Can you show me what you mean?" "Can you make a picture of what you are saying?"). The lesson plans described in Chapters 6, 7, and 8 (particularly in analytical listening lessons) contain many examples of activities based on various means of nonverbal expression of musical ideas.

CONTEXTS FOR MUSICAL LEARNING

The Importance of Contextuality

One important implication of schema theory for music teaching is that contextuality is essential for musical learning to take place. In a lesson, all ideas must be presented in context, and students must be able to understand how what they are being taught relates to that context. In a music lesson, the only viable and valid context is a musical work—ideally, a whole musical work, presented in its entirety. Using whole musical works makes it possible for students to understand what the creator and/or performer of the music intended and how he or she decided to carry out that intention. Studying a musical work is like studying someone else's musical ideas. It is important to allow the students to hear all of what the creator and performer are trying to say. (The lesson and unit plans that appear in Chapters 6, 7, and 8 provide examples of good teaching pieces and descriptions of ways in which students might interact with the works in their entirety.)

Musical Contexts for Learning

Musical contexts for teaching can be songs sung, pieces played, works listened to, or original works created by students. Everything a teacher teaches should be drawn from a musical work, and the students should be able to recognize and understand the relationship between the concept being taught and the work from which it is drawn. All music teaching should emanate from legitimate, quality musical works. Just as whole language teachers prefer to use quality literature rather than reading "exercises," music teachers need to use quality music literature in their teaching, rather than musical exercises contrived to teach particular techniques or skills. How to make decisions about which music to bring into the classroom is discussed in the section of Chapter 4 titled "Criteria for Selection of Music for Teaching" (pp. 63–66).

While music teaching must take place within whole, legitimate, quality musical contexts, this does not mean that the details of the work are never addressed. Specific aspects of a composition can be extracted from its context and examined in great detail, if warranted, but the students must understand how the extracted idea relates to and functions within the whole. For example, many music teachers begin teaching a song by asking students to clap rhythm patterns. Often, the rhythm patterns are related to something that will take place within a song they are about to learn. If the teacher asks the students first to clap the rhythms and then (once they have mastered them) sets the rhythms into the context of a song, this is *not* contextual teaching. If the students engage in similar activities in the reverse order, this can be considered contextual teaching. For it to be considered contextual teaching, the whole song would be presented in some fashion first, so that the students are able to become familiar with the complete musical context. If they have heard the song several times, and *then* the teacher presents a series of representations of rhythm patterns found in the song and asks the students to find the patterns in the song, a context has been established.

Please consider these two different approaches to the teaching of "Skip to My Lou" to a second-grade class, as shown in Boxes 2.4 and 2.5.

BOX 2.4: "SKIP TO MY LOU" (VERSION 1)

Several rhythm patterns are written on the chalkboard. The teacher asks the class to echo the rhythms as he claps them. He then claps each pattern, and, after each one, the students respond by echoing what he has clapped.

[As you read this example, clap the first few rhythm patterns listed below. Would they have any significance to you if you did not already know the song?]

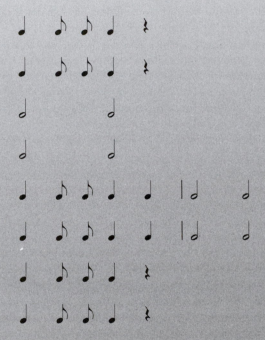

The lyrics are not written on the board, but the teacher adds them to the echo pattern near the end of the exercise.

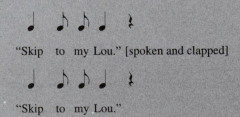

"Skip   to   my Lou." [spoken and clapped]

"Skip   to   my Lou."

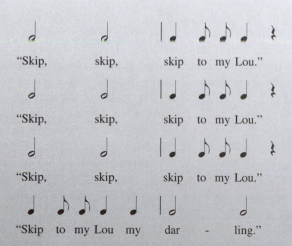

After several repetitions, the teacher moves from chanting the lyrics in rhythm to singing the melody, one line at a time, then two phrases together, and finally the whole melody, with the students echoing each version. Eventually, the song is performed with a guitar accompaniment.

BOX 2.5: "SKIP TO MY LOU" (VERSION 2)

"Class, please look at the dashes on the board. These dashes have something to do with a new song we are going to learn today."

"Do the dashes give you any clues about the song?" Students might comment that the song seems to have four parts or lines and that the first three seem to be the same and the fourth, different.

"How might you expect the last line to sound? How will it be different?" Students who are familiar with the use of these dashes as iconic representations of duration generally talk about the first three lines beginning with longer sounds, while the last line ends with the longer sounds. Likewise, they generally comment that the first three lines seem to have some short sounds in the middle but that the last line has a lot of short sounds in the beginning.

"Listen as I sing the song and see if you were right about what you thought." The teacher then performs the song, accompanying himself with chords on a guitar. As he sings, many students trace the icons in the air with their fingers, trying to make a connection between what the teacher is singing and the icons on the board.

After the teacher has sung the song once, the students discuss whether or not they were correct in their predictions about the rhythm of the song. The teacher sings the song again so the students can recheck or refine their earlier predictions. One student then points out that the dashes are not really completely accurate because the song not only has "shorts and longs," it also has "ups and downs." Others second this complaint, and they decide that they need to make the picture look more like what the song sounds like. As the teacher sings the song again and again, the students suggest ways of rearranging the icons so that they better represent the contour and direction of the melody in addition to the rhythm. [If the icons used are magnetic strips or something else that can be moved around on the board, this kind of activity becomes much easier to manage. Students can then manipulate the icons themselves until they are satisfied with their solution.]

Having heard the song five or six times, the students are satisfied with their representation of the contour and rhythm of the melody. At this point, they also know the song intimately and can sing it easily. In fact, as they worked together to graph the melody, many began spontaneously singing along with the teacher. Also, many had to sing portions of the song very carefully to themselves in order to determine how the icons should be placed to show contour and direction.

In each scenario, the students are dealing with the rhythm of the song and using aspects of the rhythm to learn to sing the song. Take a moment to think about the two scenarios. How would you answer the questions in Box 2.6?

BOX 2.6   THINK ABOUT THIS . . .

In which case are the concepts presented from the outset within a musical context?

Which case is an example of contextually embedded conceptual teaching?

In which case might you expect children to learn the song better?

In which case might you expect them to understand how the rhythm functions within the song?

Which group of second graders would be better able to play the rhythm of the melody on a drum?

Which class would you expect to sing the song more in tune?

In which case do you think students are further along on the road to musical independence?

Which method of introducing a song is more in keeping with what you have learned about the ways people learn?

In Version 1, the students may guess that the echoing will eventually lead to the learning of a new song. However, the teacher does not really mention that to the class. The class is not "clued in" to what they will be doing in today's lesson. Further, the students are expected to deal with standard music notation, even though many of them may not as yet hold a concept of its meaning. In Version 2, the teacher uses graphic icons similar to the "piano roll" notation found in many computer programs.[3] The children know from the start that the representation on the board is taken from a song they are about to learn. Even if this was their first experienced with the icons, the teacher has told them from the start that the dashes on the board will give them clues about the song they are going to learn. This simple statement invites them to become partners in their own learning from the very beginning of the lesson.

In Version 1, the students are expected to passively accept and follow the teacher's direction with no importance attached to the meaning of the experience. In Version 2, the students are immediately engaged in *solving a problem* that they need to figure out in order to proceed. From the start, they are suggesting their own theories and testing those theories. Further, they are engaged in *problem finding*. Within the first few minutes of the lesson, some of the students have also identified a new problem—that the representation shows only half of the picture, rhythm but not pitch. This was not surprising to the teacher: he had intentionally designed the problem to encourage such thinking by asking the students to focus on the rhythmic aspects of the melody, although he presented the song in its entirety with all of its rhythm and pitch aspects. Hearing the song only twice, the children immediately noticed the omission, as he had hoped they would. This enabled him to shift responsibility for that aspect of the task (representing what they heard in graphic icons) to the students, making it their responsibility instead of his.

Many music educators have observed that children seem to hear and understand melodies first in their entirety (with both rhythm and pitch); and, after instruction, they learn to isolate rhythm and pitch as the two components of melody. Thinking is holistic in nature. People conceive of whole entities long before they understand their parts (filling in the slots of the schemas). People can conceive of what a song is long before they can talk about it as a series of different pitches and durations arranged in patterns that imply an underlying chord structure, tonality, and modality. Many of the methods used in general music classrooms today start with the parts and assemble them into the whole. This way of working is contrary to students' natural ways of thinking and understanding. The kind of teaching that Version 2 portrays represents an approach much more conducive to children's natural ways of thinking.

Teaching Musical Concepts with No Musical Context

It is possible to deal with the words that talk about musical ideas without setting them into a musical context. For example, it is certainly possible to teach that some sounds are louder or faster than others without relating the lesson to musical experiences. It is possible to teach about direction (up and down) without connecting it to a concept of pitch. If there is no musical context present, teachers have no way of knowing whether their students are connecting what they are learning to musical ideas or whether they are accessing inappropriate schemas and making erroneous connections, which consequently results in misconception.

Students who can easily identify "up and down" on a stairway and visually identify "up and down" on a xylophone may be unable to correctly identify an ascending or descending scale line in a song they are singing. This could happen if a teacher uses visual imagery when teaching "up and down" but does not connect the imagery to anything aural. Students will not be able to formulate a concept of melodic direction unless they have experience with direction within the context of an actual melody. Students who can walk around the room to the beat of a teacher's drum may be unable to find and demonstrate the beat of a musical work. Students will not be able to formulate a concept of the beat of a musical work unless they have experience with beat within the context of a work. Students generally come into our classrooms already familiar with concepts of "loud and soft" and "fast and slow." If we are not teaching them about the effects that these elements can produce as they operate within a musical work, then we are not really teaching them something they did not already know. What is important to know about dynamics and tempo is what can happen to a musical work when these elements are manipulated and the effect this kind of change can produce for a listener or performer. This cannot be taught without a viable musical context.

To teach musical elements with no music present is not teaching music at all. Studying tempo or dynamics or direction in a nonmusical setting is not studying music. Most important, when extracting a particular musical element for study, it is essential that the students understand the relationship between that element and the musical work from which it is drawn. It is not enough for the teacher to have that knowledge: the students need to have knowledge of the musical context from which the particular musical elements are drawn and of their function within that context.

Even teachers who provide musical contexts for instruction sometimes neglect to make that context clear to their students. When this occurs, students need to take it upon themselves to establish their own contexts in order to understand how to proceed. The instances in Box 2.7 were drawn from a research study of teaching and learning processes in a second-grade general music classroom (Wiggins, 1998).

BOX 2.7 (VIGNETTE): AMY FIGURES THINGS OUT

As part of the lesson, the children had been asked to clap a rhythm pattern from the chalkboard. The teacher had not established any musical context for the rhythm pattern. As the children were clapping the rhythm pattern, one of the students established a metrical context for herself by representing duple meter in her speech pattern before she began.

Amy [to herself]: Let's try it again! YES no YES no YES no YES! [this last part spoken rhythmically, in an accented duple meter].

* * *

On another day, when Amy was not given specific instructions as to what she should play on the maracas in accompanying a song, she chose to fit her maraca part to the bass line of the piano accompaniment, creating a highly successful accompaniment pattern. As the piano played a beguine pattern, she played:

L   R R   L   R R

If teachers do not establish musical contexts for their students' learning, their students will establish their own contexts in their efforts to understand what the teacher wants them to do. In some instances, students like Amy will be successful at creating appropriate contexts that will enable them to understand and act. However, teachers need to realize that there is no guarantee this will occur. When the responsibility for establishing a context is left up to the students, there is also a risk that they will access an inappropriate context and therefore either misunderstand or reject what the teacher is trying to help them learn. Such things cannot be left to chance. Part of planning instruction is making certain that all information is presented in a context and presented in a way that enables the learner to understand the relationship between the new information and the context.

Social Contexts for Learning

As explained in Chapter 1, in a social constructivist view of learning, all learning is a result of social interaction with other people or a result of an individual acting based on what he or she has previously learned from other people. In classrooms, the people involved are teachers and students. This means that, in a classroom, learning takes place as a result of interaction between teacher and students and also as a result of interaction among students.

Organization for Instruction

In Chapters 3 and 4, you will learn more specifically about how musical ideas can best be taught. As Version 2 of the "Skip to My Lou" lesson demonstrated, independent problem solving is an important component of this process. In order to create a setting in which independent problem solving can flourish, it is important to look at some of the ways of organizing instruction to support such an approach that are consistent with a social constructivist view of learning.

Students need to have opportunities to work together in a variety of instructional settings—as a whole class with opportunities for support from both peers and teacher; in small groups with opportunities for peer support and, when necessary, teacher assistance; with partners; and working independently. In general, it makes sense that early experiences with a particular concept or skill will probably require large group, whole-class instruction with a significant amount of teacher guidance and support. Once students have gained experience with a particular concept or skill, it makes sense to allow them opportunities to work with less reliance on the teacher but with a strong vehicle for support, such as that provided by small group activities. As students become more and more competent, they become ready to work either independently or with the support of a partner. While this organizational plan is not a hard and fast rule, it provides a good model for instructional planning. As you will see in subsequent chapters, organizing your classroom so that students are able to work with musical ideas on their own will nurture the development of their musical independence.

Nature of Student/Teacher Interaction

During large group, whole-class instruction, the teacher generally takes on the role of leader. However, when students are working in a problem-solving situation, even a whole-class setting takes on a different feel. As students suggest and discuss theories, the teacher becomes more of a facilitator and guide (and sometimes a referee or cheerleader). In a large group instructional setting, the teacher functions as more of a resource than a lecturer. Since learning occurs when we expand or alter our schemas, it is important that the student be solving genuine, meaningful problems, not simply listening to the teacher's description of a solution. Since problem solving is the key to learning, it must be the *students* who are solving the problem. (Problem solving is discussed in detail in Chapter 3.) However, particularly in the introductory stages of a unit, when large group, whole-class instruction is likely to take place, part of the teacher's role is to be sure that the students have enough information at their fingertips to be able to solve the problem at hand and to be able to go on solving related problems, eventually without teacher help. In this sense, the teacher must adopt the role of resource.

It is important to remember, however, that the teacher is certainly not the only resource in the classroom. Students bring into the classroom varying levels of expertise in whatever the group may be discussing, analyzing, performing, or creating. The teacher is not the only one with musical expertise in the classroom and, at many points during the lesson, the "more knowledgeable other" might very well be someone other than the teacher.

In small group, partner, and independent work, the teacher becomes more of a coach than a leader but remains a resource, a facilitator, a guide (and sometimes a referee or cheerleader). In these settings, the teacher works more from the sidelines than as a strong leader working from the front of the room. In all instructional settings, teachers need to be sensitive to the extent and level of student understanding and provide scaffolding for individuals or for the group, when necessary. However, it is important to allow the students time to think and function on their own. One can keep abreast of what is going on without hovering. Students should know that, if they need help, they should seek it either from a peer or from the teacher. This kind of arrangement is far more productive than one in which the teacher circulates constantly asking each group whether they need or would like help. This kind of action on the part of the teacher can be extremely disruptive to students' thinking processes (Wiggins, 1992).

Nature of Student/Student Interaction

Regardless of the instructional setting (large group, small group, independent), students' learning is dependent upon opportunities to interact with their peers, both with and without the teacher present in the situation. Within a large group instructional setting, students should be sharing ideas and discussing with their peers. It is important for students to have opportunities to initiate ideas in large group settings as well as in less teacher-guided settings.

It is also important for teachers to allow some student/student talk during whole-class instruction. While one must maintain some semblance of order in a large group setting, insisting on silence during whole-class instruction can inhibit learning since many students are dependent upon peers for translation and clarification of teacher talk. In my research, I have captured on tape numerous moments when students engaged in large group instruction needed to rely on a momentary comment or question to a peer in order to be able to continue to understand what was going on in class. Sometimes such comments are as simple as "What page did he say?" Sometimes they contribute to a student's comfort level as a participant in an activity: "When we get to the keyboard, you'll show me what to do, right?" Sometimes students check with peers before contributing to the whole group. Sometimes students ask peers for a more detailed explanation of something the teacher has said, which can be disruptive to the group but can serve as one way the teacher can become aware that there is some confusion occurring. If a class appears chatty, it is sometimes wise to check for understanding ("Is this chart making sense to you? Do you know what I mean by this question?"). Recordings of classroom teaching and learning often reveal that student/student talk is more productive than teachers perceive it to be. In many cases, when teachers believe a class to be misbehaving, listening carefully to the student/student talk will reveal that students are confused and are seeking help from peers as to how they are supposed to proceed.

Large group settings provide models that show students how to function better in small group and independent work. Students working with peers in small groups utilize many of the same strategies they have seen used by the teacher during large group instruction. They use what they have learned in large group settings to enable them to know how to proceed when asked to solve a similar problem without teacher help. One can observe the use of strategies that are specific to the problem at hand but also general management strategies, such as students listening to one another and commenting on one another's ideas or students putting ideas up for a vote and settling disputes by determining the will of the majority.

As students work together to solve problems, their conversations include comments, questions, suggestions, negotiations, evaluations, corrections, and criticisms. Working together with peers in a small group to solve a common problem necessitates communication of both verbal and musical ideas, which helps students become more articulate in sharing musical thoughts. In small group settings, children also clarify and interpret teacher instructions for one another, just as they do in large group settings. This is particularly beneficial because explaining something to a peer often helps the "explainer" to clarify his or her own understanding in the process.

When working in small groups without teacher help, it is not uncommon for students to adopt many of the roles generally performed by the teacher in large group settings. In peer teaching, students utilize the same techniques as professional teachers do, such as modeling, correcting errors, offering praise, assessing need for help, anticipating needs, and providing scaffolding. Recordings of students working together in groups have shown that students not only provide scaffolding for one another but also exhibit expertise in knowing how and when to pull the scaffold away. Within a group, students who step forward into the role of peer teacher tend to be the ones who possess a more mature understanding of the problem or situation at hand. These students also exhibit the ability to monitor peers' work or understanding at the same time as they participate in the particular activity (for example, keeping track of what and how a peer is playing an instrument at the same time as they perform a part on their own instrument).

Scaffolding in the Music Classroom

Scaffolding takes place throughout the music teaching/learning experience, regardless of the nature of instructional setting or activity. It occurs in large group, small group, and partner work, and also in independent work when students realize they still need a bit of assistance. Scaffolding takes many forms within a music classroom. In a performance lesson, for example, scaffolding can occur when the teacher performs parts of the piece that are too difficult for the students (like an accompaniment) but encourages students to perform whatever parts they are able to manage. In a listening lesson, scaffolding can take the form of providing a framework within which the students might be able to hear more and more complex aspects of a composition. In creative activities, scaffolding might take the form of clarification of the parameters of an assignment.

Boxes 2.8 and 2.9 present two different instances of scaffolding drawn from actual classroom learning experiences. The first took place during a fifth-grade lesson in a small group setting. The second occurred as fifth-grade students took their places at keyboards to get ready to accompany a class song by playing chords.

BOX 2.8 (VIGNETTE): PEER SCAFFOLDING IN A SMALL GROUP SETTING

The following is an excerpt from a transcript of an actual lesson in which the children were trying to figure out where tonic and dominant harmonies fit in the folk song "A Ram Sam Sam" (Chapter 8, pp. 230–234). They were working in groups of four, each group gathered around an Autoharp on the floor. They had been instructed to sing the song as they strummed and to use their ears to determine which chord belonged with each phrase of the song. After listening to the teacher's directions, Louise was still uncertain of how to begin. She asked her peers for help:

Louise [who was holding the Autoharp pick]: But what am I supposed to do?

Lynn: Look up on the board . . . D and A_7.

Sheila [pointing to the bar on the Autoharp]: D is right here. D major.

Lynn: Right there.

Louise: Oh!

Lynn: Yeah.

Louise: Which is the home tone (tonic)?

Lynn: D.

Louise: O.K. [She began strumming a D chord, and the group began to sing the folk song.]

With Lynn and Sheila's assistance, Louise was able to participate successfully in the project.

BOX 2.9 (VIGNETTE): PEER SCAFFOLDING IN A LARGE GROUP SETTING

The following is an excerpt from a transcript of a performance-based lesson. The students were working in pairs on synthesizer keyboards, trying to learn to play the chords and bass line of a song they would accompany. Sam and Matt shared a keyboard. By their own choosing, Sam played the chords and Matt the bass line.

Sam [locating and playing the chords as he speaks]: This is the G chord . . . my C chord . . . and my F chord is . . . F . . . wait, wait . . .

Matt: Chill out man!

Sam [still practicing his chords]: F . . . C . . . D . . .

Matt: Wait! Help me with this one. It's C . . .

Sam: Yeah . . . F . . . that one. [He then demonstrated the entire bass line.]

Matt: Oh, F.

Sam: G . . . that one. [Points to key on keyboard.]

Matt [locating and playing the key]: G.

Sam: Yeah.

Matt: This is so easy!

Sam: A'right! A'right! [Offers praise.]

In this instance, in a matter of minutes, Sam successfully taught Matt what to play and where to play it on the keyboard. Sam's instructions seemed to make the task easy for Matt, and he shared his friend's enthusiasm at his success.

[handwritten margin notes: district teachers → "community of practice" "learning communities" classroom]

MUSICAL COGNITIVE APPRENTICESHIP

Pulling all of these ideas together should generate a workable description of what teaching and learning in a *musical cognitive apprenticeship* might look like. First, let us consider music teaching in terms of the six points discussed at the end of Chapter 1:

• *Learners need to engage in real-life, problem-solving situations.* Some aspects of traditional music teaching have always been real-life situations, such as performing in "real" bands, orchestras, and choruses, but, in these settings, it has not been the norm for students to be asked to solve problems. While many students do participate in real-life music making, these experiences can be made less real when, for example, students are asked to play music that has been "watered down" for instructional purposes. While beginners certainly need to start with music that is less complex, there is no reason to ask them to perform or listen to less than quality music.

• *Learning situations need to be holistic in nature.* This means setting all music instruction into a genuine musical context—starting with the big picture and working down to the detail, setting every detail back into its larger musical context, and making sure that the students understand the relationship between the detail and the context. The lesson and unit plans in this book are designed to help you develop a sense of what it is to plan and teach music holistically and contextually.

- *Learners need opportunities to interact directly with the subject matter.* This means planning instruction so that students engage in performing, listening to, and creating music. Any teaching "about" music, such as historical or cultural information related to the musical work, should be taught as an outgrowth of performing, listening, and creating experiences.
- *Learners need to take an active role in their own learning.* This means teaching music in ways other than large group, teacher-directed instruction; permitting ample opportunity for students to initiate and carry out original ideas; and planning instruction such that the teacher is not seen as the only holder of knowledge in the classroom.
- *Learners need opportunities to work on their own, with peers, and with teacher support, when needed.* Music instruction must consist of more than teacher-directed, large group performance of music. Students also need opportunities to work in small groups and independently within the context of performing, listening, and creating experiences.
- *Learners need to be cognizant of the goals of the learning situation and their own progress toward goals.* It is important for the teacher to establish contexts that allow students to understand relationships. Students must be "clued in" and informed about how what they are learning fits with other things they already know or have experienced. Only then will they be able to construct their own understanding and grow in independence as musicians and musical learners.

In order to teach within a musical cognitive apprenticeship, a teacher needs to know how to design instruction as problem solving (see Box 2.10). *Thinking of learning as problem solving enables the teacher to conceptualize instruction in terms of what the learner will learn rather than in terms of what the teacher will teach.* Chapters 3 and 4 are devoted to a discussion of conceiving of instruction through problem solving.

[handwritten marginal note: interpsychological – working / learning w/others; intrapsychological – understanding / independent → Vygotsky]

BOX 2.10   THINK ABOUT THIS . . .

In planning instruction, keep in mind that:

- Musical concepts are based on understanding the elements and principles of music.
- These concepts are understood through schemas that are constantly expanding and changing.
- Developing these schemas must begin with what the students already know and can express about music.
- This development must occur in the context of whole works of quality music.
- While it is important to extract details from these musical works, it is essential that the students understand the relationship between the details and the musical whole.
- These ideas are best carried out in a setting that is a musical cognitive apprenticeship.

In order to better understand what a musical cognitive apprenticeship might look like, consider this description of a music lesson that took place in a fifth-grade music classroom.

BOX 2.11 (ACTIVITY)

As you read "The Fifties Song," see how many characteristics of cognitive apprenticeship you can identify. Next, go back and compare your list to the characteristics described in Chapters 1 and 2.

THE "FIFTIES" SONG

A fifth-grade class is learning to perform a classic 1950s rock and roll song that can be accompanied by I, IV, and V_7 chords.

On one side of the room is a long table with three synthesizers side by side. Across one end of the table is a programmable synthesizer on which the teacher has recorded a suitable drum track. A semicircle of 26 chairs starts next to the table, curves across the back of the room, and finishes not far from the chalkboard in front. On the floor, just inside the semicircle of chairs, are 10 barred instruments of various sizes and ranges. (See Figure 9.1, p. 251).

The students, seated in the chairs, have been divided into teams of two. Each pair has been given sheet music for the song, including the notes and lyrics of the melodic line with chord symbols written above. On the chalkboard is a chart showing the chords. The students already know how to sing the song. Most can easily locate and read the lyrics, although for several students just finding the lyrics on the page has proposed a challenge. These students have been able to learn the song along with their peers, partially because of the support they received both directly and indirectly from peers and teacher.

During previous experiences, these students studied the sonority of tonic, dominant, and subdominant harmonies. They accompanied simple folk songs by selecting the appropriate chords and playing them on either an Autoharp or keyboard. Most are relatively comfortable finding at least C, F, and G_7 chords on a keyboard. All were comfortable and highly experienced with playing appropriate bass notes on xylophones (following a chord progression by playing only the root of the chord). All were experienced at playing chords and bass lines in time with a drum track.

Today, they will try to apply what they know to a class performance of a rock and roll song. With their partners, the students take places at instruments, two students sharing each xylophone or synthesizer. Once they begin, each pair will play one instrument for a portion of the song and then move over to the next instrument in a rotation pattern that moves everyone around the room.

As students take their places, they immediately begin practicing the parts for which they will be responsible. The pairs seated on the floor behind the barred instruments are busily removing bars that sit near the C, F, and G that they will need to play. One pair decides to leave all the bars in place because they have figured out how to play the melody of the B section of the song.

Students who have opted to begin their rotation at the synthesizer are standing behind their keyboards with their partners, checking to be sure they remember how to find the right keys to play the C, F, and G_7 chords. Some check with their partners to be sure they are remembering correctly. One girl quite easily finds the correct notes for the chords. She decides to use this time to ask her partner, who studies piano outside of school, to show her how a pianist would finger the chords. She then tries the new fingering pattern and giggles as her little finger refuses to cooperate. Her partner, who has long since mastered this skill, stands a bit taller for a moment, briefly taking pride in her own expertise.

A synthesizer player who is unsure suddenly remembers that he is supposed to begin by looking for D, the easiest key to locate. He finds a D and then, using what he knows about the "musical alphabet," locates C. He has decided to try to play the bass line. His partner reminds him that it will be easier for him to keep his place if he plays all the Cs with his left index finger and the Fs and Gs with his right. He gets his fingers set on the keyboard, looks up at the chalkboard to follow the chord progression that is written there, and begins to practice. (Please see vignette in Box 2.9 for an actual instance of this kind of peer support that occurred during a similar situation.)

Earlier, the students had sung through the song with the drum track and the teacher's synthesizer. This time, they will try to play the chords and bass line while the drum track keeps time and the teacher fills out the accompaniment a bit, in order to establish the style. The teacher starts the drum track—a 1950s rock and roll style pattern. As they make their first attempts at producing their own accompaniment for the song, the students are barely singing—using their singing as more of a tool to keep track of where they are in the song and chord progression. On this first attempt, some students are able to perform the whole progression; others lose their way, but find it again. A few get lost early in the performance and stop playing. Those who are unsure carefully watch what others are playing. One or two are able to rejoin, often with their partners' assistance. Sometimes partners, sensing that their support is needed, say the chord names aloud as they play.

The group is able to play through one verse of the song. The drum track continues and the teams of two move on to the next instrument, ready to play again. On the second verse, many of the students are more successful at finding the correct pitches and playing the right chords in the right places.

After several repetitions, the group, as a whole, becomes much more proficient. The singing is stronger as more and more students become comfortable with the chords and bass notes in relation to the lyrics and drum track. The group, as a whole, is stronger because the individuals within the group are becoming more proficient at playing their individual parts and at "getting it all together" with a sense of simultaneity and ensemble.

The goal of participation in a cognitive apprenticeship is competence and independence of the learner. Through guided participation in holistic, real-life, problem-solving experiences that involve hands-on interaction with music and opportunities to interact with both teacher and peers, students develop their own understanding of musical concepts and principles such that they move toward musical competence and independence. Over time, participating in a musical cognitive apprenticeship should enable individuals to develop the understandings and skills such that they are able to apply what they know to solve new problems on their own.

ENDNOTES

1. It is because of a listener's schema for dominant-tonic resolution that a deceptive cadence works. If one had no expectation, one would not be deceived (Meyer, 1956).
2. For an extensive discussion of the nature of musical thinking, see Gardner, 1993.
3. This kind of iconic representation of pitch and duration is used by Eunice Boardman (Bergethon, Boardman, and Montgomery, 1997; Boardman, 1988) in her "Generative Approach" to general music instruction.

SELECTED RESOURCES

Bamberger, J. 1991. *The mind behind the musical ear: How children develop musical intelligence.* Cambridge: Harvard University Press.

Bergethon, B., E. Boardman, and J. Montgomery. 1997. *Musical growth in the elementary school,* 6th ed. Fort Worth, Tx.: Harcourt Brace.

Boardman, E. L. 1988. The generative theory of musical learning, (Part II). *General Music Today* 2(2):3–6, 28–31.

———, ed. 1989. *Dimensions of musical thinking.* Reston, Va.: Music Educators National Conference.

Campbell, P. S., and C. Scott-Kassner. 1995. *Music in childhood.* New York: Schirmer Books.

Gardner, H. 1993. *Frames of mind: The theory of multiple intelligence,* 2d ed. New York: Basic Books.

———. 1991. *The unschooled mind.* New York: Basic Books.

Hargreaves, D. 1986. *The developmental psychology of music.* Cambridge: Cambridge University Press.

Serafine, M. L. 1988. *Music as cognition: The development of thought in sound* (Part I). New York: Columbia University Press.

Swanwick, K. 1988. *Music, mind and education.* London: Routledge.

Chapter 3
TEACHING MUSIC THROUGH PROBLEM SOLVING

The theories in Chapters 1 and 2 suggest that people learn best in situations in which they are asked to use what they know to solve problems. Chapter 3 describes ways of teaching music through problem solving and provides some concrete examples.

If students need to construct their own understanding in order to learn, the best learning situations are those in which they are asked to take the initiative to solve problems. If learning is a social process, then problem-solving opportunities need to be set into a social context. Therefore, as you begin to think about planning music instruction, you should be thinking about establishing a learning environment rich in opportunities for collaborative problem solving.

ABOUT PROBLEM SOLVING

Learning through Problem Solving

Solving problems requires students to use what they know, but also provides opportunities for them to construct new understandings and clarify existing understandings. Some teachers view problem solving as a way of evaluating how much a student understands: therefore, they use it more as a means of assessment than as a teaching tool. It is important to realize that the process is much more complex than that—in the process of using what they know to figure something out, students are also increasing their knowledge base. Learning theorists like Dewey, Bruner, and Gardner talk about the role of problem solving in learning as more than a means of demonstrating understanding. While students' ability to solve problems certainly provides the teacher with information about the level and depth of their understanding, what is more important is that problem solving is an opportunity to further learning.

Teaching through Problem Solving

Teaching through problem solving is more of a mindset and approach to classroom experiences than it is a "methodology." If teachers truly understand that students need to figure things out for themselves in order to learn, their way of being in a classroom and ways of interacting with students will reflect that understanding. Sometimes a problem might take only seconds to solve, as in the scenario in Box 3.1, which is drawn from an actual case.

BOX 3.1 (VIGNETTE)

The tenth-grade band was on stage for the final dress rehearsal before their winter concert. As they were playing through one particular work, their teacher stopped the group and asked quickly, "Clarinets, the people who are not with my beat, are they ahead of or behind the beat?"

Students quickly responded, "Behind," to which the teacher replied, "Then can you fix it?" and the rehearsal continued.

This momentary exchange lasted less than a minute. What makes it a problem-solving situation is that the teacher put the onus on the students to figure out what the problem was and to solve it rather than telling them what they ought to be doing. Whether teachers plan extended units requiring solutions to complex, long-term problems or simply adjust their ways of interacting with students to put the onus on them to figure things out, the more problem solving they can incorporate into their teaching, the more productive and healthier the learning experiences they design will be for their students.

Collaborative Problem Solving

When students are given opportunities to work with others to solve problems, they learn even more than they might learn working alone because they benefit from the perspectives that others bring to the situation. Interacting with others provides them with a wider range of alternatives and possibilities, helping them see things in ways they may not have thought of on their own. Since knowledge includes not only factual information but also procedural and contextual information, solving problems in collaboration with others provides opportunities for students to expand their palette of choices of procedures and contexts.

Teachers who view problem solving as a "test" of individual progress sometimes see collaboration as "cheating." It is only cheating if there is an expectation of only one right answer and a need to find out who knows that answer and who does not. A well-designed problem has a multitude of solutions, and learners can gain a greater perspective by being a part of more than one of those solutions rather than by seeking the "right" answer.

Further, collaborating with peers provides support for individual learning because it provides individuals opportunities for immediate feedback on their ideas. This puts students in the position of having to explain, clarify, or defend their ideas to the group, which causes them to think things through more carefully and often results in a higher level of understanding within the group and on the part of the initiator of the idea. Collaborative problem solving also creates opportunities for modeling. Students can benefit from observing the ways in which both teachers and peers approach problems. From working with others, students can learn new strategies and ways those strategies can be used, providing both procedural and metacognitive models.

The Nature of Good Teaching Problems

The best problems for learning are those that reflect problems that occur in real life within a particular discipline—problems that require students to deal with the ideas and understandings intrinsic to that discipline. Solving real-life musical problems means solving problems using the same *thought processes* and *procedures* that real musicians use when they solve musical problems.

Music students need to engage in the same processes as expert musicians do—performing, listening, and creating. Even the youngest students engage in these processes and do not pretend to engage in them or engage in them in some superficial way. While students will not think and act with the same level of expertise as someone who is highly accomplished in the field, the nature of their thinking and acting should parallel what experts in the field actually do.

The classroom should be a place where students feel that any and all ideas are both welcome and valued by teacher and peers, which makes multiple perspective possible. Not every idea can be expressed through verbal communication. Students need to have available a multitude of ways of expressing their understanding and ideas, including nonverbal means of expression such as gesture and movement, graphic representation, musical expression such as singing, visual expression such as drawing, and so on.

Problems should be designed in a way that allows students to draw upon relevant prior experience to make solving the problem a possibility. This is an important consideration in instructional design. Learning experiences need to be connected in ways that allow students to draw upon previous experiences to solve the problem at hand (see Box 3.2).

BOX 3.2: THE NATURE OF GOOD TEACHING PROBLEMS

In general, good teaching problems:

- Reflect real-life problems that occur in the discipline.
- Require students to engage in the actual processes of the discipline, thinking and acting in the same ways as experts in the discipline.
- Require students to deal with the ideas and understandings intrinsic to the discipline.
- Enable students to formulate an understanding of concepts in a context that is genuinely appropriate to the discipline.
- Have a multitude of solutions and require students to make choices and decisions based on their understanding of the discipline.
- Allow for a variety of ways for students to express what they know.
- Provide opportunities for support from peers and teacher.
- Require and enable students to use what they know to figure things out for themselves.

With this understanding, let us consider what teaching music through problem solving might look like.

TEACHING MUSIC THROUGH PROBLEM SOLVING

Allowing students opportunities to solve genuine musical problems may prove to be the best way to nurture musical independence in our students. Since students should be engaged in performing, listening, and creating, time spent in a music classroom should entail working to solve performance-based problems, listening-based problems, and creating-based problems. Students should be solving musical problems through engaging in vocal and instrumental performance experiences, analytical listening experiences, and compositional and improvisational experiences. Solving musical problems should enable students to have opportunities to manipulate and make decisions about musical ideas based on what they know and understand about music. Problems should be designed to enable students to develop conceptual understanding of the structural elements of music (pitch, rhythm, form, texture, timbre, etc.) within the context of a genuine musical work (not a work contrived to teach the concept).

Good musical problems involve *musical* thought, which is more than verbal thought *about* music. They should be designed such that students will need to engage in thinking in sound—in hearing musical ideas in their heads, including pitch, duration, timbre, dynamics, tempo, form, texture, and so on. Good musical problems will enable students to act on those musical ideas, either by performing the music they hear in their heads, by analyzing their perceptions of what they hear during listening experiences, or by using their musical ideas to generate original compositions or improvisations—and by evaluating their own musical ideas in all of these contexts.

Teaching music through problem solving can mean designing complex problems that require extended time to solve. Older and more experienced students, in particular, enjoy engaging in long-range, complex projects or units that require a multitude of decisions and actions on the part of the learner. Often, older and more experienced students may work with one particular problem for an entire class period or even longer. They might, for example, participate in a unit that entails a small group composition project based on understandings developed during performing or listening experiences. The performing and/or listening experiences that comprise the introductory stages might occur during one or two class sessions. Students might then tackle the compositional project for two or three class sessions, followed by a communal sharing of ideas and a culminating lesson extending what was learned during the entire unit. A unit such as this might last as long as six or seven class sessions and might include a series of interconnected problems—an initial performance-based problem, followed by an analytical listening problem, followed by a compositional problem, ending with another analytical listening problem.

Extended units of problem-solving experiences are often necessary to enable students to feel at home in music of an unfamiliar culture. Understandings developed through a long-term series of projects, including opportunity for listening and performing, are essential to the development of understanding of world musics. After extended experience with music of an unfamiliar culture, students might then be asked to improvise or compose in the style of the music they have studied.

However, teaching through problem solving does not always mean designing complex problems that require extended time to solve. It might mean asking students to engage in solving a series of small problems throughout one particular class session. Most often, this will be the case in designing instruction for young and/or inexperienced students. The very youngest students will need to work with more teacher guidance and support, and they will probably not be ready to work independently or to sustain work on a project over a long period of time. Older students with little prior musical experience will not have the knowledge base to work without teacher support although, developmentally, they may be better prepared to maintain attention to a project over a longer period of time. Also, some material is more appropriately organized into a series of smaller problems. This is often the case with introductory experiences where students are experiencing a musical idea for the first time. Such experiences are likely to be organized as whole-group, teacher-guided lessons where the teacher poses a series of problems for the class to work together to solve. In this case, the key often lies in the ways in which the teacher chooses to phrase questions. Teachers can phrase questions in ways that might elicit one "correct" answer or in ways that imply a multitude of possibilities. Teachers can phrase questions in ways that lead students to particular answers or in ways that encourage them to figure things out for themselves (see Box 3.3).

BOX 3.3 (ACTIVITY)

Which of these questions would you consider to be good, open-ended, problem-solving questions?

- Last week we said that, when a song has two different melodies, we would call the first melody "A" and the second melody . . . ?
- Listen to this song and raise your hand when you think a new section of the melody has begun.
- How can you tell when music changes its speed? What are some things you might be listening for in order to tell?
- Which part of the music in your text looks like it would sound like the music I am singing? Why do you think that?
- How many beats does a quarter note get in $\frac{2}{4}$ time?
- If the instruments sound to you like they are not playing together, what might people need to do to fix that problem?

What does a musical problem look like? Following are some sample musical problems rooted in performing, listening, and creating experiences. It is important to note that in most cases, a problem utilizing one of these musical processes connects to a new problem that utilizes a different process. In other words, listening-based problems often lead quite naturally into creating-based problems that deal with the same musical elements. Performance-based problems often lead quite naturally into listening-based problems, particularly where students listen to and analyze recordings of music they have performed. Creating-based problems are most successful when related to prior performing or listening experiences. Therefore, in the sample problems described below, you will note that they are often linked to additional problems that utilize a different musical process.

Performance-Based Problems

Performance-based problems can take many different forms, the common thread being that students solve the problem primarily through performing. In some ways, just learning to perform a new song or piece is a musical problem. However, learning to perform the work through imitation of a model is quite different from learning the work through solving problems related to specific aspects of the work. Asking learners to mimic a song line by line does not challenge their ability to reason musically as much as asking them to figure out specific aspects of the song does. Students might be asked to figure out the melodic contour or rhythmic characteristics of a new song or to figure out its form or textural make-up. They might be asked to determine the harmonic structure so they will know what chords to play to accompany their singing. They might be asked to determine appropriate dynamic or tempo changes based on the way they think the work should sound. In each of these cases, they would need to hear the song performed in its entirety many times to make decisions or solve the problems. In this way, they become increasingly familiar with the song before ever attempting to sing it themselves. In this process, the teacher is still presenting a model, but the students are learning through their experience with the details of the song and not simply through imitation of the teacher's model.

There are many ways to teach music for performance besides asking students to imitate the teacher—ways that help students to focus on particular elements of the music and to formulate their understanding of the work in terms of those elements. Even in a performance ensemble setting, students can make many of the decisions. They can make decisions about the appropriateness of a particular dynamic level, tempo, choice of chord progression, choice of phrasing, choice of accompanying instrument, or overall balance or intonation of the ensemble. In order to grow as musicians, students need to develop an understanding of *why* musicians make these kinds of decisions and *how* the decisions are made.

Example 3.1: Sample Performance Problem

The following is an example of a performance problem based on the round "Hey, Ho! Nobody Home." The problem is designed to help students understand both the contour of the melody and the texture of the round, in addition to learning to perform the melody in a round with peers.

1. Each small group of students will need a set of the three charts below. Groups will arrange the charts in the order they think best matches the melody you are singing. Sing the song as many times as the students require until each group is satisfied with its solution to the problem.'

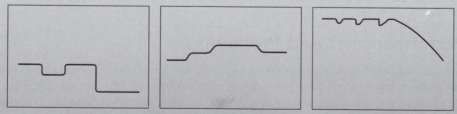

As they work together to solve the problem, students will most likely sing or hum the melody, or segments of the melody, to themselves. They will also probably need to talk quietly with their peers. This talk will reflect their understanding of the contour of the melody and their ability to describe and communicate that understanding.

2. Once finished arranging the charts, students are generally eager to sing through the melody in its entirety, often tracing their charts as they sing. It would be appropriate at this point for the whole class to try singing the song together, perhaps with teacher accompaniment. The teacher might even suggest that group members trace their contour charts as the class sings to double check their solutions to the problem.

3. This performance-based problem can easily be tied to an analytical listening problem by playing a recording of the song performed as a round and asking the students to describe what they hear. In this case, the problem to be solved is: "What do you hear in the recording that sounds different from our class performance of the song?" Students will probably point out numerous differences, which is appropriate and desirable.

4. Once students have analyzed the recording for its important points, an additional performance-based problem can be introduced. Challenge the students to sing the melody in a round as they heard it on the recording. Ask them to describe what they will have to do in order to carry this out. This is an important step because it can enable those who are uncertain to learn from strategies shared by peers and be more successful as a result.

As suggested in this scenario, these two performance-based problems and one listening-based problem can be combined to create one continuous lesson plan for the students. Upon completion of the lesson, students should have a better understanding of melodic contour and of the texture of a round. They will also have had opportunities to improve their personal skills in both graphing and singing melodic contour and in performing one melodic line against an opposing melodic line as a member of an ensemble, an ensemble that shares a common sense of underlying pulse, tonality, and simultaneity. The students are also likely to develop a far greater sense of these musical ideas than they might have in a setting where they were taught solely through imitation of the teacher. A further extension of this lesson could involve students working in pairs using xylophones or keyboards to develop original rounds. Students working from this knowledge base generally produce a melody that they then attempt to play as a round. At this level of experience, one cannot expect that the rounds will define "traditional" harmonies or even operate within a logical rhythmic organization, but the two aspects that have been studied by the students (melodic contour and canonic texture) generally appear in their work in this context.

Learning to perform music through problem-solving experiences fosters a greater understanding of the music performed and of music in general. It is important to approach performance in ways that will enable students to participate meaningfully. This means going beyond asking students to perform through imitation of the teacher—beyond echoing or chanting and then playing a part. It means providing students with the wherewithal to know how to decide what should be played or sung and how and why it should be played or sung in that way.

Listening-Based Problems

Listening-based problems also can take many different forms, the common thread being that students solve the problem primarily through listening—analytical listening, which requires listening for particular features of the work to solve the problem.

One characteristic that is unique to the process of listening is that an observer has no way of knowing what an individual is hearing unless he or she communicates it in some way. A teacher cannot tell whether a student is listening or what he or she is hearing by simply observing what the student is doing. Someone might be gazing out the window but listening very intently.

In order to deal with this in a teaching situation, it is essential that listening-based problems include at least one means of representing and communicating what students hear. Students might be asked to make a gestural or graphic representation of what they hear. They may be asked to organize "puzzle pieces" that graphically represent what the music sounds like. They may be asked to move in a way that shows what they hear. Students sometimes fill in charts with information they glean from the listening experience. They might try to represent what they hear through participating in another art form, such as language arts, visual art, drama, or dance. In each of these cases, it is essential that the focus remain on the music and on how the music expresses. One can easily maintain this focus by asking students, "What did you hear in the music that made you decide to move that way (or paint that way, or write that dialogue, etc.)?"[2]

In solving listening-based problems, students might be asked to represent their understanding of formal or textural characteristics of the work or of the organization of dynamic or tempo changes within the work. They might be asked to represent their understanding of pitch, harmonic or rhythmic characteristics, or even stylistic characteristics. Through analytical listening experiences, students broaden their understanding of the ways in which music is put together and the ways in which it operates. One of the perks of asking students to engage in these kinds of activities as they listen is that they find themselves needing to ask to hear the music again and again in order to know how to solve the problem at hand. This aspect is invaluable because repeated listenings afford students opportunities to become more familiar with the music and therefore to experience what the composer and performers are trying to express.

Example 3.2: Sample Listening Problems

 The following two examples of analytical listening problems are based on a sixteenth-century Renaissance dance, "Saltarello Giorgio" (CD, Track 1) and represent two different approaches to the same work. The problems are designed to help students use what they know about melodic contour to understand the form of the work.

VERSION 1

1. Students listen to the piece and in small groups decide how they will move (or walk) to reflect what they hear in the music. As they work, they will need to listen to the music again and again. When ready to share their ideas with the class, the different groups probably will have chosen to represent various aspects of the work—perhaps the melodic contour or rhythm, quite often the meter, and sometimes various stylistic characteristics as well. However, because the form is so obvious in this work, most students also choose to represent the arrangement of the two thematic ideas in their motions, making it easy to focus their attention on the form of the work during follow-up discussions.

2. Class discussion of the various solutions should focus on which aspects of the music the groups have chosen to portray, answering the question, "What do you think they heard in the music that made them decide to move that way?"

3. A logical follow-up experience would be to ask students to compose an original bithematic work based on what they have learned about how professional composers create a work out of two contrasting themes. Students work in small groups using classroom instruments, synthesizers, or composition software to develop a work that has an A theme and a B theme. To carry this out, each group will need to develop thematic material and decide how it will be arranged and repeated within the work.

VERSION 2

1. A different approach to the same piece is to ask students to work in a whole-class setting with a graphic representation of the rhythmic and pitch aspects of the melody. The piece consists of two distinctive melodies that appear in a typical dance form: AABBAABB. Students first consider graphic representations of the thematic material and predict what they think the music might sound like:

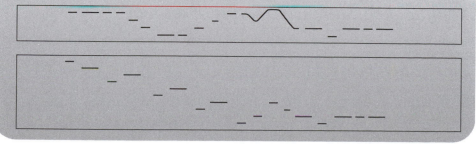

> Ask the students, "How do you think this music will sound? What makes you think that?" Students might then listen to the recording and compare their predictions to what they hear.
>
>   Focus attention on the rhythmic aspects of the melody. "Can you hear that this music is made up of mostly a pattern of long and short sounds?" [The piece has an underlying rhythmic pattern of (♩ | ♪ ♩ ♪ | ♪ ♩ ♪).]
>
> 2. Challenge the students to walk in a circle in a way that reflects the long/short pattern that is the predominant rhythmic pattern in the work. As they walk to the rhythm, can they circle to the right on the A theme and to the left on the B theme?
>
> 3. This version can be used to launch a composition project where students are asked to make up their own music that uses a combination of long and short sounds, causing them to focus on the rhythmic aspects of their work.

In listening-based problems, it is important to create a situation in which students need to hear the music played many times in order to solve the problem. This enables them to become intimately involved with the music, increasing their capacity to understand the music, and therefore, their capacity for response to the music. *Familiarity and increased understanding foster lifelong valuing.*

Creating-Based Problems

Creating-based problems can take many different forms and include the processes of composing, improvising, and even arranging. The common thread is that the students solve the problem primarily through the generation and organization of original musical ideas. Often, problems are constructed such that students are asked to work within particular parameters as they compose, improvise, or arrange. These parameters generally reflect particular elements of music, often linked to concepts learned through prior performing or listening experiences. By the nature of creative processes, students engaged in creating are solving musical problems. When composing or arranging, they are planning and evaluating solutions ahead of time—before the premiere performance of the work. When improvising, they are solving problems instantaneously as they perform.

Example 3.3: Sample Creating Problem

The following is an example of a composition-based problem based on understanding of the role of direction in melody.

Once students have experience working with melodic direction through analytical listening and performance-based activities, they may be ready to use their understanding of the concept to create an original composition. In previous lessons, they may have engaged in such activities as listening to "Leap Frog" from Bizet's *Jeux d'Enfants* (Children's Games), reflecting their understanding of the melodic direction through gesture or other movement or through graphic representation. They may have analyzed songs for passages that move "up and down," and they may have learned some songs where the melodic direction is a particularly pronounced and important aspect of the song, perhaps used to portray the lyrics.

1. Students can work in pairs or small groups to develop an original composition that is driven by melodic direction, where extremes in melodic direction are a central characteristic. Depending on the nature of their prior experiences, they might be asked to create an instrumental piece using barred instruments and/or keyboard instruments. Some students might try creating a piece using computer software, if available. (The software described in Chapter 5 works very well for an assignment like this one.) They may also be asked to write a song, setting a text where the lyrics are concerned with something related to the concept of "up and down"—or they might be asked to create original lyrics as well.

2. Once students have established how they will use melodic direction in their work, they may opt to add accompanying figures or nondirectional percussion parts.

3. In the final product, listeners ought to be able to hear how melodic direction has been used, but they should also be able to discuss other decisions made by the composers—decisions not necessarily related to melodic direction.

4. Students working on such an assignment might work during one class session to plan and practice their piece and then share their products with the class during the next session. As students share their work, the teacher should focus attention by asking, "How did this group decide to show up and down in their work?" and "What else did they decide to do? What other decisions did they make?"

BOX 3.4 (ACTIVITY)

Before moving on to Chapter 4, take some time to consider the sample problems you have just read. In each problem:

- What is the teacher trying to help the students learn?
- What are the students learning?
- What did the students need to know in order to be able to solve this problem?
- What is the problem? Can you articulate it?
- What did the teacher do to prepare the students to be able to solve the problem?
- How would the teacher know whether or not the students have understood what he or she was trying to teach?

ENDNOTES

1. Many of these ideas for designing performance problems come from Eunice Boardman, who also advocates teaching music through problem solving.
2. Many of the ideas for designing listening problems are from Lawrence Eisman, Queens College, CUNY, and Magne Espeland, Stord/Haugesund University College, Norway.

SELECTED RESOURCES

Bruner, J. 1960. *The process of education.* Cambridge: Harvard University Press.
Dewey, J. 1910. *Experience and education.* Chicago: University of Chicago Press.
Gardner, H. 1993. *Frames of mind: The theory of multiple intelligence,* 2d ed. New York: Basic Books.

PART 2
Planning for Teaching and Learning

Part 2 of this book will help you learn how to plan instruction by designing musical problems for your students to solve. Chapter 4 describes the thought processes that underlie instructional design. It will teach you how to plan a music lesson. Because many music teachers have had little prior experience designing instruction that includes opportunities for composing and improvising, Chapter 5 provides more detailed information about designing these kinds of musical problems for students.

Chapter 4

DESIGNING MUSICAL PROBLEMS

Drawing on the ideas established in Part 1, Chapter 4 will show you how to go about creating a lesson plan. You will learn about the elements of a good lesson plan and some of the thinking that teachers need to do in order to construct a successful lesson plan.

Now that you have had an opportunity to explore some musical problems, let us consider some of the thought processes that underlie the designing of musical problems. In this vision of teaching music, lesson planning *is* designing musical problems. Each music lesson should set forth a musical problem for students to solve. Thinking of a lesson as a *problem to be solved by the students* creates a situation in which the teacher must conceive of the lesson from the students' point of view. Lesson planning as *problem finding* creates a mindset that produces student-centered rather than teacher-centered lessons.

In designing musical problems for students to solve, one must take into account:

- What the students will be learning.
- What the students will be doing in order to learn.
- Through what music the students will be learning.
- How the learning will be organized.
- How the teacher will know that learning has taken place.

In order to plan a successful lesson, a music teacher needs to have a good understanding of all of these aspects of lesson planning.

First, let us consider the kinds of activities in which students might engage in a music classroom.

PERFORMING, LISTENING, CREATING

As was discussed in Chapters 2 and 3, in order to develop the kinds of skills, understandings, and sensitivities that comprise musicality and musicianship, individuals need to participate in all three means of interaction with music (performing, listening, and creating); and, ideally, these experiences should be interrelated. Further, insufficient opportunity for participation in listening and creative experiences along with performing experiences will place limits on the level of musical understanding students will be able to achieve.

As you consider the lessons and units of instruction in Chapters 6, 7, and 8, you will notice that, in many cases, an idea that is introduced through one means of interaction is followed by an experience with the same idea but through a different means of interaction. For example, students may be introduced to the idea of bithematic form (a piece constructed of two motivic ideas, e.g., AB or ABA) through a performing experience. They may then engage in analyzing a listening example for its formal structure and, in a subsequent lesson, compose an original bithematic piece. This series of integrated experiences—integrated in that the unit or series of experiences asks students to study the same musical idea through all three means of interaction with music—creates a platform for learning that is far more powerful than any single experience could be. It asks students to work with the same concept in all three arenas, enabling them to build their understanding of a multitude of dimensions and implications of the concept.

It is also important to recognize that, while the three means of interaction with music are distinct processes, there is a tremendous amount of overlap and commonality among them as well. The processes of performing, listening, and creating are intricately connected.

THE MUSICAL CONTEXT

In Chapters 1 and 2, you learned about the importance of contexts in learning. As you have seen, teaching for musical understanding requires musical contextuality. Good music teaching requires that each and every idea be drawn from or be related to an authentic piece of music. Music teachers must be certain that in each part of their lessons *all* material is drawn from an authentic musical context and that the *students* are fully aware of this connection. It is essential that the *students* understand the relationship between what is being taught and the musical work from which it is drawn.

Criteria for Selection of Music for Teaching

All music teaching should take place within the context of performing, listening, or creating experiences and within whole, legitimate musical works rather than works created as exercises to teach particular ideas. Selecting a musical context for teaching is one of the most important aspects of lesson design. Finding a good teaching piece can make a lesson almost write itself. Understanding what makes a musical work a good teaching piece is an important part of learning to teach music. Music teachers must take great care in deciding what music they will bring into their classrooms.

There are two critical criteria for selection of music for teaching: the structural complexity of the work, and its capacity to evoke aesthetic response in the listener or performer.

Capacity to Evoke Aesthetic Response

The well-known music education philosopher, Bennett Reimer, considers capacity for evoking aesthetic response to be the foremost criterion for selection of music for classroom use (Reimer, 1989). The extent to which the listener is able to comprehend the expressive characteristics of a work is directly related to his or her level of understanding of the work itself. This understanding can be interpreted as *structural understanding*. In other words, the more a student understands about the structural aspects of a musical work—how it is organized in terms of form, texture, or meter and how the expressive characteristics such as dynamics, tempo, or articulation function to produce the desired effect—the greater his or her capacity for aesthetic response. One cannot teach aesthetic response. The teacher can only help the student to increase his or her understanding of the ways in which music "works" in hopes that increased structural understanding will foster aesthetic understanding. This is the philosophy that underlies much music education practice in the United States and also provides the basis for the ideas expressed in this book.

While musics of non-Western cultures may not be organized in the same ways as Western music, most children in American schools perceive non-Western music through schemas they have developed through their experience with Western music. For example, in the musics of some cultures, concepts of meter or harmony may not be intrinsic or important. Instead, perhaps the essence lies in the organization and arrangement of particular melodic or rhythmic patterns. Students with schemas for Western music can certainly learn to use part of what they know about their own music to begin to understand how some non-Western musics are put together. Conversely, in American schools where a majority of the population has been raised in a particular non-Western musical culture, a music teacher would have to reverse the process. In that case, the teacher would have to begin with the music of the students' culture and then help them to use what they understand about their own music to begin to understand Western music. The principles remain the same—students need opportunities to use what they already know and understand to learn about new musical ideas and concepts.

Structure of the Musical Work: A "Doorway In"

In selecting musical works for teaching novice listeners, it is important to seek works in which particular structural or expressive elements are quite obvious and exposed. In some ways what we are seeking is structural simplicity—works that contain obvious expressive or structural characteristics that will immediately strike the listener. As they study and come to know the music, students will become involved with the more subtle aspects of the work as well. Therefore, it is important to find pieces that have an inviting "doorway" into their midst. For example, in Jacques Ibert's "Parade" (see Chapter 6, pp. 149–151), students first will be drawn into the obvious dynamic changes designed to suggest a

parade moving up and down the street (making dynamic change a good "doorway in"). However, through the repeated listenings necessary to complete the assignment, they will also become aware of other more subtle characteristics of the work, such as the constant beat or the instrumentation chosen to impersonate a marching band. They might even notice that the beat pauses at two places, a sort of joke that would probably not occur in a real-life parade setting. The piece was selected because it is a rich source through which students can begin to formulate understandings about decisions composers make in generating particular effects. It is a delightful work that will inspire children and will hopefully evoke in them some sort of "higher-level" understanding and response.

Additional Considerations

Additional criteria for selection of music should also be considered. Music for teaching should be representative of *a wide range of musical styles, genres, and media,* emanating from a *variety of historical and cultural settings.* Music permeates many facets of life. Experience with music of all kinds nurtures understanding of both the commonalities and differences among musics and can serve to broaden the palette of choices for students in their own lives.

In selecting pieces for listening lessons, *length* is also an important consideration. Musical examples need to be short enough to enable inexperienced listeners to comprehend all that is occurring during the work. They also need to be short enough to enable students to listen to them many times over as they work to solve the problems drawn from the pieces. In order for students to be able to experience complete musical ideas, as the composers intended them to be heard, wherever possible it is best to try to avoid using excerpts. If excerpts are unavoidable, one must be careful to extract them in a way that allows the composer to "finish a thought."

Listening pieces also need to be appealing to students, particularly when the students are young. While a broad range of musical works would fit this criterion, one might give consideration to the presence of contrast. Music with striking contrasts in dynamics, tempo, instrumentation, and so on is good for teaching purposes because it demonstrates so clearly the ways in which music functions.

Pieces selected for performing lessons should be pitched within a suitable vocal range and deal with suitable subject matter for the students. They should be challenging enough for students to be able to learn from the performing experience but simple enough for students to be able to be successful in performing the work well. Consider which aspects of the performance will be within the students' grasp. Will they be able to accompany their own singing by playing the chords on Autoharps, guitars, or synthesizers? Will they be able to successfully sing the countermelody with the melody? Will they be able to eventually perform the song without teacher assistance?

In creating experiences, children's own musical ideas form the musical context. However, it is often best to link creating experiences to either performing or listening experiences. In these cases, one would seek performing or listening experiences that would serve as good models for creative process.

A summary of these criteria is presented in Box 4.1.

BOX 4.1: CRITERIA FOR SELECTION OF MUSIC FOR TEACHING

In general, when selecting music for teaching, the work should be:

- Structurally simple.
- Capable of evoking aesthetic response in the listener or performer.
- Representative of a wide range of musical styles, genres, and media emanating from a variety of historical and cultural settings.

For listening lessons, the work should be:

- Short enough for the novice to comprehend it in its entirety.
- Short enough for repeated listenings.
- Appealing to the listener (perhaps with striking contrasts).

For performing lessons, the work should be:

- In a suitable vocal range.
- Dealing with suitable subject matter.
- Challenging enough to learn from.
- Simple enough for student success.

For creating lessons, the characteristics of the assignment should have:

- Qualities that enable it to be linked to performing and/or listening pieces that will serve as good models for creative process.

Once you have selected music for teaching, you need to consider what it is you expect the students to learn from interacting with it.

MUSICAL CONCEPTS AND PRINCIPLES

Whether engaged in performing, listening, or creating experiences, students in music classrooms should be learning musical concepts and principles and how those concepts and principles operate within the musical works they are studying. In order to understand how to design musical problems, you, as the teacher, must have a high level of understanding of the connections between musical concepts and principles and musical compositions.

In order to understand what music teachers teach, you need to think about your own conceptual understanding of music. As musicians, each of us holds a complex schema for music in our minds. What might this schema look like? Members of different musical cultures have different ways of defining and talking about music. However, in order to establish a common ground from which to begin talking about teaching and learning music, let us use as a starting point this definition: *Music is sound, moving through time and space, organized to express.* Sounds can be organized in perhaps an infinite number of ways, but musicians have been able to identify certain characteristics or elements that seem to be common to most things we call music. These elements are highly interconnected and interact with one another to produce a musical work. Western musicians generally conceive of music as outlined in Figure 4.1. Some of these concepts apply to non-Western musics as well, but some do not. What is considered central to the music varies from culture to culture. These structural elements of Western music, however, offer a starting place for teaching American students to understand the music of their world.

FIGURE 4.1

Music consists of:
    pitch (high and low)
    arranged in lines of **melody** that have:
        contour   (shape)
        direction   (up and down)
    and consist of:
        intervals   (skips and steps)
    arranged in:
        phrases
    focused around:
        a **tonal center** (home tone)
    functioning within a particular:
        modality   (major, minor, Dorian, pentatonic, non-Western
                        scales, etc.)
    combined to produce or imply:
        harmony   (related to the development of a sense of simultaneity
                        and ensemble)

Pitched and nonpitched sounds also have:
    duration or **rhythm**   (long and short) (also sound and silence)
        dependent upon an understanding of steady **beat** (also related to
        development of a sense of simultaneity and ensemble)
    in which some beats have:
        accent   (strong and weak)
    the arrangement of which results in:
        meter   (heard as groups of twos or threes)
and move through time characterized by:
    tempo   (fast and slow)
    volume or **dynamics**   (loud and soft)

> **timbre** or **tone color**   (sound source)
>   acoustic sounds: instrumental, vocal, body percussion,
>   environmental
>   synthesized sounds: electronic sounds
> **articulation**   (smooth and choppy)
>   (how the sound sources are played)
>
>
> *and are organized by:*
> **texture**   (thick and thin—for younger students)
>   number and arrangement of voices
>   monophony, polyphony, homophony—which includes melody and
>   accompaniment as well as chordal motion
>   (also related to the development of a sense of simultaneity and
>   ensemble)
> **form** (repetition and contrast)
>   (same and different—for younger students)
>   basically concerned with melodic or thematic structure of the work
>
>
> *combined in ways that produce:*
> **style**
>   a result of combination of all of the above qualities and characteristics
> **affect** (the way the music makes you feel)
>   a result of combination of all of the above qualities and characteristics

American music teachers have been basing instruction on musical elements since Bruner (1960) first suggested a vision of curricular design that was based on the structural elements of a given field of knowledge. Since that time, music instruction has been designed around musical elements but methods of teaching have not always led students to *conceptual* understanding of these elements, which was Bruner's intent. Contemporary learning theorists, like Gardner (1991), talk about knowledge as conceptual understanding and the knowledge base of the various subject areas consisting of not only concepts but also principles (see Box 4.2).

BOX 4.2 THINK ABOUT THIS . . .

A great deal has been written for music teachers about musical concepts but very little on musical principles. Perhaps musical principles include things like simultaneity and ensemble, or balance, or tension and release, which are certainly part of musical understanding. These principles seem broader than the specific elements, as they seem to connect to more than one of the elements. Simultaneity and ensemble are related to rhythm and texture but also to pitch in terms of intonation. Balance is also related to ensemble. Tension and release are an important part of harmony, but are also linked to rhythm, dynamics, tempo, and even form. Can you think of other musical principles that seem to override and connect the musical elements? These would be important understandings for students to develop as well.

As students formulate their understanding of these structural elements and principles of music and of how they are interrelated within a musical work, they are building their *conceptual* understanding of music. These are the understandings a student needs to hold in order to understand how to make music, hear music, create music, and read and write musical notation. These structural elements and principles of music are *what* music teachers in all kinds of music classes need to teach their students.

The Interactive Nature of Music

We can break a musical work into many different parts and talk about it from many viewpoints. We can discuss its form, texture, tonality, or harmonic structure. We can talk about the setting of lyrics, style of performance, or the nature of the articulation or phrasing. We can discuss use of tone color, range, and tessitura or the change in dynamics, tempo, or meter. We can understand a piece of music from so many different vantage points, each one a valid part of the whole work. However, the effect of a whole musical work depends on the ways in which *all* of the elements of music interact within that whole. Music is never *only* loud or *only* fast. The essence of a piece of music is in the ways in which all of its different aspects come together—that a particular passage is soft *and* high *and* staccato *and* in $\frac{5}{4}$ time *and* in Dorian mode, and so on. If this is the way music "works"—if this is its essence—then we must take this into account when we teach music.

This means that we should not play a series of excerpts to show students what fast or slow music sounds like. In order for them to really understand the role of tempo in a work, they need to study how the tempo is related to other aspects of the piece. In order for them to understand the effect of a particular choice of tempo, they must experience the work on more than just a superficial level. Musical elements must be taught within the context of a whole musical work, and students must have enough time to experience all the ways in which the particular element operates within that piece. Further, it is not enough for students to learn to merely identify loud and soft or fast and slow. It is important for them to begin to understand that these are some of the tools musicians use to express musical ideas—to understand that people use music as a vehicle for expression.

A "Doorway In"

Finding a "doorway in" is an analogy designed to help teachers plan instruction to enable students to develop a structural understanding of music—an understanding that will empower their ability to listen to, perform, and create music, and enrich their capacity to understand what the music expresses. It is an image to help teachers choose music from which to teach and create lessons that will maximize student understanding of the music and of the ways in which music operates.

In order to understand this analogy, let us again consider the structural elements of music presented in Figure 4.1. Any piece or song that students might listen to, perform, compose, or improvise is likely to contain *all* of these elements, which is precisely why we teach the elements. However, in a given work, it is likely that some of the elements will be more pronounced and more obvious than others. In some cases, it is one particular element above all others that drives a particular work. When this is the case, it generally makes the piece an excellent choice for teaching. For example, a work that is basically one huge crescendo or one long accelerando or is driven by extreme contrasts in tone color and range would be quite easily understood by inexperienced listeners. A work in which a simple melody is clearly organized in a particular textural plan, such as a round or canon, can be understood easily by inexperienced performers. Inexperienced composers find it easier to create original works when asked to focus on one particular element, such as developing a piece that moves from soft to loud or from slow to fast.

However, remember that in each of these cases, although one particular structural element may appear to drive the whole work, *all* of the other elements are operating within the piece as well. A composition that is basically one huge crescendo will also have a particular harmonic structure, rhythmic structure, organization of thematic material, and textural organization and will be performed with particular tone colors, articulation, phrasing, dynamics, and so on. A simple round also operates within a particular meter, tonality, harmonic structure, and so on. Students composing their own music that moves from soft to loud will still have to make decisions about tone color, thematic material, texture, meter, tempo, and so on.

The point is that the one obvious structural element that appears to be driving the work can be considered a "doorway in" to your students' understanding of the whole work. It is necessary to begin somewhere. Why not begin with the most obvious feature? Music teachers have actually been taking this approach for many years. The general music textbook series are full of lessons in which students listen to a sampling of works that have very obvious features in common or where two contrasting works are studied (one that is very slow and one that is very fast, or one that moves in twos and one that moves in threes). A cursory trip through a musical experience that shows students only the most obvious features of several works does not allow them to formulate an understanding of why a composer might make such a choice. To really understand the work, they must have opportunities to study it more closely and in greater depth. Pieces with one or two obvious features are excellent teaching pieces because those particular features can easily be used as a "doorway in" to a deeper understanding of the work and of music in general.

In a listening lesson, after students have identified or responded to the most obvious feature, ask them, "What *else* do you hear?" Encourage repeated listenings. Encourage them to share and discuss all of what they hear and how all of those things work together to produce a particular effect.

In a performing lesson, once students have mastered the most obvious feature (e.g., able to sing a round), ask them, "What *else* can we do to make this piece exciting and interesting?" Encourage them to evaluate their own performances and consider and experiment with options.

In a composition lesson, once students have shared their finished products ask, "What *else* did they do?" (besides what the assignment required, that is). Encourage students to analyze and discuss the musical decisions made by their peers (e.g., "Their piece did start slowly and get faster like it was supposed to, but they also had a 'tune and a background' and they started quietly and got louder too."). Analyzing one another's musical decisions helps provide a wider palette of choices for students in subsequent composition assignments. The more they understand about choices peers have made in carrying out assignments, the more they are capable of doing it on their own the next time they have the opportunity to do so.

In listening lessons, the "doorway in" is an obvious feature of the work to be studied, one that all students are likely to hear easily during the first listening experience. If you plan your lessons so that students will need to listen to the work again and again, they will come to know the greater complexities of the work and have a better chance of understanding it on a deeper level.

In performing lessons, the "doorway in" is an obvious feature of the work to be studied, one that all students are likely to hear and understand easily during the first performing experience. If you plan your lessons so that students will need to perform the work again and again, they will come to know the greater complexities of the work and have a better chance of understanding it on a deeper level.

In creating lessons, the "doorway in" is an obvious feature of the work to be created, one that all students are likely to be able to understand and carry out easily during the creating experience. The very nature of creative process necessitates the manipulation of all of the elements of music. Students cannot create a work without making decisions about virtually all of the structural elements. However, these may not all be conscious decisions. For example, they may not know about meter, but they will create within a particular meter just because of their life experience in the music of their world (which means, for children raised in American pop music culture, the meter will likely be duple). They may not know about harmonic structure, but they will create pieces that operate within the tonal system that is familiar to them just because of their experience with the music of their world (which means, for American children, the tonality will likely be major). If you plan your lessons so that students have opportunities to create original music, they will become more and more proficient at operating within music systems and come to know the greater complexities of music in general.

Providing students with opportunities to become intimately involved with the pieces they listen to, perform, and create enables them to develop a broader and deeper understanding of the ways in which music "works," which greatly enhances their opportunities for understanding what music communicates.

ORGANIZATION FOR INSTRUCTION

As was discussed in Chapters 1 and 2, classroom instruction should take place through a variety of settings, including teacher-guided, whole-group instruction; small group work; and pair and independent work (see pp. 37–40). In planning a lesson, you need to think about how instruction will be organized in a general sense, but you must also remain open to other options and possibilities that might arise during the teaching/learning process. The purpose of using a variety of organizational settings is to provide students with the optimal conditions for learning at all times. The lesson and unit plans in Chapters 6, 7, and 8 provide examples of what it is to teach through a variety of instructional settings.

ASSESSMENT

Assessment should be an ongoing process occurring throughout the teaching/learning experience. It is through assessing student understanding that teachers make decisions about the effectiveness of their teaching and about what should come next. In a classroom, assessment takes place on both formal and informal levels throughout the teaching/learning experience. Informally, teachers monitor student understanding throughout the lesson and make decisions about pacing, readiness for new material, and the need for reteaching. Formally, teachers design particular activities to seek specific information about the level and extent of student understanding of a particular concept.

Assessment is an integral part of planning on several levels. First, in order to know how to plan instruction, teachers need ways of assessing the prior knowledge students bring into the classroom. Second, throughout the teaching of a lesson, teachers need to be aware of the extent of the class's understanding of what is being taught in order to know how to proceed at each point within the lesson. Third, teachers need ways of determining the extent of individual students' understanding within the class, for both teaching and accountability purposes. Fourth, assessment of the overall level of understanding of the group (class or grade level) can be a part of determining what should be taught next in the curriculum.

Assessing Students' Prior Knowledge

Students grow up in a world full of music. They enter the classroom knowing more about music than they are able to articulate and more than they are aware of knowing. Part of teaching is helping them to recognize what they already know and using that knowledge to explore more complex issues. How, then, does the teacher find out what students already know? One good starting point is to think carefully about what *you* know about the music of their experience. Teachers are generally aware of the kinds of music their students are apt to be listening to outside of school. Thinking about the most obvious characteristics of the music of your students' lives will provide some good places to begin instruction.

In your initial planning, however, it is important to create opportunities where students will be able to share with you what they already know. These might be listening experiences in which you ask students to tell or show you what they hear, from which you can deduce what they do not yet hear. They might be creating experiences, in which students have opportunities to show you what they already know about constructing a piece of music and what they do not. They might be performing experiences, in which students show their competence and prior experience through their level of success in performing a work. You will learn what students know and do not know by engaging in musical processes with them.

Throughout these experiences, it is important to listen carefully to what students say and do. If you do not understand what they are saying or doing, ask questions. Ask questions that will cause students to think and respond with explanations and details rather than one-word answers. Carefully observe students in both their verbal and musical interactions. You can learn an enormous amount about student perspective by just "tuning in" to your students and to what they are doing and saying during music experiences. Examples of some entry-level assessment experiences appear in Chapter 6, on pp. 121–123.

Building Assessment Techniques into Lessons

In designing lessons, it is essential to build into your planning numerous opportunities through which you will be able to find out whether or not students are understanding what you are teaching. This ongoing assessment must take place throughout the lesson. It may take the form of formal and informal teacher questions and student answers or student questions and teacher answers. Opportunities for the teacher to learn about student perspective arise during student/student interactions as well.

Teachers also monitor student progress during lessons by observing what students do as they participate in making or listening to music. Listen to the music they make and watch the ways they move as they make it. Be aware of who is singing and/or playing accurately; who needs more support; who can find the beat, meter, B section, and who cannot. Use your eyes and your ears; connect with students to try to understand the situation from their perspective. If they are having problems or are unsure, can you figure out the cause? Can you provide support to help them to become more successful?

You can build more formal means of assessment of student understanding into your lesson plans by including activities that, by their nature, reveal the extent of student understanding. Such activities include composing or improvising within specific parameters; creating graphic representations of what they have heard, performed, or composed; moving in ways that reflect their understanding of music they have heard, performed, or composed; or performing music in a specific way. More specific suggestions are shared in the lesson and unit plans in Chapters 6, 7, and 8.

Formal Assessment of Individual Progress

While it is important to have a sense of where the whole class is in terms of understanding and progress, it is also important to be aware of the progress and extent of understanding of individual students within the group. This is important to the teaching process but also because, as a professional, you are accountable for knowing about the progress of your individual students. This is the information you will be asked to share with parents at some point in the semester, either through parent-teacher conferences or through formal grades or report cards.

Most general music teachers have a student load that makes this seem like a daunting task. However, it is less daunting for teachers who make an effort to incorporate assessment strategies into their teaching as a matter of routine. Teachers who make it a point to constantly interact with individual students and to be aware of what students are doing and saying in their classes find it easier to assess individuals. Also, teachers who plan instructional time to include small group and independent work have many more opportunities to get to know their students as individuals.

In designing more formalized assessment, it is important to use *authentic assessment* techniques. That is, assessment activities should be real-life problem-solving experiences designed to enable students to demonstrate their understanding of musical ideas in a musical context.

One of the most authentic ways to document student work is through *portfolio assessment*. You may be familiar with this technique because professional assessment of teachers is often done through portfolios. In a general music classroom, a students' portfolio may not take the form of an actual folder of papers because much of the students' work is oral and aural. One idea is to use audio- and videotapes to capture student work (with parental permission). Videotaping a whole grade level's work on a particular composition assignment can provide an excellent overview, which can be helpful in planning the next phase of instruction. It also provides an opportunity for the teacher to look at the work of individuals in the context of the work of their peers, which can be helpful in determining what "successful" work for a particular assignment might be. There is also information to be gained by recording work-in-progress in addition to finished products. Such tapes can provide valuable information about the ways students are thinking about a particular concept as they work. If students generally work with the same small group of peers, you can keep an audiotape as a kind of portfolio for each group, dropping it into the tape recorder whenever that particular group performs an original work or recording a performance of the whole class. At some point, the students in each group can be given an opportunity to listen to their tape and comment about the decisions they made as they worked and their own progress as represented by the tape. That tape can then be sent home as an audio-portfolio to be shared with parents. An important aspect of this is students' self-assessment. This is probably a more important aspect than the teacher's assessment because, ultimately, it is the students who need to know their own strengths and weaknesses and where they need to grow.

Another technique that is commonly found in classrooms is an *assessment rubric*. A rubric lists criteria that will be assessed and a description of various levels of proficiency in the various criteria. The rubric is then used by either teacher or students to describe student work. For examples of assessment rubrics, please see pp. 168 and 191 in Chapter 7 and pp. 206, 215, and 226 in Chapter 8.

Students can also engage in self-assessment and assessment of peers using a rubric in the shape of a target (see Figure 4.2).[1] For example, they might be asked to decide whether a particular effort is "on target," "off target," "near the edge," or a "bull's-eye."

FIGURE 4.2

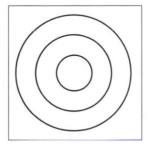

This approach can be used to assess work in performing, creating, or listening settings. A class would first have to decide what constitutes "on target," "off target," and so on. This might be done by asking the students to describe the characteristics of successful work and contrasting that with the characteristics of less than successful work. These descriptions could then be posted prominently in the classroom while the students are working and could ultimately become the rubric through which the teacher assesses students' understanding or proficiency.

Assessment and Curricular Decisions

There is an integral relationship between the assessment of student understanding and the planning of instructional goals. Teachers need to use what they learn about the extent of understanding of the group as a whole to determine what to teach next. In this way, assessment can drive curricular planning. Teachers need to provide themselves with vehicles for reflecting on the overall progress of students in their program. Audiotaping and videotaping lessons and student products is one way to achieve this. Teachers also need to spend time carefully reflecting on curricular goals and on how effective they think a particular lesson or unit was in reaching those goals. Thus, even on the level of the individual music lesson, assessment of students plays a key role in determining what and how you will teach. This process will become more clear as we examine the nature of lesson planning.

LESSON PLANNING

To summarize, in a music lesson students will be (*a*) learning musical concepts and principles through (*b*) engaging in performing, listening, and creating experiences (*c*) set into viable musical context, (*d*) in the context of a whole group, small group, pair, or independent instructional setting with (*e*) a variety of means of assessment built into the lesson. With that understanding, you are ready to begin thinking about how to plan a lesson (Box 4.3).

BOX 4.3

To design a lesson:

1. Decide which musical element(s), concept(s), or principle(s) will be your focus ("doorway in").
2. Decide which musical work(s) you will use (musical context).
3. Decide the primary means of interaction (performing, analytical listening, creating).
4. Choose an appropriate organizational setting.
    a. Teacher-directed lesson in a whole class setting.
    b. Independent work in small groups, with partners, or as individuals.
5. Consider how you will know whether or not the students have learned what you set out to teach (means of assessment).

In designing a lesson, one must take all the factors shown in Box 4.3 into consideration. But where does one begin the process? Most often, teachers begin either with a musical work they have identified as a good teaching piece or with an idea of what they would like to teach (Steps 1 or 2 in Box 4.3). Ideally, a teacher would like to be able to identify a need in his or her students—through assessment of student understanding, identify an area that needs enhancement or extension. In an ideal situation, you would start with Step 1 ["Decide which characteristic(s) or organizational element(s) of music will be your focus"] and then proceed to look for a good teaching piece to use as a context for the lesson.

However, there will be times when you might come upon a great teaching piece and the piece itself will become the starting point for the planning of the lesson. You may think to yourself, "This would be a great piece for teaching form [or texture or meter or whatever]," and you may begin designing a lesson inspired by the particular musical work. There is nothing wrong with working this way (beginning with Step 2). The danger lies in deciding to carry out the lesson in class at an inappropriate time. What you choose to teach on a particular day must be determined in relation to what has come before and where you are headed. Therefore, there will be times when you may discover a wonderful teaching piece, set it into an exciting lesson plan, but need to put it on hold until your students are ready.

While, in most cases, the starting point for developing a lesson will either be the concept you are trying to teach or the music through which you will teach the concept, there are also times when the nature of the activity could be your point of entry. A colleague might ask whether students could perform or compose a song for an upcoming school assembly program, or you might look through your plan book and realize that students have spent quite a bit of time composing during the last two months and are probably ready for a lesson that involves a large-group singing experience. In these cases, the nature of the classroom activities might serve as a starting point for planning. In this same way, the nature of the instructional setting might become a deciding factor. Perhaps the students have spent quite a bit of time working in small groups; it might be a good time to bring everyone together into some kind of large-group activity with more teacher support. The starting point for planning a lesson, therefore, could be Step 3 ("Decide what will be the primary means of interaction in which the students will engage") or Step 4 ("Choose an appropriate organizational setting").

Most important, decisions about what to teach next should be driven by a need determined through assessment of the students' understanding during previous lessons. Deciding what to teach and when to teach it is directly related to information gleaned through assessment (Step 5, "Consider how you will know whether or not the students have learned what you set out to teach"). As a professional, you will use this information to guide you in knowing what to teach next. However, as a novice teacher, you may not find it as helpful a place to begin learning how to plan lessons. As you begin the process of learning to design lessons, the easiest points of entry are probably Steps 1 and 2, the content and context of the lesson.

Planning the Problem

Once you have selected a musical work and decided what you will teach from the work, it is time to design the lesson. To be an effective lesson, what you design should be an experience in which the students are asked to solve a problem. Remember that good musical problems require students to engage in musical thinking—to hear music in their heads and make judgments and decisions about what they hear. Remember also that good problems allow for a variety of ways for students to express what they know. Students will not be able to express in words everything they hear and know in the music. They will need opportunities to express what they hear and know through a number of nonverbal means, including musical performance, graphic representation, gesture, movement, and use of manipulatives, charts, signs, pictures, and so forth.

Once you have decided (*a*) what the students will be learning, (*b*) what the students will be doing in order to learn, (*c*) through what music the students will be learning, (*d*) how the learning will be organized, and (*e*) how the teacher will know that learning has taken place, it is time to write out the plan so that it can be put into action. The steps in Box 4.4 might be helpful in guiding your thinking in this process.

BOX 4.4

- Design a musical problem emanating from one musical concept, element, or principle drawn from a musical context.
- Create a need to know (from the student's perspective).
- What groundwork will be necessary for students to be able to solve the problem?
- How will the students work to solve the problem?
- How will they share their solutions to the problem?

We have already discussed designing the musical problem itself. Once it has been designed, how does the teacher put it into motion? First, you should understand that students are motivated to do what they perceive as important. Including students in their own learning process can motivate them. In other words, students are often reluctant to engage in a particular activity just because the teacher asks them to do so. If they know *why* they are being asked to do something, their energies become more focused on the task at hand. This can be accomplished by sharing with students your own thinking about why they are being asked to engage in the particular activity.

For example, say that students in a fourth-grade class have just completed the culminating activity in a unit on tempo change. They have spent two class periods composing original instrumental pieces that have at least one slow section and one fast section. In assessing the students' work, the teacher has noticed that, while they were successful in showing their understanding of tempo and tempo change, in general their thematic material was relatively unimaginative. Most students chose nonpitched instruments, and most used the same rhythm pattern for both their slow and fast sections. From his assessment of the student work, this teacher has decided that these students need more experiences with melodic contour and variety. He might begin the lesson by saying:

> Boys and girls, the pieces you wrote last week were wonderful. You really showed that you understand the effect a tempo change can create in a piece of music. Your ideas were very exciting. One of the things I noticed was that in most of the pieces, students chose to play instruments that could not play a tune. Most of what you played had interesting rhythms but your music did not go up or down in any way. So, I think it would be a good idea for us to look at some songs—songs that use repeated rhythm patterns in the same way you did in your pieces but where the rhythm patterns move through all different pitches. Some of the rhythm patterns go up and down; others skip all over the place. Let's look at what professional musicians do to use repeated rhythm patterns in more interesting ways. This might give you some ideas you might want to use the next time you compose your own music.

The effect of this kind of interaction is to create a need to know from the students' perspective. This is critical to the success of a lesson. Students need to know what they are supposed to be learning and why. If this information is shared with them, they can participate willingly and honestly and become partners in their own learning process. What is even more exciting is when, as a result of working on a particular problem, students themselves comment that they need to learn more about an aspect of music. However, it usually takes some experience for students to reach this point.

Once students understand why they are being asked to engage in the particular activity, it is time to lay the groundwork necessary for them to be able to solve the problem. Most often, this takes place in a large-group, teacher-guided setting. It is the time when directions are given or preliminary activities take place. During this time, the students must be provided with enough information to enable them to work to solve the problem. It is a time for making connections to prior experiences, a time for making certain that everyone knows what to do and how to do it.

The next phase of the lesson is usually where the bulk of the time lies, where the students work to find solutions to the problem at hand. It is important for the teacher to keep in mind that, while the problem may have been designed around one particular focus or element (the "doorway in"), the students will probably need to make decisions about many other elements of music in order to solve the problem. Therefore, the teacher must remain "tuned in" to student questions and comments that may seem to deviate from the intended purpose of the lesson.

The final stage of the process is generally the time when students share their solutions to the musical problem. A great deal of teaching often takes place during this part of the lesson. As students share solutions, the teacher needs to ask questions like: "Why did you make that choice?" "What did you hear in the music that made you decide to walk that way? (draw that shape? choose that puzzle piece?)" Exploring student solutions to problems can reveal a tremendous amount about the depth and breadth of their understanding. Celebrating student solutions can be tremendously rewarding for students and certainly motivates future learning.

It is important to recognize that some problems may take students two minutes to solve and some may take two weeks. The process, however, is generally the same. A lesson may contain a series of shorter, but related, problems to be solved, and students might move from one to the next during one class session. On the other hand, some lessons (particularly those that involve original musical thought, like composition lessons) might actually take several class sessions. Older students, in particular, thrive during long-term problem-solving projects. They tend to enjoy the autonomy and opportunity for decision making independent of a teacher. Long-term problem-solving projects give students a sense of ownership of the music classroom and of the music curriculum. Exploring the sample lessons in Chapters 6, 7, and 8 should give the reader a better understanding of the wide variety of problems that students can be asked to solve. At this point, suffice it to say that whether a problem is long term or momentary the process used to design the lesson is essentially the same.

In writing out lesson plans, you might find the format suggested in Figure 4.3 to be helpful.

80

Figure 4.3: Lesson Plan Format

Materials:

Recording, Song, or other Musical Context

Instruments

Charts, Supplies, Props

Lesson assumes:

What prior knowledge or experience is this lesson building upon?

What are you assuming the students already know, understand, are able to do?

Standards or Guidlines: (National, State, District, etc.)

Grade:

Organization:

How will the bulk of the work be organized?

Whole group? Small groups? Pairs? Independent work?

Objective:

To help students formulate an understanding of _____ or expand their understanding of _____ or use what they know about _____ to _____.

Connection to prior knowledge/experience:

Connect to something students already know or have done.

Groundwork that enables:

Lay the groundwork that will enable the students to solve the problem.

Pose problem(s):

What will the students be doing and why?

Students solve problem(s):

How will the students work to solve the problem(s)?

What processes will be involved?

Students share and discuss solutions:

How and when will the students share and discuss their solutions to the problem(s)?

Assessment:

How will you know they have understood? What will give you a window into the nature and depth of their understanding?

(Should be ongoing throughout lesson. Should reflect the specific objectives of the lesson.)

Extension:

In what ways might the students carry these ideas further? extend or expand their understanding? apply these ideas to new situations?

Assessment of Lesson Planning

The ability to assess the success of a lesson is something that all teachers need to develop. Even a highly experienced teacher does not know whether a lesson will be successful until he or she has put the lesson into practice. As a professional, you will probably design lessons that may be taught to several different groups of students (e.g., four different fifth-grade classes). A particular lesson might work very well with one group of students and not nearly as well with another. Over time, teachers learn to assess and evaluate their own lessons so that they know which plans have potential for success and which plans need to be improved upon or eliminated.

Once working in the profession, teachers have very little opportunity to get feedback about lessons from either peers or supervisors. While teachers occasionally are observed by peers or supervisors, most of the time they need to be able to evaluate the success of their own teaching, reflect on what needs to be improved, and make the improvements on their own.

As students learn to teach, it is also important that they learn to critique their own lessons. The assessment rubric included here (see Figure 4.4), or something similar, might be used by an instructor to comment on and assess students' planning and teaching or might be used by students as a vehicle for self-assessment.

FIGURE 4.4   **LESSON PLAN ASSESSMENT RUBRIC**

	not present in lesson	present in lesson	present with good understanding	present with sophisticated understanding
The lesson is designed to enable students to better understand an essential element of music.				
The lesson is constructed as a real-life problem for students to solve.				
The problem is set into or drawn from a musical context.				
The musical context is appropriate (aesthetic qualities, structural simplicity, length, age level, range, etc.).				
Sufficient groundwork is established to enable students to solve the problem.				
Students engage in performing, creating or listening in order to solve the problem.				
Means of assessing student understanding are present throughout the lesson.				

With this mindset of how to conceive of a musical problem-solving lesson, let us now look at some sample lessons. The lesson plans described in the next three chapters are categorized according to the level of students' prior experience. At this point, you might also want to try constructing some of your own musical problems (perhaps in the ways described in Boxes 4.5 and 4.6).

BOX 4.5 (ACTIVITY)

Working together with your own peers, try to write out one of the lessons described in Chapter 3 using the lesson plan format. This may give you a better understanding of this vision of planning instruction.

BOX 4.6 (ACTIVITY)

With a partner, plan a musical problem for your peers to solve. In class, lead your peers in carrying out the problem. Using the lesson plan format, can the class construct a lesson plan based on what you have done?

ENDNOTE

1. This target idea comes from Loretta Ackroyd, a general music teacher in the Farmington Hills Public Schools, Michigan.

SELECTED RESOURCE

Wiggins, G., and J. McTighe. 1998. *Understanding by design.* Alexandria, Va.: Association for Supervision and Curriculum Development. This resource addresses assessment issues.

Chapter 5

A CLOSER LOOK AT CREATIVE PROBLEMS

In your own school music experience, it is likely that you had little or no opportunity to compose or improvise original music in your general music classes. To help you better understand the possibilities for your own students, Chapter 5 focuses on creative process, providing a closer look at issues related to planning and carrying out composition and improvisation lessons in classrooms.

The processes of creating music are found less often in music classrooms than are performing and listening. As a result, you probably have had less personal experience with this aspect of music teaching in practice. This chapter is designed to help you establish a context for understanding composing, improvising, and arranging in a music class setting.

ABOUT COMPOSING

Any time students engage in preplanned performance of original musical ideas, they are composing. Compositional ideas are those that have been planned to the extent that the students would be able to replicate their performance upon request. Students in music classes can compose both songs and instrumental pieces.

Many people view engaging in the process of composing original music as something that is set aside for a select few. Many believe that the amount of expertise required to compose music makes it something that children cannot do. Most children are not ready to write novels, either, but schools do consider the process of writing to be a basic element of the curriculum. In the same way, while students may not be ready to compose a symphony, they can certainly learn to engage in the process of creating original musical ideas.

Composing is one form of thinking in music. Musical thought is part of what Howard Gardner means by musical intelligence. Musical thought is more than thinking *about* music; it is thinking *in* music. Opportunities for thinking in music are essential to music education process. They are part of what helps students to formulate their understanding of music.

If students are in a music program that includes opportunities for performance only, with no opportunities for listening or creating, it is comparable to being in a language arts program in which students have opportunities to read but not to speak or write. Language arts teachers understand the strength of teaching reading, writing, listening, and speaking in combination, each experience strengthening the others. In our field, we need to think about the powerful connections among performing, listening, and creating experiences and about how each experience strengthens our ability to participate successfully in the others.[1]

Composing with Instruments

Students can compose original music using classroom instruments, band or orchestral instruments, piano, guitar, synthesizers, compositional software on a computer, or even "found sounds." While students create interesting and successful pieces using instruments generally found in music classrooms (barred instruments, assorted percussion, recorders, Autoharps, and so on), bringing real-world instruments into the classroom as additional options for student use brings a certain amount of credibility into the classroom as well. Orchestral instruments can be used in schools that have established instrumental programs. This is an opportunity for students who are learning to play these instruments to encounter different kinds of playing experiences. In this case, students would play their own instruments, which they would bring to school for the purpose.

In today's culture, guitars and synthesizers are powerful tools in the music classroom because their presence aids in the perception of what happens in the music classroom as "real music." Many school music experiences are perceived by students as "school music" and not "real music." Teaching through problem solving—and enabling students to function in ways that musicians function—generates a feeling among students that they are learning "real music." Using the tools of the students' culture (guitars and synthesizers) adds dramatically to this perception. Further, students need to have experience playing synthesizers in live performance settings—playing together with peers— before they would be able to use them effectively in a MIDI[2] station, which is likely to be an option for older students. Finally, because of their wealth of timbres, synthesizers seem to be rather inspiring to young composers. Music that students compose on synthesizers is often very different from the more rhythmic works they generally produce on classroom acoustic percussion instruments. Synthesizer pieces are often "gluey" conglomerations of layers of sound organized in very different ways from percussion pieces. Synthesizers also provide an easy way to bring non-Western timbres into the classroom, because of the wide variety of synthesizer programs available. Students also become much more conversant with harmony in their compositions when they compose at keyboard instruments, including synthesizers and piano.

Instrumental Composition Problems

Instrumental composition problems are most successful when based on prior listening and performing experiences. Generally, it is best to structure composition assignments around a particular parameter or structural element of music ("doorway in"). Students can be asked to create a piece in a particular form (AB, ABA, rondo, variation on a theme, etc.) or a particular texture (round or canon, solo line with accompaniment, etc.). They might be asked to use dynamics as an organizer (starting softly and getting louder) or tempo (make a slow section, a fast section and a transition between the two) or meter (make a piece that starts in twos and then changes to threes).

When designing compositional problems, it is important to keep in mind that whatever the parameter ("doorway in") set forth by the teacher, the students will have to make decisions about all the other elements of music in order to create a musical work. For example, students working to create a piece that utilizes dynamic contrast will still have to make decisions about motivic material (pitch and rhythm), meter, tempo, form, texture, tonality, modality, and so on. While not all of these decisions will be conscious ones, it would not be possible to create a piece of music without attending to all the elements, which is, of course, why we consider them to be the elements of music.

Because consciously thinking of all these things at one time would be very inhibiting to the creative process, students find it easier to solve compositional problems that involve fewer specifications established by the teacher. It is often difficult and intimidating for students to focus on preestablished limitations for several elements at the same time. An assignment to create a piece that has a particular form and texture, that uses a particular rhythm pattern, and that moves in a meter of three contains too many parameters to be helpful to the students. They are apt not to know where to begin. At some point in the process, they will need to develop original motivic material and need to feel they can think freely in sound in order to do so. Students do not "happen upon" motivic material. Research into children's compositional processes as they work with peers to create original works in general music class settings has produced a great deal of evidence that supports the idea that students first hear a musical idea in their heads and then try to figure out how to play on an instrument what they are hearing (Wiggins, 1992, 1994, 1995, 2000/01). For example, if a teacher were to limit the pitches available to the student, she might create a situation in which students are seeking pitches they hear in their heads but are not permitted to use for this particular composition.

Whatever the assignment, it is best if the students first consider ways a "professional" has chosen to solve that particular compositional problem. Before composing an ABA piece, students should study examples of songs or pieces that have two contrasting themes. They should listen to a work that is in ABA form and be sure they understand how that work is organized. Before improvising or composing layered polyrhythms similar to those found in some African music, students should spend time listening to one or more accessible African pieces to be sure they understand how the works are organized. Using the students' understanding of their own performance and listening repertoire as a basis for compositional projects helps them to know how to proceed when composing on their own. Looking at the decisions made by professional composers or performers helps them to be better decision makers in their own work. It also furthers their understanding of the listening and performing experiences. It is important to recognize that student success in compositional experiences is often reflective of the extent of the preparation that led up to the assignment. If students have trouble with or are unable to complete an assignment, it is important for the teacher to consider whether or not he provided the students with sufficient prior experience to ensure that they would know how to proceed. When students are unsuccessful in solving compositional problems, it is often the fault of the teacher. Preparatory work for a compositional project should make the assignment so clear that they are "chomping at the bit" while the teacher is explaining it. Before they begin, students need to feel as though they already know what to do in order to be successful.

In sharing final products, it is important to celebrate and validate all efforts. It is also important for the teacher to use this time to assess the work that the whole class (or grade level) has produced with an eye toward future planning. Students are generally quite satisfied with the work they have produced. If there are shortcomings, it is best to address these in future lessons, possibly through performing and listening experiences. Then, when it is time to once again engage in a compositional project, remind the students to attend to whatever the shortcoming was. The goal here is not to produce a perfect product but rather to learn through the process. If student work on a form piece generally lacks textural variety, you might point that out to the students, in a general sense rather than singling out individual student work. It might make sense, then, to teach a performance-based and listening-based unit on texture, followed by a compositional experience that focuses on textural variety. As you continue working this way, the overall level of student compositional products should gradually improve over time. This will be reflective of their growing understanding of how a piece of music is put together and is far more productive than asking students to rework one particular assignment—an assignment they view as already "finished."

With a group of your own peers, try the activity in Box 5.1.

BOX 5.1 (ACTIVITY)

With a group, compose a piece in ABA form for classroom instruments, with optional introduction, bridge, and/or coda. Share the finished products with the whole class. During the sharing, try to comment about what you heard in each group's music but also about what it was like to participate in the experience. As a participant, what kinds of decisions did you have to make? What kinds of musical decisions were made? Were all of your decisions conscious? In what ways were you operating like a musician? Do you think this would be a worthwhile experience for students in your own class? Why or why not?

Notes on Small-Group Composition Projects

Generally, it is preferable to permit students to choose their own group members. From prior experience both in and out of the music classroom, students seem to be able to seek out peers who have a work style similar to their own and who think as they do. If the social dynamics of a particular group seem to be problematic during one project, you can be sure those students will choose not to work together for a subsequent project. If their energies are focused on the project and on success in carrying it out, they will find a way to make this happen. Students are eager to be successful and will solve their own social problems as one way of achieving that goal.

In general, groups should contain somewhere between four and six students. Students often find that they need at least four people to create and perform ideas of any complexity. More than six people tends to create a situation where there are simply too many ideas being suggested to make the work feasible. Even groups of six often inadvertently become two groups of three, as the ideas flow.

Decisions about how much time to allow for students to complete a composition assignment are difficult to make, especially in a school day where there never seems to be enough contact time for music. However, you should keep in mind that students are able to find more complex solutions to compositional problems if they are given a longer period of time in which to work. *The sophistication of students' projects and the depth of their commitment to them will be reflective of the time allotted for creative process.*

Free Instrumental Composition

"Free" instrumental composition is a way of describing projects in which the teacher does not set any parameters for the compositions. For students who have never composed, the instructions "Make up any music you want to" could be immensely intimidating. They might not know where to begin. However, for students who have spent the school year composing music to fit specific parameters, it is a welcome charge. Students working in a composition-based program often generate numerous thematic ideas throughout the semester that they have rejected because the ideas did not fit a particular assignment or because a peer preferred to use a different idea. Such students generally welcome an opportunity to use these ideas or related ideas. Therefore, as the semester or course draws to a close, you might allow your students some time to use the classroom instruments to compose whatever they would like. You may be surprised at the complexity of what is produced.

Songwriting

Songwriting is quite easy for students of all ages because children grow up surrounded by songs. They know a great deal about how songs are put together. Very young children may not be able to articulate what they know about songs; but, when asked to create one, they know that songs have verses and refrains, that the title of the song is often found in the refrain, that the text generally rhymes, that songs are sung while instruments play a background part, that songs can be fast or slow or happy or sad or scary or funny, and so on. While students may not be able to articulate what they know, with teacher support they can certainly make up a song that has these characteristics.

Older students who have had experience writing songs with teacher support often learn to become quite independent in the process. They become a community of composers in much the same way that language arts teachers refer to their students as a community of writers. For these students, composing becomes a vehicle for personal expression, which makes the music classroom a very exciting place to be.

Songwriting for Beginners

The first time students work together as a class to write an original song, they will require the most teacher support. In subsequent songwriting experiences, they will be able to assume more and more of the responsibility until they are eventually able to compose a song on their own. While some children may be able to function independently at the outset, it is important to set forth a general process that will enable more-hesitant students to participate and succeed as well.

With first-time songwriters of any age, the easiest place to begin is generally with the lyrics. More-experienced composers may choose to begin with other elements such as an interesting bass line, an accompaniment pattern, a drum part, or a melodic idea. Experienced composers often talk about form or performance style while they are creating lyrics. They will often speak a line of lyrics and then, immediately, set it into a melodic context or compose melody and lyrics simultaneously. However, first-time composers who are unaccustomed to the process seem to feel most comfortable generating most of the lyrics before beginning work on the music.

You might begin by asking students to brainstorm a topic. One that is interesting and relevant to the majority of students in the class is best. Depending upon the way language arts is taught in the school, students will use different approaches to creating a poem for the text. Some will begin with an opening line; others will continue to brainstorm ideas and relevant catch phrases and then assemble the suggested ideas into a poem. Students usually do not need to be taught that song lyrics are poetry. Their life experience has taught them that, and they generally fall quite naturally into rhyme schemes and metric speech. If not, it is helpful for the teacher to repeat ideas suggested by the students in a somewhat rhythmic fashion. The students generally will follow suit, and subsequent ideas often will be suggested with attention to the rhythmic flow and number of beats per line. Ideas suggested by the very youngest students may not fall into these kinds of patterns. If that is the case, you can take either of two approaches: *(a)* work with the students to compose a free-flowing through-composed song or *(b)* help the students fit their ideas into a more rhythmic pattern. Either way, it is important to be sensitive to the flow of ideas emanating from the group. The song must be a product of the students' ideas and not the teacher's. It is not the product that is important, but the process. Listen carefully to the students and tune in to their perceptions of how the song should sound. Be certain the song is *their* song.

Once a set of lyrics has been generated, the next step in writing a song will vary from situation to situation. It is not uncommon for individual students to subtly or intentionally suggest a melody, a portion of a melody, or even a stylistic characteristic that represents their vision of the song. A whole class does not really write a song simultaneously. What they produce will be a product of the ideas individuals have suggested within the group process. It is important to be sensitive to the ways in which students articulate ideas. They may reveal their own perception of how they want the song to sound in the ways they suggest or talk about the lyrics or the drum part they are thinking about or the modality they hear. Often, it works well to just ask, "Now that we have our words, how do you want them to go? Any ideas about how the song should sound?" If you give students a bit of time to think, you may be on your way within minutes as suggestions emerge from the group.

With first-time composers, however, such questions may be met with silence and, perhaps, some nervousness or hesitation. ("Does he think *I* know how the song should go?") In that case, the teacher needs to take more of the initiative. Because the goal is for the students to generate an original melody, it sometimes works best for the teacher to suggest at this point some alternative accompaniment patterns that the group might use. These can be played on any instrument that can establish a harmonic structure for the song—piano, synthesizer, guitar, Autoharp, etc. When students are very hesitant, you might begin by suggesting an accompaniment pattern that you think is highly inappropriate for their text. This sometimes prompts them, in rejecting what the teacher has suggested, to propose alternatives that they find preferable. If not, try playing several different accompaniment patterns—perhaps chanting some of the lyrics over each—and letting the students vote on the one they prefer.

Once an accompaniment pattern has been agreed upon by the group, play a rather standard chord progression (I–IV–V$_7$, I–ii–vi–V$_7$, etc.) in that pattern and ask the students to chant the text while you play.[3] As the melody emerges from the group, be sensitive to the possibility of altering or abandoning your original chord progression. You might start the group chanting but should allow the group to determine the "lay of the text" over the accompaniment. If there are discrepancies, point them out and come to some sort of consensus ("These people seem to be putting a pause after this word, and these people are not. Which way do you like better? Let's try them both and decide.") Once they have agreed on an accompaniment pattern and on how the text will fit the pattern, ask the whole group to sing the song. Explain that you understand that they will all be singing different tunes at the same time and that that is the intent in this initial stage. Ask them to sing their melodies again and again. After a while, some sort of consensus should arise from the group. Students generally gravitate toward one or two ideas that can then be set forth and voted upon. Once they have agreed on a melody, the song is essentially finished. This entire process may take one or two classes. Experienced composers can usually compose a song in as little as 20 minutes because they tend to think about lyrics, melody, and accompaniment as all one entity.

Once the song is complete, you might use a subsequent class period to develop an arrangement of the work. You might record the work on either audiotape or videotape, perform it for another class, or share it in a schoolwide performance. It is helpful to present each student in the class with a written copy of the song. Using music notation software, the teacher can generate a printed version that includes melody, lyrics, and chord symbols. Where the composer's name would be written, it could say, for example, "Class 3-B." For very young children, the teacher might generate a printed version that is written in icons instead of musical symbols. Since younger children are new to reading words as well as music, be sure lyrics are printed clearly. Encourage the students to perform their song from the printed page and to take the music home to share with their families. This is actually a very effective way of teaching note reading because the motivation is so high and because the songs students write tend to have predictable melodies, few leaps, and lots of repetition.

Please note that I am suggesting that notation of the songs take place *after* the song is created. Songwriting should not be viewed as a lesson in symbolic notation. Students who are new to music reading are not yet capable of thinking through that medium. They need to think in sound and to hear in their heads the way they want the song to sound. They do not yet know how to think through symbols. Further, teachers should not establish inappropriate parameters emanating from notation issues or issues of musical convention, such as determining how many measures each line of the song should last. The song needs to flow as a product of the musical ideas of the students. They will communicate the way they want the song to sound by the way they decide to sing it. Students generally do create songs that operate within the Western tonal system because that is the music of their experience. However, it is not uncommon for them to sing their songs in ways that reflect key or meter changes or an occasional three-beat measure within a duple song. The teacher should endeavor to represent the students' ideas accurately and not edit them to conventions. Children's rhythms are often syncopated because this is a common characteristic of the music of their experience. Teachers need to print the rhythms as the children sang them and not edit those rhythms to create music that can be used for a notation lesson using only rhythms the students already know how to read. This is not the purpose of such a lesson. Songwriting is a real-life experience, and students have a right to have their ideas portrayed accurately—as they would be in real life.

Printed copies of original songs can be bound into songbooks, using equipment commonly found in language arts publishing centers. Original songs also can be preserved and shared through audiotape. Tape duplication is an inexpensive process. Producing tapes of student work in a school recording studio parallels the real-life experience language arts teachers try to establish with their publishing centers. Keep in mind that publishing a book of original songs that reflects more of the teacher's work than it does the students' own creative process does not constitute a real-life problem-solving experience. Unless the students have engaged in genuine compositional thinking processes and procedures, the fact that a real-life book has been published is meaningless to the students' learning. It is not the activity that must be authentic, it is the process.

Children who compose original songs see themselves as a community of composers in much the same way as language arts programs encourage them to see themselves as a community of writers. You might find this community of composers to be quite prolific. Once children know that they are capable of writing songs, they generally continue to do so on their own. Students who grow up composing original music see the process as an important and integral one in their lives. It becomes one of their primary vehicles for expressing the things they care about. When important events happen in their world or in the world in general, students often choose to write songs about them—and want to have the songs performed in public places as a means of sharing what the event means to them.

When a school music program becomes a community of composers, students tend to view everything they do in the music class as teaching them more about writing their own music. Incorporating composing—and particularly songwriting—enables students to envision the music curriculum from a very personal point of view. It becomes an extremely powerful force in their lives.[4]

Examples of Class Songs

All about Puppies

First-Grade Class

TV Madness

Second-Grade Class

T   V   Mad-ness,   T   V   Mad-ness,   Fun   to watch and   see,

T   V   Mad - ness,   T   V   Mad - ness,   Fun   for you and   me.

Use   your im - ag - i - na   -   tion.   When you   watch   T   V.

When the show   is   o   -   ver,   Be   what you want to   be.   Or you could

be   a   couch po - ta   -   to ____   Just   ly - ing   there all   day.   Or

when the   next   show is   o - ver   You could   go out - side and   play.

Weird Week

Third-Grade Class

Stuck in the Stuffing

Fourth-Grade Class

Chicken Pox

Dream Your Future

Fifth/Sixth-Grade Class

Dreams can mean man - y things. We might dream of hav-ing wings

Or of be-ing the great-est of kings, What-ev - er your im - ag - i - na - tion

brings. What will hap-pen to - mor - row? What will

be? What will life bring to - mor - row? We shall see.

Dreams can be the way you live. Dreams can make you want to give.

Dreams can pre-dict what the fu - ture will hold. They can in-spire you

wheth-er you're young or old. What will hap-pen to - mor - row?

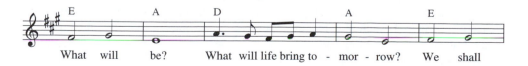

What will be? What will life bring to - mor - row? We shall

Songwriting for More-Experienced Students

Students who have had experience writing songs in a large-group setting with teacher support soon become competent enough in the process to pursue it in small groups, with a partner, and in independent work settings. Actually, in practice, more-experienced students find it increasingly difficult to compose as a class because, as they become more proficient in the process, there are simply too many ideas being expressed to make the situation manageable. The teacher can easily recognize when students have reached this point because, when too many ideas are set forth, they tend to argue about whose ideas should be used. More-experienced composers become quite possessive about their musical ideas and are less likely to want to give them up to produce a work by consensus. This is not really problematic. Rather, it is a clear signal to the teacher that the students are ready to work on their own so that everyone's ideas can be developed and carried through.

When students work in small groups and as individuals to compose songs, the classroom becomes a flurry of activity. Groups and individuals progress through the process at different rates, depending upon flow of ideas and work styles. This makes it possible for the teacher to be available to most students at the time he or she is needed—different students will have different needs at different times during the process. For example, some groups or individuals will work with a tremendous amount of independence and not seek assistance until they are finished with their songs and are ready for help recording or writing them out. They may even develop their own accompaniment for their song. Other students will be more hesitant and require support from the outset ("We can't think of anything. Can you help us?"). Students rarely have *no* ideas, even though they may claim that to be the case. You might respond to such statements with, "Show me what you have so far." More often than not, students *do* have ideas but are not sure how to begin to work with them. Some students will get started on their own, select a topic, generate most or all of their lyrics, and then seek the teacher's assistance in getting started setting the text. Such students require the same kind of support as might be provided to the whole group in writing a class song. They may need the teacher to establish a harmonic progression and/or accompaniment pattern while they chant their lyrics and develop a melody that fits with the accompaniment. During small-group songwriting experiences, teachers are likely to be providing support for uncertain students in the beginning of the time frame, helping more independent students set their texts in the middle of the unit, and helping most everyone with finishing touches toward the end of the unit. That students finish their pieces at all different times actually makes it easier to have time to tape record those who are finished and time to notate the music.

Songs written by individuals can be treated in much the same way as class songs. They can be notated and distributed to the composers and shared with others. They can be audiotaped or videotaped or performed in concerts. In making recordings, student composers can be asked to "hire" singers to perform their work and be responsible for teaching their song and arrangement to peers. In many cases, at least in the early stages of independent songwriting, the teacher will need to be a member of the ensemble that performs each work—generally providing harmonic support. However, many older students study piano and guitar outside of school and are often capable of developing an accompaniment for a student song. Students might also opt to develop accompaniments on classroom instruments or perform their songs *a cappella*. Synthesizers and drum tracks can give student songs a contemporary flair. Older students may be ready to create accompaniments for songs using sequencing techniques in MIDI stations. Students working under these circumstances may enter into the process from a slightly different angle, beginning with drum tracks, bass lines, and chords, and then developing song material that fits with the background they have created. There is no right or wrong way to write a song. The ideas suggested here are designed to get students started in the process. With experience, they will develop their own preferences for how to proceed.

Composing with Computers

There is already a great deal of composition software available for computers, and, as time goes on, there is likely to be much more. As computers become more and more commonplace in music classrooms, teachers need to be able to decide which software is appropriate for their students' needs and which may not be as useful.

One important criterion is the amount of student input involved in using the program. Beware of software that composes *for* students instead of allowing students to compose *using* the software. Some programs allow students to organize chunks of music, but do not permit them to generate original thematic ideas. Good compositional software should enable students to generate motivic material, set it into a context, and manipulate it within that context. A program like *Making Music* (Subotnick, 1995) requires no MIDI setup and enables students to engage in all of these processes. Students can create thematic material by simply moving the mouse—up for a sound that goes up and down for a sound that goes down. If students move the mouse sideways for a long or short time, they hear a long or short sound and see it represented on the screen by appropriate graphics. Using the mouse, students can enter the pitch and duration data that they want to use. The computer plays the music as they create it and represents the music on the screen in iconic "piano-roll" notation. Students can select a timbre from a palette of sounds, and each timbre is represented on the screen by a different color. They can hear their melodies at any time by clicking on "play." Once students have created a melody or set of melodies they like, they can create accompanying sounds or edit the music in just about any way conceivable. The material can be rhythmically augmented or diminished, melodically inverted or played in retrograde, played louder or softer, faster or slower, or with a new timbre. Students of all ages will enjoy experimenting with a program such as this. This particular program is designed so that students do not have to be able to read words or music to compose with it. Its originator, a composer himself, set out to create a medium in which people could "finger paint in sound" (Subotnick, 1995, 32–33).

Once students become more experienced composing with computer software and they know more about what it is to create a musical work, they may want to use software that will give them more control over the specific pitches and durations that they use in their pieces. At this point, then, they are ready to use simple sequencing/printing software, such as *Freestyle* (1994), which requires a MIDI setup with computer and synthesizer. A program such as this one will allow students to play the music they want on the keyboard and see it represented on the screen in either iconic "piano-roll" notation or traditional music notation. Students can easily flip back and forth between the two forms of notation throughout their work process. They can select timbres (any that are in the keyboard) and, like *Making Music*, each timbre appears on the screen in a different color. Students can easily edit their music on screen by clicking on a note or icon and dragging it higher, lower, longer, or shorter (always accompanied by the sound the note or icon will make, so the decision can be made by ear and not eye). Students can learn to develop thematic material, percussion parts, chordal accompaniments, and so on, and set them all into a portion of the program that allows them to organize the larger form of the work. Student work can easily be played back at any time and saved to disk. Most sequencer programs also print out notated versions of pieces, and this is true of *Freestyle* as well. The program will print out exactly what is on the screen, including options for creating a title, lyrics, and other commonly used markings.

It would seem that using computers to compose original music may be one of the best uses of technology in music classrooms. When students are working in small groups to compose, it is easy to set up the situation in which some students are working at computers and others at instruments. This is an ideal way to integrate technology into music teaching—an appropriate and authentic way because composing, sequencing, and printing are ways that musicians actually use computer technology. This is a far more effective means of helping students to understand the role of technology in music production than using computers as a platform for theory, note-reading, and ear-training exercises (which are not part of what professional musicians really do with technology and may not be appropriate activities for a general music curriculum).

Schoolwide Publication of Original Compositions

You may decide to produce a songbook and audiotape of student work in a format that can become part of the school library or classroom libraries. Classes of younger students can compose class songs for the book in March, for example. During that month, those songs can be transcribed and recorded. Also in March, older students could begin to work in small groups, pairs, and as individuals (their choice) to compose either songs or free instrumental compositions. Throughout March and April, these, too, would be transcribed and recorded as they are completed. Students who finish their projects early can become performers of other students' work, as needed. Some might write a second work during the same time period. By the end of April, all work has been produced, recorded, and transcribed, giving you whatever spare time can be found during the month of May to duplicate and assemble songbooks and duplicate cassette tapes. Professional audiotape duplication is very reasonably priced and language arts publishing centers often have teacher assistants who can help create the books. In June, you can share the music schoolwide in the remaining music class sessions. During these sharing sessions, you are likely to find your students "glued to" the songbooks listening eagerly to their peers' music—commenting, praising, and (after a while) sight-singing the songs along with the recordings. Individual students become celebrities overnight, with their songs resounding in the hallways and on school buses. Students begin talking about what they might do differently for next year's songbook. This project has the potential to be the most influential and driving force in the whole music program because the students become that passionate about their desire to produce a product that represents to everyone who and what they are. The value students place on having the right to use music as a vehicle for personal expression can override anything else we can do for them as music teachers.

ABOUT IMPROVISING

Any time students spontaneously perform original musical ideas in real time, they are improvising. While compositional ideas are preplanned so that students would be able to repeat their performance on request, improvised ideas are planned *during* performance and are therefore more difficult to replicate. Students can be asked to improvise original musical ideas under many different kinds of circumstances, some more structured than others.

When asking students to improvise, it is important to be accepting of whatever is produced but also to take the time to discuss and acknowledge particularly successful improvisations. This provides students with models that will help them to build an understanding of the goals and objectives of participating in improvisatory music making. Learning from peers is a powerful influence in this kind of setting.

Anyone can improvise original music. Improvising is just "thinking out loud" in sound. What prevents most of us from doing it is inexperience and fear. Keep in mind that students have not yet developed inhibitions about improvising music. Children will freely generate musical ideas when given the opportunity.

Like composing, improvising is a form of thinking in music. Opportunities for thinking in music are essential to music education process because of the role they play in helping students to formulate their understanding of music.

Unstructured Improvisation

Students might engage in free, unstructured kinds of improvisation where they use a variety of sounds to produce a particular effect, such as in a whole-class improvisation of a scary Halloween piece or the like. When engaging in such experiences, teachers should encourage students to watch and listen to classmates carefully and to try to fit the sounds they are making with the sounds others are making. After a few different attempts, encourage discussion about how the versions differed. Encourage exploration. Encourage leadership and initiative on the part of the students.

Improvising with Voices

Students can also learn to improvise vocally. You might establish a simple repeating chord progression either on the piano or as sung chords. Once students are familiar with the sound of a chord progression (by ear), they can easily sing melodies that fit with that progression. They will make decisions as to which pitches to sing by determining what feels comfortable. To help students feel more secure, the whole class might improvise melodies simultaneously. Eventually, you might ask one row at a time to "take a solo" until individuals feel comfortable enough to work on their own.

More-Structured Instrumental Improvisation

While instrumentalists can engage in free improvisatory activities, it is also important for them to learn to work within particular chord progressions as well. In a general music classroom, students as young as fourth grade can use synthesizers, Autoharps and/or guitars to establish underlying harmonies while individuals perform melodic improvisations on xylophones or resonator bells. You might set up the bars so that each student has only the pitches of one chord. It then becomes the responsibility of that student to keep track of when that particular chord is being played by the other students. The students learn to hear the harmony shift and to know where their part fits into the whole. Keep chord progressions short and simple, but allow each chord to last long enough for soloists to have time to think. Students generally have much less trouble figuring this out than you might believe they will. Most have grown up within the Western tonal system and function within it with ease and comfort.

 Essential to the study of most world music traditions is opportunity to improvise in the style of the music studied. For example, students might listen to and analyze a Ghanaian xylophone piece (featured on pp. 148–149 and on CD, Track 4). Then, they can use their understanding of the structure of the piece as a basis for creating original improvised music.

Ideas for Improvising Experiences

A good starting activity is to ask students to "set the mood" for a song by improvising an introduction or a coda. This can be done by a few individuals or by the whole class on classroom instruments or synthesizers or even using vocal and body sounds. Young children also enjoy telling stories through music. This kind of experience can be more than creating sound effects to accompany a story (which is usually more of a language arts lesson than a music lesson). Children might read or hear a short story and then decide how to tell the story without words so that the story becomes an organizational plan for the musical improvisation, which makes it a genuine musical activity rather than a language arts activity.

Older students enjoy engaging in "conducted" improvisations where one student gives signals and cues to a group of players (or the whole class), indicating how the music should be played. Student conductors do not need to use conventional conducting signals. They can use signals that have been agreed upon by the group. They might make up signals that represent cues, cutoffs, dynamic changes, tempo changes, solo vs. ensemble performance, etc. Throughout the experience, the improvisers in the group decide what they will play on their instruments (motivic material). The conductor makes decisions as to who will play, when they will play, how fast or loud they should play, when they should stop, and so on. Older students also enjoy working from a movie theme idea, where they create the background music for a particular mood or scene. Another way to begin is to ask performers to sit in a circle where they can see one another and one another's instruments clearly. A volunteer might suggest an opening theme, either a melodic or rhythmic idea. Using eye contact and other forms of nonverbal communication, students work with the theme within the circle, imitating it, changing it, adding to it in a spontaneous fashion.

It is important to establish a classroom atmosphere in which it is commonplace for students to invent original musical ideas. For students who have opportunities to improvise original music, their capacity for initiating original ideas grows over time and through experience. With this comes a growth in musical understanding and capacity for musical thought (see Box 5.2).

BOX 5.2 (ACTIVITY)

With your peers and using general music classroom instruments, try some of these suggestions for improvisatory experiences. How does it feel to have such an opportunity? Do you think your students would enjoy having the same opportunity? What kinds of musical decisions does one have to make during these kinds of experiences?

Sample Improvisation Problem

The following is an example of an improvisation problem based on a scene from a familiar story.

Students are generally very familiar with the nature of background music because of its extensive use to establish mood in movies and television shows.[5] In this experience, they will create background music for a particular scene from a novel. Choose a novel they know well.

Many fourth-grade students are familiar with the novel *The Lion, the Witch, and the Wardrobe,* by C. S. Lewis. The story is about children who like to play inside a turn-of-the-century wardrobe. As they do, the back of the wardrobe opens (or perhaps their imaginations open) revealing a magical land called Narnia. The first time one of the children in the story sees Narnia, it is night and the ground is covered with snow. Her attention is drawn to a solitary lamppost casting its light upon the snow. All is very quiet and serene. Suddenly, a horse-drawn carriage enters the scene.

1. Students sit in a circle facing one another, each seated behind an instrument of choice. They will improvise background music from the moment the back of the wardrobe opens revealing Narnia up until the time the horse-drawn carriage enters the scene. It may be wise to ask the students for suggestions as to whose instrument might be suitable for the sound of the door opening, for the light of the lamppost, and for the arrival of the carriage. This will give the group "landmarks" that will help them to function as a unit within the improvisation and know when the music needs to change. Once these sounds have been agreed on, let the opening door begin. Because the mood has been established by the story, the students are generally quite comfortable and secure in contributing to the overall effect. The group improvisation will progress until the carriage appears, and then will quietly die away, as individuals drop out one by one. Sometimes the group just stops suddenly when the carriage sound appears.

2. Once they have experienced this kind of improvisation, students generally get the idea that music can set a mood. They often suggest other moods for the group to portray next. They might want to improvise a "scary" soundtrack or one for an adventure movie or chase scene. As they do, it is helpful for the teacher to make suggestions regarding strategies and procedures that the

students might find helpful. The teacher might suggest that students do not have to play all the time—that it is all right to play for awhile, complete an idea, drop out for awhile, and come in again when it seems appropriate. Students should know that, once they have finished what they want to say, they should stop playing and listen for a while. This tends to give the work more variety of texture and dynamics. The teacher might suggest that individuals look and listen carefully to what their fellow students are doing and try to play something that fits with what someone else is playing. This makes the work more cohesive. In general, students will make spontaneous evaluations of the group's work and strive to make each successive improvisation more unified and more interesting than the one that came before.

ABOUT ARRANGING

The process of arranging music is really a part of the process of composing music. It refers to taking musical ideas created by someone else and organizing or reorganizing them in a way that generates a new musical work that is different from the original. It is quite a useful tool for teaching music. Students who work with musical ideas in this way need to know and understand the ideas intimately in order to be able to engage in arranging. Therefore, experiences in arranging musical material tend to nurture a greater understanding of music that is performed. This is because students generally need to have achieved a certain level of proficiency in performing the musical material in order to be able to arrange the material. Working with musical material in arranging often creates a situation in which students need to know more about the melodic, rhythmic, or harmonic structure of the material as well. (A sample arranging problem can be found on pp. 201–205.)

PROMOTING AND INHIBITING CREATIVITY IN THE CLASSROOM

It is possible to design and carry out compositional projects in ways that enable students to initiate and develop musical ideas.[6] Unfortunately, it is also possible to inadvertently design or carry out projects in ways that might actually hamper students' ability to initiate and develop musical ideas. Well-designed creative experiences should enable students to communicate what they understand about music and allow teachers to assess the extent of their level of understanding. They also should have the potential to promote and motivate the creation of music as a vehicle for personal expression.

Enabling and Hampering Creative Process

You will need to understand what constitutes an assignment that enables student creativity and what constitutes an assignment that restricts or even prevents student creativity. Much work has been done in the field of language arts to teach teachers how to "get out of their students' way" and to allow them to express themselves with language—to express what they really know and understand about their world. Music teachers need to look at what they have learned and take it to heart (see Box 5.3).

BOX 5.3 (VIGNETTE)

Fifth graders in an inner-city classroom were given the following language arts assignment: "Write three paragraphs about tornadoes. Each paragraph should have a topic sentence. The first paragraph should tell what you know about tornadoes. The second should tell what a tornado is like. The third should tell what to do if a tornado comes."

One student wrote: "When a tornado happens, the sky gets very dark and there is no noise."

Another wrote, "A tornado is swirling air rising from the ground."

Both students were having trouble getting from their opening statements into the particulars of the teacher's assignment. Upon seeking the teacher's assistance, both were given instructions as to how to make their opening sentences conform to the parameters of the assignment. As a result, neither produced a particularly memorable product.

What might these students have produced had they been allowed and encouraged to continue their beautiful imagery? What might the teacher have done to nurture this? What is really important here is what the students are thinking and trying to communicate, not the parameters of the assignment. The teacher needed to ask questions about what the students know, think, or feel about a tornado. To the student who said "the sky gets very dark," the teacher might have asked, "What color was the sky? Was it black? Was the sky completely dark? Was it just parts of the sky? What else do you know about tornadoes? What else could you tell me if I didn't know anything about a tornado?" In order to answer questions such as these, the student would need to think carefully and deeply about what she already knows about tornadoes—what she knows and would like to communicate to someone else. She would be thinking about the subject matter and about how it might best be expressed, not about the requirements of the assignment.

In this case, the structure of this assignment and the nature of the teacher's actions when the students sought help actually limited student creativity.

We can find parallels to this scenario in some kinds of instrumental composition assignments. Asking students to compose a piece that is 20 notes long is like writing a 100-word essay and spending more time counting words than thinking about content. Asking students to compose music using a particular rhythm pattern is like being asked to use a particular vocabulary word in a sentence. Composing a piece using only the pitches sol, mi, and la is comparable to making up a story that uses 10 spelling words. While these kinds of writing and composing assignments may present certain challenges, the challenges are not creative challenges. Assignments such as these are not likely to result in fine literary or musical works. Students become too focused on the parameters of the assignment to concern themselves with the quality of the product or with what it will express. In the same way, music assignments with restrictive parameters can cause students to focus on extramusical, nonexpressive aspects of the project. The assignment itself can hamper rather than enable or promote creative process.

This is not to say that teachers are intentionally restricting their students. However, because of some of the instructional decisions they make, a number of teachers inadvertently do restrict the potential creativity of their students.

Restricting Options to Make Things Simpler

Some teachers design restrictive assignments in an effort to make the project simpler for students. In this effort, they are actually asserting a kind of control over the situation—a control that may ultimately restrict their students' creativity. Asking students to work from a particular rhythm or tonal pattern can fit into this category. Some teachers approach song composition by asking students to write a short poem and then decide which words in the poem should be quarter notes and which should be eighths. Students working on such an assignment can be found arbitrarily distributing quarter and eighth notes over the page (making visual decisions, rather than aural ones). The next instruction in such an assignment often involves tone bells or xylophone bars, where students are asked to choose one of the given pitches (usually pitches of a pentatonic scale and often not even all five) to be played for each note they have written. Children generally approach this like a puzzle, randomly assigning pitches to the notes written on their page of poetry. When asked to perform their final work, children who have worked this way are usually unable to sing the song they have written. If they have had ample experience decoding our rhythm system, they can often play it with reasonable accuracy, but more as a sort of rhythm exercise than as a song. This is not creating; it is puzzle solving.

Students who are given a genuine opportunity to compose a song can sing it accurately with all the nuances and meaning they have intended the song to express. They truly possess the song because they have created it—and they do not forget it. Students who make up a song by fitting together puzzle pieces do not own the song. They need the teacher's help to sing it because they do not know it. Students who genuinely compose a song know it intimately. A better assignment might be to ask students to make up a song that expresses something they want to express. They may choose to start with lyrics or with decisions about the overall style, texture, or form. Students can use what they come into our classrooms knowing about songs to compose original songs, even in kindergarten. The very youngest children will need more teacher assistance, but it is important to lend assistance only when it is needed—and to stay out of the way when it is not.

Assignments Derived from Detail or Whole?

The creative process is a holistic process. Giving an assignment that stems from (or asks students to) focus on isolated patterns would seem to be contrary to the nature of creative process. One of the intrinsic problems with asking students to focus on specific rhythms or pitches when they compose is that, left to their own devices, students' primary decisions in composing tend to be the broader, more holistic decisions. In beginning a compositional project, students' initial decisions most often reflect broader concepts, like style ("Let's make it a rock song"), form ("You be the verse, and we'll be the chorus"), textural organization ("Me and Steve are gonna be the tune and you guys be the background"), or affective characteristics ("Let's make it real scary!"). Students often develop thematic material at the outset and use a particular motif (with a particular rhythmic and pitch structure) as the basis for a work, but they generally do not choose to begin with an isolated rhythm pattern or series of pitches, unless instructed to by a teacher.

Requiring Notated Versions

Requiring students to produce notated versions of original works can be detrimental to their process as well, as can be seen in Boxes 5.4 and 5.5.

BOX 5.4 (VIGNETTE)

A middle-school teacher asked students in a keyboard class to work in pairs to compose a piece as a culminating project for the course. The students were to write their pieces down on manuscript paper. Writing notated music on paper was a new experience for these students, something they had studied for the first time during this particular semester. Most students began work on the assignment by playing their keyboards. Many immediately found melodies or chord sequences they liked. They worked for quite a while, playing various permutations of their thematic material, as students generally do. However, the same comments could be heard throughout the room. "We can't do that! We don't know how to write that down!" So, in one team after another, the students stopped creating: either they began drawing a random collection of notes on their papers and trying to figure out how to play what they had just written, or they began trying to play something that they would know how to write. By the time the project was over, each team had produced some notes on their paper and each could play what they had written, although haltingly and, more often then not, inaccurately. The pieces they produced had only quarter notes and eighth notes. Most were unaccompanied, angular melodies— a far cry from the syncopated rhythms and interesting chord progressions they had played before they remembered they had to write their pieces down.

Requirements to "write your piece down" can limit creativity, even when nonstandard notation is acceptable and encouraged.

BOX 5.5 (VIGNETTE)

In a fourth-grade classroom where the children were asked to work in small groups to compose a piece for xylophone and percussion, the teacher asked the children to write down the letter names of the pitches of the melodies they composed. The children in the group that I was studying behaved in a similar way to the middle-school keyboard students. Each of the group members immediately thought of a motif for the work. For about five minutes, each student practiced and subtly altered his or her own motif, looking for the preferred version. Once they began sharing ideas and trying to put their ideas together, one group member remembered that they needed to be able to write their melody down in letter names. Immediately, the interesting, syncopated ideas were lost, and the girls began a slow, painstaking process of playing one pitch at a time and writing it down. One girl tried again and again to play her original idea slowly enough to be able to write it down, but she was unable to, and eventually abandoned the melody. The problem was that none of the group members had conceived of her melody by letter name. Each was using a xylophone to realize a melody she wanted to play. Letter names had nothing to do with the process; the students had been engaged in thinking in sound.

In each of these cases, the classroom teacher had no idea of the early permutations of the original melodies. They heard only the students' performances of their finished products and, therefore, assumed that the assignments were successful ones. I was privy to the earliest ideas in one case because I happened to be sitting among the children and in the second because I was recording the group interaction as part of a research study (Wiggins, 1998). It was not until I had studied students in my own classroom in this way that I realized how many wonderful ideas they were "throwing away" because they did not fit the teacher's parameters. It was a hard lesson for me to learn as well.

When designing an assignment, it is important to consider whether the assignment truly reflects the concept or principle the students are supposed to focus on and does not contain elements that detract from that focus. If students are to focus on using a variety of tone colors or dynamics, do not ask them, for example, to write down their melodies. The students will fixate on writing down melodies (and, of course, play melodies they can easily write down) and forget all about using a variety of tone colors or dynamics. (Besides, it is not uncommon for pieces designed to show variety of tone color or dynamic contrast to have no melodies at all, but to be contemporary-sounding conglomerations of sounds.) Beware of assignments that pull students in more than one direction at the same time. They will end up focusing on one idea and forgetting or abandoning the other.

Teachers also need to think about what they do during the times when students make their work public by sharing the finished products or works in progress with peers or teacher. An Australian researcher, who has studied quite extensively in Australian and British classrooms the ways in which teachers interact with students during composition projects, found many examples in which teachers encouraged students to alter their work (Hogg, 1993, 1994, 1995). Some of the teachers she observed actually recomposed student work, clearly indicating to the students that what they had done was wrong. The actions of the teacher in response to student work are critical. Students need to feel that their ideas are valid and important in order for the experience to enable future work. Criticizing and altering student work can give students the impression that they are composing music for the teacher—and not for themselves. They tend to lose ownership of the work, which is a critical part of the importance of engaging in compositional process in the first place.

THOUGHTS ON CREATING WITH STUDENTS

Learning to teach music in ways that invite and validate students' musical ideas is not as difficult as it may seem, but it does require a shift in perspective. It is important to recognize that students enter music classrooms full of musical ideas. You will need to organize instruction in ways that will enable students to share what they already know about music and enable you to identify the things they do not know. Analytical listening lessons can provide clues to those ideas students know and those they need to learn. Students' ongoing evaluation of their own performances can provide clues as well. However, the best tool for finding out whether or not students understand a particular musical concept is a creative assignment. Students who understand a musical idea can easily operate within the assignment and use it to generate an original piece.

Students need opportunities to make music on their own—without unnecessary teacher controls. If we permit our students such opportunities, we will see them soar in ways none may have thought possible.

ENDNOTES

1. Many of my ideas about designing compositional problems have been published in various MENC publications, including *Composition in the classroom* (Copyright ©1990 by Music Educators National Conference); *Synthesizers in the elementary music classroom* (Copyright ©1991 by Music Educators National Conference); "Teacher control and creativity," *Music Educators Journal* 85(5):30–35 (Copyright ©1999 by Music Educators National Conference); "Learning through creative interaction with music," *General Music Today* 8(3):11–15 (Copyright © 1995 by Music Educators National Conference); and "Composition as a teaching tool," *Music Educators Journal* 75(8):35–38 (Copyright ©1989 by Music Educators National Conference). All used with permission.

2. MIDI stands for Musical Instrument Digital Interface. It is the name of the universal language that digital instruments speak.
3. This idea comes from Lawrence Eisman.
4. For more detailed information about this process, please see Wiggins (1990).
5. In our culture, the most prevalent experiences people have with instrumental music are in conjunction with visual images. Most of the music of our students' lives is either vocal music or background music. Teachers need to be aware of this when working with instrumental music in the classroom and be sensitive to students' lack of experience in this medium.
6. This section is based on my article, "Teacher control and creativity," *Music Educators Journal* 85(5):30–35. Used with permission.

SELECTED RESOURCES

Campbell, P. S. 1998. *Songs in their heads: Music and its meaning in children's lives.* New York: Oxford.

Sundin, B., G. E. McPherson, and G. Folkestad. 1998. *Children composing* [(in English) (Fax +46 (0)40-32 54 50)]. Malmo, Sweden: Lund University, Malmo Academy of Music.

Wiggins, J. 1990. *Composition in the classroom: A tool for teaching.* Reston, Va.: MENC (Music Educators National Conference).

Wiggins, J. 1991. *Synthesizers in the general music classroom: An integrated approach.* Reston, Va.: MENC.

Wiggins, J. H. 1992. *The nature of children's musical learning in the context of a music classroom.* Ph.D. diss. University of Illinois at Urbana-Champaign.

Wiggins, J. H. 1994. "Children's strategies for solving compositional problems with peers." *Journal of Research in Music Education* 42(3):232–52.

Wiggins, J. H. 1995. "Building structural understanding: Sam's story." *The Quarterly Journal of Music Teaching and Learning* 6(3):57–75.

Wiggins, J. H. 2000/01. "The nature of shared musical understanding and its role in empowering independent musical thinking," *Bulletin* (Council for Research in Music Education) 143(Winter):68–93.

Computer Software (available in Mac and PC formats)

Freestyle. 1994. Cambridge, Mass.: Mark of the Unicorn, Inc.

Subotnick, M. 1995. *Making Music.* Voyager CD-ROMs.

Interactive Website

"Morton Subotnick's Creating Music" <http://www.creatingmusic.com>

PART 3
Lesson and Unit Plans

Part 3 provides examples of lesson plans for students of different ages and levels of prior musical experience. The intent is to help expand your understanding of teaching music through problem solving. It includes lessons for both younger and older beginners, for students with some musical experience, and for students ready to solve complex musical problems. Each chapter also provides a broad overview of issues related to teaching students of the various age and experience levels. Additional lesson plans can be found on our website at www.mhhe.com/wiggins.

Chapter 6

DESIGNING ENTRY-LEVEL MUSICAL PROBLEMS

Chapter 6 provides important information about teaching young children. It also includes examples of lesson plans for beginners of all ages. Additional material can be found on our website (www.mhhe.com/wiggins).

As students begin musical study for the first time, it is important that the experiences they encounter both establish a basis for further study and invite and intrigue them to be motivated to pursue further study.

Musical problems for inexperienced students generally have certain qualities in common whether they are designed for students who are 5, 12, or 18 years old. Beginners of all ages need to start with the most accessible and least-complex musical concepts—concepts that can be understood without extensive prior experience with other concepts. It is best to begin with basic experiences with the effects produced by the manipulation of the more obvious elements, such as dynamics and tempo, and with a basic understanding of the role of steady beat, duration, register, melodic contour and direction, and articulation (see Box 6.1).

BOX 6.1: SOME ENTRY-LEVEL MUSICAL CONCEPTS

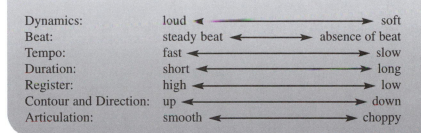

Dynamics:	loud ◄─────────────► soft
Beat:	steady beat ◄──────► absence of beat
Tempo:	fast ◄───────────────► slow
Duration:	short ◄──────────────► long
Register:	high ◄───────────────► low
Contour and Direction:	up ◄─────────────────► down
Articulation:	smooth ◄─────────────► choppy

Once students have formulated a basic understanding of how these ideas operate within a musical work, it is then appropriate to build on and extend their understandings to include more specific aspects, such as intervals, tonal center, and phrases as they occur within melodies; more in-depth experience with long and short sounds and silences; and basic experiences with form, texture, timbre, dynamic change, and tempo change (see Box 6.2).

BOX 6.2: SOME MIDDLE-LEVEL MUSICAL CONCEPTS

Intervals:	skips ◄───────────► steps
Tonal Center:	home tone
Melody:	phrases
Duration:	sound ◄───────────► silence
	more than two durations in one work
Texture:	thin ◄───────────► thick
	number and arrangement of voices
Form:	repetition ◄────────► contrast
	(*same*) (*different*)
Timbre:	instrument families, classroom instruments
Dynamics:	crescendo ◄──────► decrescendo
Tempo:	accelerando ◄──────► ritardando

The most complex musical concepts are those that are based on a more encompassing understanding of these simpler ideas. For example, to understand meter it is necessary to understand steady beat and accent. To understand form, it is necessary to understand melodic contour and phrase. To understand harmonic structure, it is necessary to understand tonal center. A person needs to have a working knowledge of all the elements of music in order to understand style or what creates the affective qualities of a work. In general, higher-level musical experiences deal with broad, encompassing ideas concerning the whole work and how a multitude of ideas operate within that work to produce a particular effect (see Box 6.3).

BOX 6.3: SOME COMPLEX MUSICAL CONCEPTS

Meter: heard as twos or threes or some combination of the two.
Harmony: tonality, modality, relationship between melodies and chords.
Timbre: experience with a broad spectrum of acoustic and electronic instruments, and use of voice.
Form: experience with specific forms, such as call-and-response, binary, ternary, rondo, theme and variation, ground bass.
Texture: specific textures, such as canon (round), melody and accompaniment, chordal, monophonic, homophonic, polyphonic.
Style: the nature of all of the elements in the work and of how they are combined in the work.
Affect: the way the music makes the listener or performer feel.

Young students (grades K–2) need to spend a considerable amount of time exploring very basic musical concepts. They need to participate in a multitude of experiences singing songs, playing classroom instruments, moving to music, listening to and creating music, and representing their understanding of musical ideas through nonverbal means such as movement and graphic representation. Active, physical engagement is particularly significant for young children because it is an important part of the ways they learn.

In some of his earlier work, Bruner (1971) suggested that, as people learn, they need to experience things first on the *enactive* level (physically experiencing and representing the idea) and then on the *iconic* level (expressing understanding through graphics or verbal descriptions that do not yet include appropriate labels). Once they have shown, through these other means of expression, that they understand the concept, they are ready to work with the concept on the *symbolic* level (using the appropriate, agreed-upon label for the concept). This perspective is very useful in the music classroom. For example, young children need to move their bodies, arms, and hands to show the shapes of melodies. Once they have understood how to represent melodic contour through movement, they can transfer that understanding to graphic representation of melodic contour. However, they need to have had numerous experiences working with contour through enactive and iconic representation before they attempt to represent that understanding with conventional music notation. Students who attend music class only once or twice a week may not be ready to transfer their understanding of contour and direction to the symbolic level until the end of the second or beginning of the third grade. Many do not read standard notation comfortably until at least the fourth grade. However, from a very young age, they can make rich use of the other means of expression to engage in sophisticated discussions of the ideas behind the symbols.

Upper elementary, middle school, or high school students who have not had the benefit of strong, well-rounded music learning experiences earlier in their school careers should be considered older beginners. These students need to explore very basic musical concepts to establish a platform from which to consider more complex issues. However, depending on their prior experience, older beginners may be able to deal with more than one of the basic ideas within one lesson and progress rather quickly to more complex ideas. It is important to remember that inexperienced students of any age will not be able to leap headlong into understanding conventional musical symbols without a thorough understanding of what those symbols represent. Older beginners may also need to physically move in order to understand a particular musical concept (e.g., beat or meter), and they will certainly appreciate being permitted to explore musical ideas without needing to be conversant with specific musical terminology. They will, no doubt, be able to progress to working with conventional symbols more quickly than younger students might, but iconic representation will help them speak freely about what they are hearing or performing and feel more at ease sharing their personal musical ideas when creating. Iconic representation can remove the barriers so often experienced by those who have had little prior opportunity to learn music. It can empower older students to explore musical ideas with greater confidence.

Another difference between the ways older and younger students approach entry-level ideas is in the musical material selected for the lessons. In all likelihood, the songs a 5-year-old enjoys will not be exciting to a 12-year-old or young adult. One of the challenges of teaching older beginners is in finding literature that interests and appeals to them but that is also simple enough to teach basic musical ideas. Fortunately, it is really only song literature that poses this problem. Music that teachers select for listening experiences is not necessarily composed for listeners of any particular age. Age also poses no problem in creating activities, because individuals are free to create original music that suits them.

ENTRY-LEVEL EXPERIENCES FOR YOUNG STUDENTS

Singing

In general, it is important for the youngest children to engage in children's music of their own and other cultures, such as finger plays, play party games, hand-clap games, and the like. These kinds of activities are invaluable for helping students find steady beat in familiar songs and for requiring them to move their hands, feet, fingers, or whole bodies to the beat of the song. Songs that are short and repetitive with a relatively limited pitch range help young singers learn to sing on pitch because they are generally easy to master and because the repetition enables students to become comfortable with the melodies. Many students sing incorrect pitches simply because they do not take the time or were not given the time to learn a song accurately. Children who know songs well can generally sing them well. These kinds of activities also teach young children to sing and move with others in an ensemble setting and help them learn to attend to what others are doing and to be sure their own singing and moving fits with the group.

In general, teaching from songs that have simpler, "catchy" lyrics allows young students to concentrate on the musical aspects of the song while they are learning and performing it. Lengthy songs with a large number of complicated lyrics are less appropriate for teaching musical ideas to young children because the lyrics require so much of their attention. Also, young singers who do not yet read words need to rely on their ability to memorize lyrics in order to perform a song.

Young children enjoy singing songs in which they can make up their own lyrics or motions for particular parts of verses or stanzas. These kinds of activities help them develop ownership of song material in the music classroom. In addition, because they delight in singing such songs again and again (so there will be many opportunities for personal participation and recognition), they learn the songs better and better. Performing— and particularly singing—should occupy a greater percentage of the time in classes for young children because the students need to develop a broad base of personal, enactive experience with music in order to be able to engage in more sophisticated experiences later on.[1]

Moving

Movement is an integral part of the musical experiences of young children. Besides using gesture and whole-body movement to communicate their understanding of musical ideas, students need to engage in enactive experiences in order to *develop* an understanding of musical ideas. For example, in addition to finding beat in songs, students need to have many experiences moving to the long and short durations of songs in order to establish a basis for understanding rhythm and its functions. They need opportunities to move in ways that reflect the shape of a line, lilt of a phrase, or overall mood of a work. Young children experience and interpret the world in a very physical way, and their musical experiences should be no exception. Physical interaction with music helps them to understand how it works, even though they may not be able to articulate what they are beginning to understand.

Playing

Young children also learn a great deal from early experiences playing classroom instruments. Playing instruments can be seen as an extension of moving to music. Students need to enact steady beat or rhythms before playing them on instruments. They can learn to play a steady beat or short pattern on nonpitched percussion instruments to accompany class singing. Students most easily learn patterns that are part of songs they are singing (like playing the short-short-long pattern of "rolling home" over and over again to accompany class singing of "This Old Man"). To get to this point, students might have walked the pattern of "rolling home" each time it came in the song. They might then have transferred the rhythm of "rolling home" to some sort of hand motion that shows the short-short-long pattern. (It is preferable to use a motion other than clapping, which does not adequately show long sounds. Sliding the hands together works well, as does using a sound like "ch-ch-

chhhhh.") Once they are comfortable with the short-short-long pattern, some students might try executing the pattern over and over again while others sing the melody of the song. Eventually, individuals will be ready to transfer the pattern to a drum to accompany class singing. As they do, observant students might note that the pattern also fits with the phrases "This Old Man" and "he played one."

Young students can also play simple barred instruments to accompany class singing. It is often easier for them to hit the bars of larger instruments because they require more of a gross-motor arm motion than the more controlled wrist motion necessary for playing the bars of a glockenspiel or the finger motion required to play a keyboard. They can easily learn to play steady beat and simple rhythm patterns to accompany class singing using single pitches, open fifths, or other intervals that work to accompany a particular song.

Creating

Young children are natural creators of music. They often sing to themselves as they play, sometimes creating long involved passages of musical and textual ideas. Researchers (e.g., Davies, 1992; Campbell, 1998) who have studied children's musical musings as they play have found that individual children often develop favorite thematic ideas that appear in various permutations within their spontaneous songs. Music teachers can capitalize on the ease with which young children generate original musical ideas and encourage those ideas in the context of classroom activities.

Young students might use instruments to improvise appropriate introductions, bridges, and endings for songs they are singing—suggesting alternatives, making decisions about orchestration, dynamic levels, tempi, and the like. It is important to nurture in young children an understanding that they have the right to make musical decisions. It is important to ask them to use their judgment and to respect their opinions. ("How shall we sing this lullaby?" "What instrument do you think we can use to represent the bear in this song? How do you think we should play it?")

They can also use voices and instruments to improvise simple musical ideas, such as musical conversations, and to create thematic material representing a character in a story or background sounds establishing a mood. For the most part, improvisation tends to be a more appropriate activity for young and inexperienced students than composition because composing often requires a knowledge of broader, more-encompassing aspects of music. However, young children are very familiar with songs and can easily work together as a group with teacher guidance to create original songs.

Listening

Young children should have many opportunities to listen to music of all styles and genres, from all sorts of historical and cultural contexts. Listening pieces for young children should contain obvious features that will be easily accessible to the listener, such as extreme dynamic or direction changes, or sudden tempo changes. Children should have opportunities to demonstrate what they hear in the music, generally through movement but also through graphic representation and conversations about the music. They might all move together as a large group with teacher guidance or as individuals within the group, finding their own ways of moving to reflect what they hear. Whenever possible, listening experiences should be tied to performing and creating experiences.

Notating

For the most part, young children's work with notation of musical ideas should be through iconic representation. They should not be asked to work with symbols until they have a firm understanding of the concepts that the icons and symbols represent. In these early stages, they need to engage in numerous enactive and iconic experiences with steady beat and with long and short sounds in connection with contour and direction. These are the skills and understandings a student needs to develop in order to know how to sing a song accurately and to understand the ways pitch and duration are conventionally notated. The experiences that will foster aural skills will also lay the groundwork for the development of basic music reading skills.

Technology

It is appropriate for young children to engage in early experiences with technology. If synthesizers are available, they can be used to augment timbral choices for projects like introductions, bridges, and codas for songs. Professional-caliber synthesizers generally offer many choices of timbre that have a "sound-effects" quality. With essentially no knowledge of playing keyboards, young children can easily plan ways of organizing and layering such sounds to create a desired effect, providing an interesting background for acoustic instrument parts. They can also improvise interesting melodic or rhythmic ideas on synthesizers without having to know very much about the keyboard itself or about keyboard technique. They can transfer to the keyboard simple accompanying parts, such as open fifths played on xylophones. Transferring such patterns to keyboard requires more fine-motor coordination because students need to use their fingers instead of their whole arms to play the pattern.

The youngest students can also begin to explore simple composition software, such as the program described in Chapter 5 (pp. 99–100).

Nature of Problems for Young Children

Lesson plans for younger students often consist of a series of shorter and simpler problems rather than one long-range, encompassing problem. The youngest students generally do not engage in extended units of study because they do not yet have the maturity to maintain interest and intensity in a long-range project and because the basic concepts they are learning are often best taught through a series of shorter experiences.

It is important to provide a variety of activities within each class session to maintain young students' interest and excitement but also not to shortchange them by changing activity too soon or too often. While young children enjoy engaging in a series of intriguing experiences, they also enjoy spending enough time with each experience to get everything out of it that interests them. They like playing games again and again so that many students can have a turn. They like singing and playing songs again and again because they revel in the repetition and familiarity and because it may mean more students will get a chance to play the drum, choose a partner, or be the leader. Due to limited contact time allotted by school schedules, music teachers sometimes feel the need to rush through activities. Children need time to think and learn, so it is sometimes better to cover less material in greater depth, which allows students more time to explore.

Younger students will probably spend more time engaging in teacher-guided activities than working independently because they have less musical and social experience upon which to draw. In these formative years, they will be learning, with teacher guidance, many of the skills and understandings that will enable them to work more independently and with others as they progress through their school years.

It is appropriate for young beginners to engage in early enactive experiences with more complex elements, nurturing awareness of broader issues, laying groundwork for more specific work in the future. For example, while very young students may not be ready to consider musical form as a concept, they can certainly begin dealing with form on an experiential level by engaging in such activities as circling to the right during the A section of a play party game and to the left during the B section. While it might not be appropriate to discuss the melodic differences in detail or even to label the sections "A" and "B," the students may be able to talk about, in their own words, why the group has decided to move one way and then the other.

ENTRY-LEVEL EXPERIENCES FOR OLDER BEGINNERS

Older beginners also need to develop a basic understanding of entry-level concepts, although they probably will not require as much time to master each idea as young students might. In all likelihood, the prior experience and proficiency of a group of older beginners will span quite a wide range of diversity. With older students, it is important for the teacher to begin by assessing prior knowledge in order to understand what students already know and what they need to learn. It is important for the students to be privy to this information as well. Nothing alienates older students faster than not acknowledging what they already know and bring to the situation.

Older students also need to engage in singing, moving, playing, creating, listening, notating, and experiences with technology; but, from their viewpoint, listening is often the most comfortable and least threatening place to begin. Therefore, a listening experience is often a good initial assessment tool. Boxes 6.4 and 6.5 are examples of first-day activities that work well with older students.

BOX 6.4: WHAT DO YOU HEAR IN THIS MUSIC?

The Problem:
Select a piece that is intriguing and exciting, preferably one with many changes.
One piece that works well for this experience is Rossini's *William Tell* Overture
[the allegro vivace or perhaps the entire overture]. As the music is playing, students are invited to write a word or two that describes something they hear in the
music. They can write about anything they hear and can use any words they
choose to describe what they are hearing at any moment during the piece. This is
important because a piece may be loud at one point and soft at another, making
both "loud" and "soft" appropriate answers. The only requirement is that each student must write at least one comment during the piece.[2]

Materials:
• Place sheets of chart paper in various parts of the room. If students are seated
  in a circle, place four to six sheets of paper on the floor inside the circle. If students are seated at desks arranged in clusters, place one sheet in each cluster.
  On each sheet place two or three markers.
• Or invite students to go to the chalkboard, grab a piece of chalk, and write
  something that reflects what they hear.

Sharing Solutions:
With *William Tell,* students generally write words that reflect musical elements
(loud, fast), specific instruments they hear, and associative images the music
brings to mind (horse race, "The Lone Ranger"). Encourage any and all responses.
Ultimately, the intention is to consider all responses and then to group and catego-
rize them in a way that makes sense to the students. You might hang all the papers
across the front of the room and then, together, step back and consider what has
been written. Students usually group instrument sounds together (which the
teacher might label as "timbre" or "sound source"), affective responses together
(the words that describe how the music makes people feel), generally leaving a
random collection of musical elements uncategorized. With teacher guidance, the
students can seek similarities among these elements and group these ideas as well.

Assessing:
The net result will be a working list that reflects those aspects of music of which
the students are already aware. The teacher can then introduce the idea that there
are a number of ways that sounds can be organized to produce music. The class
has identified some of these ways. There are others as well. This is what this
course will be about—learning the ways sounds can be organized to create music
and how music "works." The teacher might choose to begin by either expanding
upon an element the students seem very familiar with or by exploring an element
they seem to know little or nothing about.

BOX 6.5: HOW IS THIS MUSIC ORGANIZED?

The Problem:
People who make the music that is recorded on CDs need to make certain decisions about how the music will be organized. They have many different choices as to how this might be accomplished. Students will listen to four or five examples and see if they can decide which musical features were used to plan and organize the music. In some cases, these decisions were made by the composer who originally wrote the music. In others, it might reflect the decision of an arranger or even of the performer.

In solving this problem, students might work:

- Independently, writing down their thoughts as they listen, and sharing them with the class after each recording is played.
- In pairs or small groups, generating a collaborative theory about how the music in each recording is organized. (Generally this method is preferable because it gets students talking with one another about their musical ideas from the outset.)

Materials:
Choose a diverse sampling of music in which each work is organized by one or two particularly obvious features. Try to cover a wide range of styles, genres, cultural contexts, and organizational features. This lesson should serve to open the door to future work, helping the students to understand what they already know and what they may still need to learn about music.

Musical examples for such a lesson might include a rock song with a repeating bass line or other obvious pattern, a Native American song accompanied by a single drum, a particularly intriguing jazz solo, a contemporary choral work that utilizes unusual vocal sounds and effects, and perhaps an example of a work that represents a fusion of two musical cultures.

LESSON PLANS FOR YOUNGER (AND OLDER) BEGINNERS

Since singing is an individual's first way of making music, many early lessons, particularly for young beginners, are based on singing experiences. Teaching new songs through problem-solving experiences generally creates a situation in which students are able to hear the song sung in its entirety several times over before they are expected to sing it. This process enables students to learn songs in a more holistic manner, creating many opportunities to hear the whole song before attempting to sing the parts that make up that whole. This way of teaching songs parallels what whole language teachers do to familiarize students with the flow of the sound of language as they begin to read. With beginning readers, language teachers read whole stories and encourage students to join in on obvious, repetitive portions of the text until they can eventually repeat the entire text, partially from memory and partially from an emerging understanding of the symbol system. Holistic teaching of songs involves creating numerous opportunities to hear the song in its entirety until students begin spontaneously to sing the portions they know and, eventually, possess the entire song. The problem-solving activities also help to focus student attention on specific aspects of the melodic contour and rhythm, promoting a more complete understanding of the specifics of the song within the whole and enabling them to sing it accurately and with ease.

The sample lesson plans that comprise the bulk of this chapter are written in greater detail than a teacher would write in daily planning. The intention is to enable the reader to develop a better understanding of how teaching through problem solving might be carried out. In a sense, the lesson plans in Chapters 6, 7, and 8 serve the same purpose as the box vignettes in Chapters 1 through 4. They provide glimpses into real-life music teaching to clarify the ideas set forth in the opening chapters.

Iconic Representation of Beat

The first lesson is an example of a first experience with iconic representation of beat. It would logically follow a series of enactive experiences finding and moving to beat in a variety of settings, during both listening and performing activities. In this first lesson plan, the concept of steady beat is used as a "doorway in" that will enable students to explore the rhythmic concept of sound and no sound (rest), contour and direction (pitch) of the melody in relation to the steady beat, and affective qualities of the song. The icon magnets used in this and other lessons can be cut from $8^{1}/_{2}$-x-11 sheets of laminated magnet, available at sign stores, print shops, and educational supplies stores.

After playing a familiar listening example or singing game in which the children have previously moved to steady beat, talk with students about how they know when to move their feet, hands, or bodies. What do they hear in the music that tells them when to move? Musicians call that feeling a steady beat. [Steady beat is a very difficult concept to describe in words, even for an expert musician. Listen carefully to how they describe the feeling of beat. They will probably use gestures and nonverbal expressions like "dut-dut-dut" or "bum-bum-bum" in order to explain what they feel.] "Sometimes musicians use symbols to show what music sounds like. Today we are going to use these red magnets to try to show steady beat." [Place a series of magnets in a row on the board.] "Let's listen to the music (or sing the song again) and try to follow the magnets in a way that shows the steady beat." [Touch a magnet for each beat while singing or listening.]

Reviewing an earlier experience of moving to the beat of a listening piece or song will help students remember and identify the feeling of steady beat. With teacher support, they will learn to represent that feeling with the icons and learn to "track" the icons within the musical context of the song or piece. Once students understand what the icons represent, the icons become a tool for engaging in the remainder of the problem-solving experiences of this lesson.

Figure 6.1: Lesson Plan: Iconic Representation of Beat

National Standards[3]: 1, 2, 5, 6
Grade: K or 1

Materials:
- "Engine, Engine Number Nine."
- Thirty-two icon magnets of one size and color to represent a duration that moves with the beat.
- Four icon magnets of the same size in white, or other neutral color, to represent rests.
- Classroom instruments (including electronic instruments, if available).

Lesson assumes:
- Considerable prior experience identifying and representing understanding of steady beat through movement, finger plays, play party games, moving to other kinds of songs, and moving to listening examples.
- Considerable experience singing songs with general awareness of duration and contour of a melodic line.

Organization:
Whole-group performance problem.

Objective:
To help students expand their understanding of steady beat and apply that understanding to the performance of a student-accompanied song.

Connection to prior knowledge/experience:
- Play either a familiar listening example or familiar singing game in which the children have previously moved to a steady beat.
- Teacher graphically represents students' suggestions on the board.

Pose problems: Students will:
- Use what they know about moving to steady beat to point to the icons in a motion that reflects their understanding of the steady beat of a known song or piece.
- Transfer that understanding to a new song, "Engine, Engine Number Nine."
- Use what they understand about beat to figure out what happens on the last beat of the song, which contains a one-beat rest.
- Use what they have learned from prior singing experience to figure out the contour and direction of this melody.
- Perform the song with instrumental accompaniment and movement that reflects their understanding of steady beat, rest, contour and direction.

Students solve problem: Students will:
- Identify and iconically represent beat of song.
- Consider iconic representation of rest (in context of song).
- Adjust icons to represent pitch (contour) as well as beat.
- Transfer their understanding to pitched instruments.
- Use their understanding of the beat and contour of the song to both sing and play an arrangement of this song.

Groundwork that enables:
- Connecting to the prior listening or singing experience establishes the groundwork for this lesson.

Students share and discuss solutions:
Occurs throughout because of the constant interaction between teacher and students, and among students.

Assessment: Students will be able to:
- Track the icons with the beat of a known song,
- Show understanding of "rest" through verbal comments about the white magnet and subsequent singing and playing.
- Show understanding of contour and direction through manipulation of magnets and subsequent singing and playing.
- Show understanding of steady beat, rest, and contour and direction through ensemble performance of the song.

Engine, Engine Number Nine

American

En-gine, En-gine Num-ber Nine,   Go-ing down Chi - ca - go Line.

If   the   train goes   off   the track,   Do you want your   mon-ey back?

This lesson is described in greater detail than the ones that follow to help you develop a frame for how iconic representations of musical sounds can be used in your teaching:

- Students move to the beat of the known work. With advice from the students, the teacher represents that beat in icons. Students point to the icons during a second experience with the known work. The teacher then rearranges the icons[4] as follows:

The teacher explains that the icons will be a kind of picture of the sound of the new song they are going to learn. Students will track the four rows of icons (by pointing from their seats) while the teacher sings the new song. "Listen carefully as I sing this song. Follow the magnets with your finger—one magnet for each beat you feel. See if you can tell why I put the magnets into four rows instead of one long row." After several repetitions, most of the students should figure out that the four rows represent four different lines or phrases in the song. Invite students to sing the song, tracking the icons as they do.

- Replace the final magnet in each row with one that represents a rest, using white or another neutral color. "To make this picture look more like what the song sounds like, I am going to take off some of the red ones and put up white ones instead. Can you figure out why I decided to make some of these white?" Students and teacher sing and point again. [Students generally comment that there are no words where the white ones come.] The teacher helps the students to understand that, in music, the beat never stops—but sometimes the singing stops. When there is a beat that has no singing, we will represent it with a white magnet to show that there is still a beat there.

- "Does what we have here really look like what we are singing? Do our voices do just what the magnets do?" [Some students will realize that the magnets do not show that their voices move up and down to sing the song.] "Can we make the magnets go up and down in the way our voices do?" With advice from students, the teacher places the icons in each row to reflect the skips of the melody:

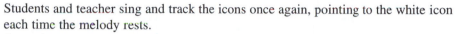

Students and teacher sing and track the icons once again, pointing to the white icon each time the melody rests.

• Set up barred instruments (larger ones are better for very young students) so that the bars near to E and G have been removed (making it easier for small hands to aim for the right place). Invite volunteers to try to play the song on the xylophones. From the icons, the students realize there are only two pitches in the song. Their performances will reflect a variety of levels of "correctness" with some playing the melody accurately, some realizing only the steady beat in some way, some acknowledging the rest, and so on. Each attempt provides a window through which to learn about the sophistication of individual students' understanding of the earlier part of the lesson. All of their attempts will function as accompaniments to the class singing, enabling everyone to feel successful in the overall experience.

Identifying and Representing Duration and Pitch

Once students understand that steady beat can be represented in icons and that that representation can be translated back into sounds they sing and play, they are ready to explore representations of duration and pitch of songs. Since children's conception of melodic ideas contains understanding of both pitch and duration, it is possible to deal with both aspects within the frame of one lesson. In other words, to be able to conceive of and sing a song, children need to understand that the melody is made up of a series of different pitches and that those pitches may last different lengths of time. The ability to perform a song with accurate pitches and durations does not mean that a student is able to articulate an understanding of these ideas. But the ability to sing a song does require an understanding of these concepts on some level. Problem solving through enactive and iconic representation can help bring these understandings to the forefront.

Before engaging in this lesson, students should have had numerous experiences enactively reflecting the contour of melodies and rhythms of melodies. This lesson builds on earlier enactive experiences and provides an early experience in iconic representation of both pitch and duration of a simple melody. Basic understanding of duration and pitch is used as a "doorway in." Once inside the door, students also experience steady beat and the affective and cultural aspects of the song.

Figure 6.2: Lesson Plan: Identifying and Representing Duration and Pitch

National Standards: 1, 5, 6, 7, 9

Grade: 1 or 2 and up, depending upon prior experience

Organization:
Whole-group performance problem.

Materials:

- "Paw Paw Patch".
- Icons of two different lengths and colors representing duration in the phrases of the song, not yet indicating pitch.

Lesson assumes:

Students have had basic, introductory experiences working with iconic representation of duration in the context of a melodic line (perhaps two or three lessons using icons). This is a first experience with iconic representation that contains two durations.

Objective:

To help students expand their understanding of long and short sounds and skips, steps, and repeated tones within the contour of a melodic line.

Connection to prior knowledge/experience:

- Relate to prior experience using icons to represent pitch and duration of a song they know, like "Engine, Engine Number Nine."
- Either review a familiar song with iconic representation first or begin by presenting icons for this new song and asking students to talk about what they already know about this new song, just by looking at the icons.

Groundwork that enables:

Using understanding developed during previous experiences with iconic representation of duration and pitch, students will solve a new problem. The teacher may need to remind the students of these earlier experiences at the outset of the lesson in order to help them to know what strategies to use.

Pose problems: Students will:

- Theorize about what they expect this song to sound like, based on prior experience with iconic representation of songs.
- Figure out some of the relationships between the lyrics and the rhythm of the song.
- Arrange the icons to reflect the pitch aspects of the melody as well, with teacher support.
- Perform the song as an ensemble in the context of a folk dance. The movements of the folk dance are typical of American folk dance, and reflect the form of the song (different motions for each stanza). Movements also require understanding of steady beat (underlying pulse).

Students share and discuss solutions:

Students share and discuss ideas with peers and teacher throughout.

Students solve problem: Students will:

- Listen to the song, consider the icons, and theorize about how they are connected.
- Adjust icons to represent pitch (contour) as well as beat.
- Transfer their understanding to performance of the song.
- Learn a traditional folk dance that goes with the song.

Assessment: Students will be able to:

- Show understanding of long and short sounds and skips, steps, and repeated tones within the contour of a melodic line through their comments during the discussions about the nature and location of the icons and their ability to sing the song accurately.
- Show understanding of steady beat and the form of the song (form on an enactive level only) through their participation in the dance.

Extensions:

- As students become more familiar with iconic representation of pitch and duration, they might try solving a similar problem with peer support (in small groups or in pairs) and eventually on their own.
- You might also integrate experiences with computer programs that deal with this kind of representation of melodies (such as *Making Music*).

128

Paw Paw Patch

American Folk Song

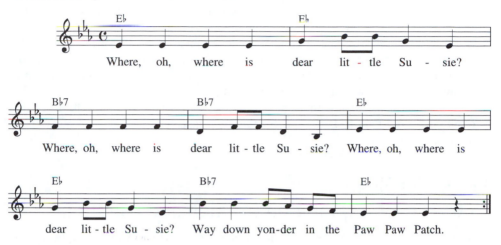

Where, oh, where is dear lit-tle Su-sie? *(etc.)*

2. Come on boys, let's go find her. (3×)
   Way down yonder in the Paw Paw Patch.

3. Pickin' up paw paws, puttin' 'em in her pocket. (3×)
   Way down yonder in the Paw Paw Patch.

For this lesson, the icons could be arranged all on one level grouped by phrase, in two rows with two phrases per row, or as below:

As the teacher sings, students listen to the song and discuss their theories in relation to what they hear in the song. ("What do you think this song might sound like?" "How do you know?")

• The patterns of the first three phrases are the same, the last is different.
• Some of the magnets are smaller and a different color from the rest.
• These seem to represent sounds that move more quickly (short sounds).

Talk about long and short sounds, perhaps linking to earlier experiences moving to long and short sounds of songs and pieces.

"Does this picture show everything about the way the song sounds?" [No, it shows only the longs and shorts, not the ups and downs that the voice makes when singing the song.] "What do we need to do to make it look like the way the song sounds?" [Move some higher and lower.] Invite students to suggest theories as to where the magnets should be placed. Together with the teacher, the magnets are moved to better reflect the contour and direction of the song. When complete, students and teacher sing the song together. [During the problem-solving stage, all singing should be unaccompanied so that the children can focus intently on the melodic contour. Once the problem is solved, the teacher may opt to add an instrumental accompaniment of guitar, piano, Autoharp, synthesizer, etc. As a result of the careful listening during the problem-solving stage, the students have had ample opportunity to get to know the melody well, enabling the accompaniment to augment the ensemble without causing confusion.]

Once the students know the song well, they might learn a simple folk dance that is often performed with it. Directions for this folk dance can be found on our website at *www.mhhe.com/wiggins.*

For Older Beginners:
Entry-Level Exploration of Pitch and Duration

Now that we have looked at several basic introductory experiences for young beginners, let us consider how similar material might be shared with older students. This next lesson assumes that students are at least middle-school age, perhaps older. As it appears here the lesson may actually move too quickly for sixth-grade students. This version is probably more appropriate for high school students or adults. Middle school students can work in a similar fashion, but they may not progress through all of the steps at quite the same rate—material may have to be spread out over several experiences.

Figure 6.3: Lesson Plan: Entry-Level Exploration of Pitch and Duration for Older Beginners

Materials:

- Sheet music of an unfamiliar song.
- Student worksheets: Introducing, Exploring, Notating, and Creating Melody.
- Pencils and paper.
- For extension: Audiotape recording of four or five simple melodies, each one more complex than the one that comes before.

Lesson assumes:

- Experience making and listening to music outside of school.
- Prior knowledge of the three songs used in the lesson.

Organization:
Pair or small group work.

Objective:
To help students use what they know about music to explore the role of pitch and duration in a melody, and the ways musicians manipulate and notate these phenomena.

Connection to prior knowledge/experience:
Show students a page of unfamiliar sheet music. Encourage them to share with you what they understand about what is written on it and what they do not know. The activities of today's lesson should help them to understand more about what is printed on the page.

Groundwork that enables:
Assumes no prior experience with these kinds of activities.
Lesson is designed to provide the groundwowrk for future, more complex experiences.

Pose problems: Students will:

- Work with peers to discover how to represent, iconically and symbolically, the pitches and durations of familiar melodies.

Students solve problem:
Students may work with partners or in small groups to complete the series of activities on these worksheets.

Students share and discuss solutions:
Sharing of ideas occurs throughout.

Assessment: Students will show their understanding by their ability to:

- Notate simple familiar melodies in iconic representation and make some connections between the icons and standard music notation.
- Create original melodies.
- Figure out how another student's melody sounds by interpreting an iconic representation.

Extensions:

- At home, listen to each melody on the tape. Work with them one at a time. Play each one again and again. Sing it to yourself until you are very sure of how it sounds. Next, try to represent it in dashes and numbers. Each melody is more challenging than the one that comes before. See how many you can do.
- Compare your representation with those of others in the class. Talk about differences that may arise. How were some people hearing the music that was different from the way others were hearing it? The class should try to agree upon one representation for each of the melodies on the tape.
- This is a good time to begin to explore a computer program that utilizes both iconic and symbolic representation of melodies, like *Freestyle.*

STUDENT WORKSHEET I: Introducing Melody

1. Sing the *melody* of "Mary Had a Little Lamb" to yourself. Can you sing it in your head without singing aloud? If not, try singing it aloud several times and then singing it in your head.
2. Sing it to yourself again, but this time think about the *shape of the melody.* Melodies have what musicians call *shape* or *contour,* which is a way of describing the ways the melody moves up and down. The aspect of melody that deals with the "ups and downs" is what musicians call *pitch.*
3. With paper and pencil, try drawing the shape or contour of the melody of "Mary Had a Little Lamb." If this is difficult for you or you are unsure, try tracing the shape in the air as you sing the song to yourself.
4. Compare your drawing with what other students have drawn. Are there similarities and/or differences? Talk about any differences with other students. Sing and trace one another's pictures. Can you rectify the differences and agree on one picture that represents the contour of this song?
5. Please look at this visual representation of the melody (Students should not see this visual representation until they have completed steps 1–4.):

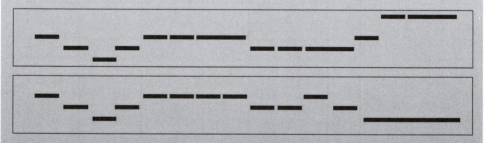

   Compare what you have drawn to this representation. Do you see similarities and/or differences?
6. What *besides pitch* is represented in this picture? This picture shows the contour of the melody, *and* how long each sound in the melody lasts. Musicians talk about the length of a sound in terms of *duration* or *rhythm.*
7. Did your own picture of this melody contain any references to duration? Did you think about that aspect of the melody as you were drawing its shape? If you were thinking about it, this would not be surprising because both duration and pitch are part of what makes up a melody. In a melody, there is usually a collection of pitches arranged in a certain way, and often those pitches are of several different lengths.
8. Look at the picture on the worksheet again. Sing the melody to yourself and trace the dashes as you sing. Notice that the first few dashes seem to move down and back up in what musicians call *stepwise motion*—each pitch seems to be right next to the one that came before.

9. Sing and trace the song again, listening carefully to yourself and looking carefully at the arrangement of the dashes. Can you find the places where both the dashes and your voice seem to skip over a step? Musicians call this kind of motion a *skip*. Pitches in melodies tend to move along in either skips or steps. Sometimes the same pitch is repeated several times. Can you find the places where this occurs in this melody (and in your voice)?

10. Musicians have several ways of naming pitches. Sometimes they use letter names to differentiate between pitches. Sometimes they use numbers. Sometimes they use a system you may know about, where there is a syllable assigned to each pitch like "do" from "do-re-mi." Each of these systems has a purpose. For our purposes right now, we will begin with the simplest system to understand and operate within—numbers.

11. Suppose we call the lowest pitches in this melody (the dashes closest to the bottom of the page) the number "1." Can you figure out what number the melody would have to start on? Can you assign numbers to each of the dashes? Remember that, if the pitches repeat, they would get the same number, and, if they skip, you will need to skip a number. Write a number near each of the dashes.

12. Now, try to sing the melody using the numbers instead of the lyrics of the song. If you understand this introductory material, you are ready to move on to the next section, which will apply what you have just learned to more complex melodies.

STUDENT WORKSHEET II: Exploring Melody

1. Try to draw a contour map for "Row, Row, Row Your Boat." Try to represent both the duration and contour of the song, using dash icons.
2. If the lowest pitch in the song is "1," can you figure out how to sing the song in numbers?
3. Try to draw a contour and duration map, including pitch numbers, for the melody of "America." What makes this melody different from the other two melodies?

STUDENT WORKSHEET III: Notating Melody

(containing notated versions of the three melodies)

1. Look at the ways musicians generally notate these three melodies. Are there things about the ways the notes move that remind you of the pictures and/or dashes you made?
2. Now let's look back at the sheet music we saw at the beginning of the class. What do you understand about this that you did not know before?

STUDENT WORKSHEET IV: Creating Melody

1. Working with a partner, create your own melody. Remember that your melody can move in skips or steps or repeated pitches and that sounds can last different lengths of time. You might find it helpful to use numbers to organize your thinking and planning. You definitely will need to sing to yourself and your partner to share ideas and to develop and agree on a melody that you both like.
2. When you find a melody you both like, try to write it down in dashes (showing duration) and numbers (showing pitch).
3. When you are ready, trade melody lines with another set of composers. See if you can figure out how to sing one another's melodies from the dashes and numbers you have drawn. If the people trying to sing your melody are singing it differently from the way you want it to sound, look at your representation and make sure it says what you want it to say. Among the four of you, see if you can develop a version that looks like what you want it to sound like.

Exploring Contour and Direction through Listening

The lesson in Figure 6.4a is designed to enable young students to apply general understandings of contour and direction in the context of a listening experience. Older students may be ready to move on to analytical listening experiences with form (such as those outlined in the next chapter) without these kinds of preliminary experiences. The lesson plan uses contour and direction as a "doorway in" to enable students to explore the characteristics of the melody of Musorgsky's "Ballet of the Unhatched Chicks" and how those characteristics create the mood of the work. This is also an introductory experience with the relationship between melodic contour and form.[5]

Figure 6.4a: Lesson Plan: Exploring Contour and Direction through Listening

National Standards: 6, 7

Grade: K and up, depending upon experience

Materials:

- Musorgsky: "Ballet of the Unhatched Chicks" from *Pictures at an Exhibition* (CD, Track 2).
- Graphic charts (Figures 6.4b and 6.4c).

Organization:

Whole-group analytical listening problem.

Lesson assumes:

- Prior experience representing melody and duration with icons and some experience moving to simple music in ways that reflect form.

Objective:

To help students apply basic understanding of contour and direction to a listening experience.

Connection to prior knowledge/experience:

The charts themselves are intriguing.

Groundwork that enables:

Prior experience with graphic representation of songs prepares students to solve this set of problems.

Pose problems: Students will:

- Predict what they think the music might sound like (according to what they see on the charts), based on their prior experience with iconic representation of contour and direction.
- Listen to the work and, with the teacher, follow the graphic representation. Encourage students to pretend they are actually touching the chart as they follow along.
- Talk about what they heard in comparison to what they thought they would hear. Often, they ask to repeat the listening experience because the charts and music are intriguing. They also generally find the music funny, which was probably part of the composer's intent in this work.
- Consider differences between the graphics on the two charts and, based on that and their listening experience, deduce that the charts represent two different musical ideas that do not sound alike.
- Listen once more to see if they can figure out the pattern of the ideas. ("How many times do you hear each card? In what order do they appear? Can you keep track in your head?") Students should eventually be able to describe the pattern, although they are not yet ready to use the label "AABA form."

Students solve problems:

Students will interact with teacher and peers, and with the music, to solve this series of problems.

Students share and discuss solutions:

Occurs before and after each listening.

Assessment: Students will be able to describe what they hear through:

- Their movements as they follow the charts.
- Their comments about the work.
- The follow-up movement activity (in "Extensions" section).

Extensions:

- On another day, students might try moving in a way that reflects what they hear in this piece. Their movements will probably reflect aspects of the rhythm, contour and direction, form, and character of the work. Students enjoy returning to a work they have come to know well.
- If students have access to a program like *Making Music*, this might be a good time to use the computer program to explore creating melodies—in particular, two contrasting melodies, that will also appear on the screen with different graphic representations, similar to the charts used in this lesson.

135

FIGURE 6.4B

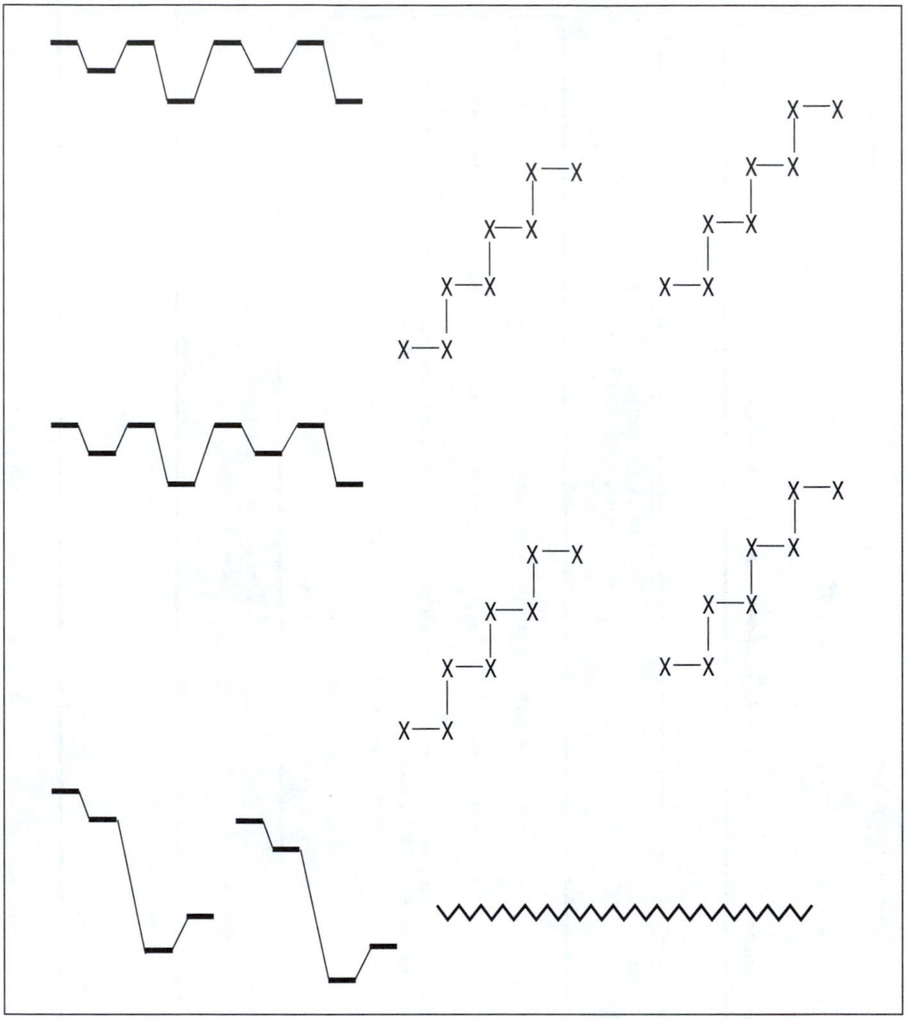

FIGURE 6.4C

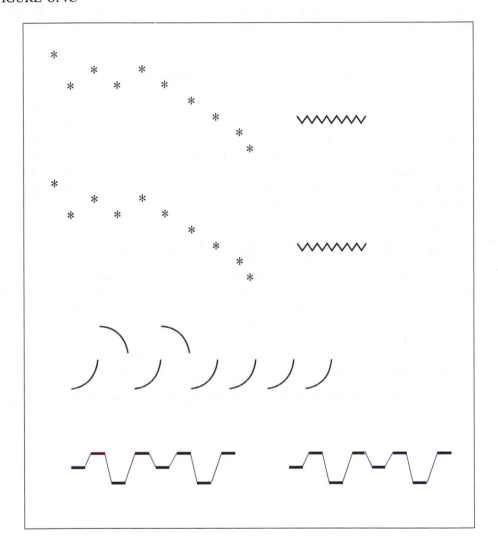

When using charts such as Figures 6.4b and 6.4c, students generally find the charts themselves to be intriguing. It is helpful for very young students to sit relatively close to the charts because it helps to focus their attention on them. You might hang them on the chalkboard side-by-side and ask students to sit on the floor nearby.

As students work with songs as represented in icons (e.g., "Paw Paw Patch"), they are also engaging in preliminary experiences with "phrase within melody." Lessons can be planned that draw attention to this aspect of melody, particularly songs that are accompanied by motions in which the motion changes for each phrase. You might bring further attention to this phenomenon by asking students to walk as they sing a song, changing direction or walking in a different way for each phrase. Whatever motion you decide to incorporate, if it is demonstrating phrase, it should be as motion that flows through time so that students are able to feel the passage of time throughout the phrase. In a lesson described later on in this chapter (pp. 155–158), students will also have experience "speaking" in sound to create original musical phrases.

Using a Song to Develop a Class Performance

The lesson in Figure 6.5 builds on earlier experiences with contour/direction and duration and uses what young students understand to develop a whole-class performance of a song. This lesson might also be a first experience with representing more than two durations in one song. In solving the problem, students will need to consider how elements of pitch and modality operate within the song to produce a particular affective quality. Based on their understanding of that affective quality, they will be asked to generate original musical ideas. Older students probably will not need to have as many experiences working with contour/direction and duration as young students will, but this kind of activity can be adapted to a song more appropriate for older students and the experience used as a basis for developing a class arrangement of the song.

Figure 6.5: Lesson Plan: Using a Song to Develop a Class Performance

National Standards: 1, 2, 3, 4, 7, 9

Grade: 2 and up, depending upon experience

Materials:

- "The Ghost of John."
- Icon charts representing duration (four different lengths and colors) and contour within phrases of the song (one chart for each phrase).
- Classroom instruments (including electronic instruments, if available).

Lesson assumes:

- Extensive prior experience working with songs that contain two different durations, a short sound and a long sound that lasts twice as long.
- Students have had many experiences working with iconic representation of pitch and duration and understand the sounds that the icons represent, that is: (1) that the icons represent how long the sound lasts, (2) that the location of the icons in relation to other icons represents the distances between the pitches, and (3) that their placement indicates melodic contour and direction.
- Prior experience accompanying class singing with steady beat patterns played on instruments.

Objective:

To help students expand their understanding of duration by working with the rhythmic elements of a song that contains four different durations.[6]

Organization:

Whole-group performance problem

Connection to prior knowledge/experience:

"Halloween is coming soon! Today we are going to try to make some Halloween music. How might you expect it to sound? We need to be thinking about some of the things that can make music sound eerie and scary. But before we make it sound like that, we need to know the Halloween song. In order to learn this new song, you will need to solve this puzzle. We will need four volunteers. Who would like to come up and hold these charts so that everyone can see them?"

Pose problems: Students will:

- Work together as a class to put the iconic representations of the phrases in the correct order, according to what they hear. (Engaging in this activity with their peers will help them to understand how the song is put together and also to know how to sing it accurately.)
- Arrange and perform the song with an instrumental accompaniment.
- Work together to organize and improvise a "scary" introduction and coda for the song, creating an appropriate setting for the song.

Students solve problems:

- Students listen to melody and "unscramble" charts.
- Students sing song.
- Students develop and perform a "scary" arrangement of the song.

Groundwork that enables:

In this whole-group, teacher-guided lesson, the teacher will have opportunities to support student strategies throughout the lesson and therefore does not need to provide all the information necessary to solve the problems at the start of the lesson. The students have worked with iconic representations of phrases of songs during earlier lessons. The only new aspect is that the phrases will not be presented in order.

Students share and discuss solutions:

There are really three different problems comprising this lesson. Since all are solved within the context of a whole-group, teacher-guided lesson, students are really sharing their proposals for solutions throughout the lesson.

Assessment:

- Students will show the depth and breadth of their thinking about duration, contour, and direction in their interactions with the teacher and peers throughout the arrangement of the cards.
- Students will show their understanding of the modality and affective quality of the song by their ability to sing the song with an appropriate feeling and develop an appropriate introduction and coda.

139

The Ghost of John

Martha Grubb

Have you seen The Ghost of John,

Long white bones with the skin all gone? _____ Oo _____

_____ Would-n't it be chil - ly with no skin on?

Since this is the first time this kind of activity is presented, you may require a more detailed explanation of how it would be carried out.

The chart holders "mix up" until the order in which they are standing does *not* match the order in which the phrases appear in the song. The teacher sings the first line of the song several times. It is important that the teacher sings the pitches and durations as accurately as possible. The students figure out which person is holding the pattern the teacher is singing. "As soon as you know, please raise your hand. Don't say it out loud, so everyone can have a chance to figure it out."

Once there are many hands raised, ask, "Who is holding the chart that looks like what the first part of the song sounds like?" When they have located the opening phrase, ask that person to stand at the head of the group (farthest to the left, as one would read it on a page). Even at this point, the teacher should not indicate whether or not the students are correct. This is their problem to solve. Instead, sing the song one more time, this time tracing the icons as you sing. The students should know immediately whether or not they are correct.

If they are correct, it is time to locate the second phrase. It is important to sing the melody from the beginning each time so that the children will be able to hear the phrases in context. As they look for the second phrase, sing through both the first and second phrases repeatedly. When they have agreed on a choice, line up phrases one and two and sing them one more time, this time inviting a student to trace the icons as you sing. (By now, many of the students may have already begun to sing with you, but they will probably sing softly to themselves as they think.)

Continue in this manner until the students agree that all four phrases have been put in the correct order. In unscrambling the charts, the students will be working together as individuals within the group—suggesting ideas, commenting on one another's ideas, testing suggested ideas—until all are agreed on a solution. The teacher will provide support by singing the phrases, tracing icons at appropriate points, assisting when needed, and managing the group discussion process (inviting children to share their ideas in an organized manner).

Once the puzzle is solved, ask all the students to trace the icons in the air (from their seats) as they try to sing the entire song. At this point, they will have heard and thought about the melody so many times and in so many ways that they will probably all be able to sing it through quite accurately.

Next, begin to work on the arrangement. "We need to make some background music for this song. First, we need some people to play instruments while we sing. If someone plays these two pitches (open fifth of the tonic and dominant) on the xylophones while we sing, it will sound just fine. Let's try it." Ask several students to play the open fifth repeatedly on several lower-pitched barred instruments or on the piano (on the first and third beats of each measure). Before the singing begins, the instruments should play an agreed-upon number of times (four works well, but if the children suggest an alternative number, try that too). It also works well if the last open fifth coincides with the last word of the song ("on"), but the children may have a different idea of how they would prefer to develop this arrangement.

Try out the various suggestions of how the open fifths might be played in relation to the melody and ask the students to agree on one version. Throughout the consideration of possibilities as to how they would like the song accompanied, you might invite several different groups of children to the instruments so that many individuals have opportunities to accompany the class as they consider options. Often, it is appropriate to invite the initiator of a suggestion to come up and try his or her idea and to teach it to others so they can try it too.

Once they have decided on their arrangement, it is time to add an introduction and coda. With young children, it is usually best to have choices of instruments already sitting in full view. With electronic instruments, unless you have time for the students to make the choices during class, it is usually best to choose an appropriate "scary" or "eerie" sound for each keyboard ahead of time. Ask the students to consider the options you have suggested and decide which sounds they would like to use and how they should be played. Focus the discussion on organizing the sounds: Which one might go first? Should it be played alone? Should it be played loud or soft? Fast or slow? Should we start with one and add the others one by one? Should the loudness change as we add (or take away) instruments? Let the children's suggestions guide your questions. Be careful not to press your own visions of the arrangement on them. Allow them to decide what will happen during the introduction and ending. After all, there is no right or wrong solution to the problem. If it works for the students and they are pleased with the results, then it is a viable solution.

Once all parts of the arrangement are decided, try performing it as the students have suggested. After the performance, ask them what they think of it. Does anything need to be fixed? changed? practiced? Does it sound like they wanted it to? Does the sound match what they thought it was going to sound like when they planned it in their heads (making them aware of their own musical thinking)? Are they satisfied with what they have produced? If so, then perform it for the classroom teacher when he or she returns, or for the next class, or the class next door, or for the children themselves.

Analyzing and Creating a Melody

This next set of lessons may span two or more class sessions, depending on the length of the sessions and the maturity of the students. Students will first use skips, steps, and repeated tones as a "doorway in" to an exploration of contour, direction, and duration in melody. They will then create original melodies. In carrying out the compositional portion of this lesson, students will need to make decisions regarding form, texture, dynamics, tempo, and other elements as well.

First, teach a lesson in which students focus on skips, steps, and repeated tones within melody. Which melody you decide to use will depend on the age and maturity of your students. One good example is the song "Lo Peter," which is part of a childrens' game from Ghana (CD, Track 3). The lyrics of this song have no literal meaning. They are Ghanaian children's interpretation of the English text:

> Row Peter, row Peter, row Peter, row Peter,
> Send my letter to my lover like the way I want it.

Cultural crossover such as this is not unusual in previously colonized nations. The game is quite popular among Ghanaian children today.[7]

Lo Peter

Ghanaian Game Song

Develop charts that represent the melody in icons. Charts for "Lo Peter" might look like this:

Using some of the techniques you have already learned, help your students explore the skips, steps, and repeated tones in this song. Through a problem-solving activity related to the icon charts, the students will learn to sing the melody. Once they know the melody well, they might engage in a performance activity using the melody. In this case, they can play the game associated with the song. Directions for playing the game can be found on our website *(www.mhhe.com/wiggins)*. Those playing the game should clap the beat as indicated in the previous musical example. Older students might improvise additional percussion parts to accompany the game, such as those suggested in the following example. The bell part could be played on an agogo bell, a cowbell, or a *gankogui* from Ghana, if one is available.

Lo Peter

Ghanaian Game Song

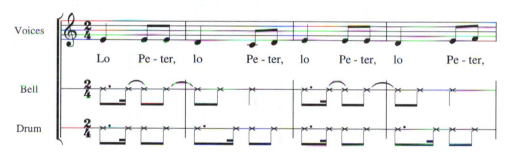

As an extension of this lesson, students might engage in the following composition project. This is an excellent first-time composition project for inexperienced composers (see Figure 6.6).

Figure 6.6: Lesson Plan: Creating a Melody

Materials:
- "Lo Peter," a children's game from Ghana, or any classroom song that has obvious patterns of skips, steps, and repeated tones in the melody.
- Icon charts representing melody.
- Classroom instruments.

Lesson assumes:
- Much experience singing melodies.
- Experience with melodic contour and direction.
- Some prior experience playing barred instruments.

National Standards: 1, 2, 4, 6, 7, 9
Grade: 2, 3 and up (with a different song)

Organization:
Whole-group performance problem.
Peer-supported composition problem.

Objective:
To help students expand their understanding of skips, steps, and repeated tones by composing their own melodies.

Connection to prior knowledge/experience = Groundwork that enables:
- Talk with the students about a song they know that has obvious patterns of skips, steps, and repeated tones within the melody or introduce a new song that has these characteristics.

Pose problems: Students will:
- Theorize about how they might play skips and steps on a barred instrument, based on their experience singing this song and others with similar characteristics.
- Work with a partner on a shared instrument to make up their own music that has skips and steps.

Students solve problems:
- Talk with the students about big skips and little skips and also about repeated tones. Encourage volunteers to try to play skips, steps, and repeated tones on a barred instrument that everyone can see.
- Talk about how musicians put lots of skips and steps together to make a melody or tune. You might play a song they know on the barred instrument, so that students can see the mallet making skips and steps as they hear the melody played.
- Students work with partners (or in groups of three or four, if there are fewer instruments available) to develop their own music that contains skips, steps, and repeated tones (essentially to create a melody).

Students share and discuss solutions:
- In the first portion of the lesson, ideas are shared in the large group setting.
- In the compositional portion, ideas are shared between partners and then with the whole group, in the discussions of the finished products.

Assessment: Students will show their understanding through:
- Their discussions of the icon charts.
- Their accurate performance of the song.
- Their original melodies and discussions of peers' melodies.

For this composition project, you will need enough barred instruments and mallets for each set of partners to have one instrument and two mallets. If the number of instruments is limited, it is possible (but a bit more challenging) to carry out this lesson with three or four students sharing one instrument, but each student would still need to have one mallet.

With very young students, it is best to explain the assignment before sending them to instruments. You might say something like, "You are going to have a chance to make up your own music that has skips, steps, and repeats. Each team of partners will have their own xylophone. You may remove some of the bars (to make skips) if you would like, but you might decide to use all the bars. Make a plan with your partner. You can make any kind of music you want, but it has to have some skips, some steps, and maybe some repeats. Any questions? Then please choose a partner and walk quietly to the instrument you would like to play. (With young children, it is most efficient and safest for the teacher to scatter xylophones around the room before the children begin.) When I turn off the lights, that means you need to stop playing so you can hear directions. Please try to be finished when the big hand on the clock gets to the "6." Then we will play our music for each other." For the very youngest students, allow 5 or 10 minutes for this independent work. Older students will appreciate having more time to work.

As the students work to create melodies, the teacher should remain available but should not interfere unless support is needed by individual students. Circulate throughout the room and make yourself available for questions and assistance, but it is better not to "hover." Give the students some space and independence. Encourage them to solve their own problems. The more you can stay out of the picture, the more surprising you might find the results. Second graders bring to music classrooms a significant amount of experience with the melodies of their worlds, and they work from that experience in creating their own.

As students share their solutions to this compositional problem, there will be many spontaneous comments about the work produced. If this is a first compositional experience, encourage the students to make positive and supportive comments to their peers and about their peers' work. It is not essential that comments be made about each and every composition (other than praise for success). At this early stage, it is important to generate a feeling in the classroom that making up music is something that everyone can do, and everyone can do well. There will be plenty of opportunity in later years to work on refining students' creating skills. At the outset, what is most critical is to help students develop a positive attitude about themselves as initiators of musical ideas.

Evaluating work produced through an open-ended assignment such as this one can inform the teacher of individual levels of understanding and can help the teacher to gauge where students are along a continuum of understanding of what it is to make music with others (e.g., sense of simultaneity and ensemble, sense of underlying pulse, sense of balance). The products produced through this assignment will represent a wide range of levels of understanding. It is important for the teacher to perceive this information because it is very useful in planning instruction and designing future lessons. It is also useful in assessing where individuals lie within the group, as far as understanding and performance skill are concerned.

In their solutions, some students might choose to work in a sort of question/answer format, taking turns with their partner (or partners). Some might choose to have both partners play at the same time, creating either a consonant or dissonant work depending on the decisions made by the students. Some develop complicated "routines" where the partners each have different responsibilities within one unified melodic line. In some ways, this last interpretation of the assignment requires the most sophisticated level of musical understanding. In some cases, it will be evident that the partners are engaged in producing a jointly understood musical idea. In other cases, where students are really working on a less sophisticated level of synthesis and understanding, individuals will perform their ideas simultaneously, but the ideas will have nothing to do with each other. In evaluating compositions such as these, it is important for the teacher to carefully watch what each individual is playing in order to adequately assess individual understanding of the concepts. In many of these cases, while the piece sounds quite cacophonous and disorganized, each individual has actually carried out the assignment but may not yet understand how to set his or her ideas into ensemble with a peer.

Samples of Student Work[8]

Original Composition Using Skips and Steps
COMPOSED BY TWO SECOND GRADERS IN FEBRUARY

Original Composition Using Skips and Steps
COMPOSED BY TWO SECOND GRADERS IN FEBRUARY

Original Composition Using Skips and Steps
COMPOSED BY TWO SECOND GRADERS IN FEBRUARY

 As a follow-up to this composing experience, students might enjoy listening to a Ghanaian xylophone piece played on an instrument called a *gyil* (CD, Track 4). On this instrument, hollow gourds placed under the bars serve as resonating chambers, and spider webs on the gourds produce a buzzing sound with each stroke. The piece, titled "Kpaa ma," is an example of a Bewa song of the Asante people from Ghana. Bewa literally means "you come" and is played recreationally at any social occasion in which many people are gathered together. Occasions may include, but are not limited to, the instoolment of a chief, harvest festivals, naming ceremonies, marriages, and other religious services. In these settings, everyone sings and dances, but the instrumental music is performed by specialist musicians. The melody of "Kpaa ma" contains four short phrases based on a pentatonic scale. The structure of these phrases is A, B, A', B'. The "A" phrase is based primarily on steps, the "B" phrase primarily on skips. The performer introduces the entire melody and then improvises. In the version of the piece on the CD, the improvisations are all based on the B phrase. Traditionally, improvisation on this melody would continue for a longer period of time and then lead into another Bewa melody. The shorter example that appears on the CD was created by the performer specifically for this lesson to make it possible for novices to study and understand the music and still preserve its integrity.

Experiencing and Creating with Dynamics

In the lessons in Figures 6.7 and 6.8, the element of dynamics is used as the "doorway in." Once "inside" the music, students will explore other compositional techniques used by the composer to give the impression that a parade is passing by.

Figure 6.7: Lesson Plan: Experiencing Dynamics (Part I)

Materials:

- Jacques Ibert (1890–1962): "Parade" from *Divertissement* (CD, Track 5).
- Chalkboard.
- Chart paper and markers.

Lesson assumes:

Experience finding and moving to beat and familiarity with the idea that music can be louder and softer.

National Standards: 6, 7, 9

Grade: 2 or 3 and up, if handled differently

Organization:

Whole-group, teacher-guided listening problem.

Objective:

To foster understanding of how dynamic change can generate a particular effect.

Connection to prior knowledge/experience = Groundwork that enables:

- Talk with the children about what it is like to watch a parade pass by, focusing on the idea that when the parade is far away the music is very soft, gets louder as it approaches, and fades as it leaves. If a composer wanted to create the same effect in a concert hall, how might he or she ask the musicians to play their instruments?
- Talk about how to play instruments softly and loudly.

Pose problems: Students will:

- Step to the beat of the recording, their feet reflecting the dynamic levels they hear (tiny steps when the music soft, larger or higher steps as it gets louder).
- Construct a diagram that reflects the dynamic plan the children heard in the music. It is best to theorize on the chalkboard and produce an agreed-upon version on the chart paper, to be saved for the next class session.
- Talk about what else they hear in the music. Listen again for other elements that make the music sound like a parade.

Students solve problems:

Students work together with teacher as described.

Students share and discuss solutions:

Ideas shared throughout.

Assessment:

Students will be able to describe what they have heard in the music through movement (stepping motion), iconic representation (diagram), and verbal description.

After connecting to students' prior knowledge, you might introduce the listening experience by saying something like, "This is a recording of some music where the composer tried to create the effect we have been discussing. Please stand and march in place to the music, lifting your feet really high when you think the music sounds loud and hardly lifting them at all when you think it sounds soft." [Students usually want to do this for more than one listening.]

Encourage the children to describe what they have heard. Ask them to construct a diagram that looks like what they heard. [They can give directions to the teacher who can draw the diagram on the board.] The diagram should reflect the terraced dynamics of the first part of the piece and the decrescendo of the latter part. Be sure to accept the children's suggestions. The diagram must make sense to *them*. Each class will probably construct a slightly different version. As long as the crucial elements are present, whatever they suggest will be fine. It may be necessary to listen to the piece again as you construct the diagram.

In preparation for the next lesson, you might say, "Next time you come to music class, you are going to have a chance to work together with some friends and try to make up your own music that uses louds and softs just the way this music does. How will your music sound? How will you play your instruments?"

Before working on their own pieces, there might be other things they can learn from this composer. "Let's listen one more time and see what else this composer does to make this music sound like a parade." [Students generally point out the steady beat, the strong drum beat, the trumpets, and other characteristics that make the orchestra sound like a marching band.]

Figure 6.8: Lesson Plan: Experiencing Dynamics (Part II)

Materials:
- Jacques Ibert (1890–1962): "Parade" from *Divertissement* (CD, Track 5).
- Chart containing diagram designed by the class during the last session.
- Assorted classroom xylophones, drums, and other percussion instruments.

Organization:
Small-group, peer-supported composition problem.

Lesson assumes:
- Participation in the previous analytical listening lesson.
- Sufficient prior experience playing classroom instruments to know how to play them independently.

Objective:
To provide an opportunity for students to expand their understanding of the use of dynamic change to generate a particular effect by using that understanding to create an original work that utilizes similar compositional strategies.

Connection to prior knowledge/experience:
- Hang the diagram in a place where everyone can easily see it. Remind the students of what they did last week. Ask the students to briefly describe what their diagram means in terms of dynamic plan, just to be certain that everyone remembers what they are supposed to do. You might play "Parade" one more time before they begin, or have it playing as they enter the classroom.

Groundwork that enables:
The previous lesson establishes the groundwork for this lesson. Ask the children to make up their own music that generates the same effect as they heard in "Parade." Be sure the children's diagram is in view. Remind them that their music is to follow the diagram (start very softly, get a little louder, then even louder, then the loudest part, and then gradually fade out and stop). Other decisions as to what they are to play or how the group is to be organized are up to the individual groups of children.

Pose problem: Students will:
- Work in small groups to compose original pieces that follow the same dynamic plan as reflected in the diagram. (A group size of four or five students usually works best, providing enough diversity of ideas, but still being a manageable size.)

Students solve problem:
Students work together for 10–20 minutes to invent an original piece. The teacher should be available to the students at all times, but should stay out of the way when not needed. (If these are first-time composers, you can anticipate that difficulties are more likely to arise out of organizational and social situations than from difficulties with the musical ideas.)

Students share and discuss solutions:
Groups share and discuss their pieces with the class.

Assessment:
Students' compositional processes and products will reflect their understanding of the function of dynamic change in a musical work. Their compositions will also reflect numerous other areas of their musical growth, including their concepts of simultaneity and ensemble, and their understanding of the roles of texture, form, beat, meter, melodic contour, rhythmic motifs, and so forth. Videotape or audiotape recordings of compositional products can easily become part of a portfolio of student work that can be used for assessment and record-keeping purposes.

Extension:
- Try adding some dynamics and dynamic changes to songs students already know, and consider the kinds of effects that are produced.

In carrying out the lesson described in Figure 6.8 with young children (second grade), it is probably best to group the instruments in five or six different areas of the room and ask the children to move to the area of their choice. It is difficult for second graders to choose an instrument from a storage shelf, carry it to a work area, and get organized. Moving the children to the instruments is easier. If possible, provide a balanced selection of instruments in each area, such as one drum, one barred instrument with several mallets (so that more than one student can play), and three assorted small percussion instruments.

It may take young and inexperienced composers only about 10 minutes to create their pieces. More experienced composers have more ideas and therefore require more time. When everyone is ready, share the products. Encourage the students to talk about what other students have chosen to do.

In organizing discussion of shared pieces, it helps to speak about the works in two ways. First, ask whether or not the students followed the parameters of the assignment and, briefly, how they carried that out. Second, ask "What else did they do that was not part of the assignment?" Possible questions for discussion:

- Does the piece follow the plan represented in the diagram? How did the group choose to follow the plan?
- How did the performers know when to change loudness levels? Did they use some kind of signal or plan?
- How do you think they knew when to stop?
- How was this group's piece different from that one?
- What other kinds of decisions did the group members make? What did they do besides change how loudly or softly they played? (These questions reflect "What else do you hear?" in addition to the parameters of the assignment, which served as the "doorway in" to this experience.)

Avoid critical or judgmental questions like, "Did you like this piece?" That is not the point of a lesson of this nature, although spontaneous applause and praise is always welcome.

Piece Based on Ibert's "Parade"

**COMPOSED BY FOUR SECOND GRADERS IN APRIL
(TWO STUDENTS SHARING ONE XYLOPHONE)**

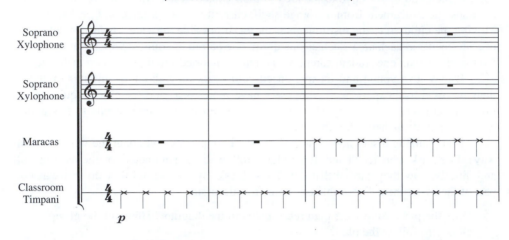

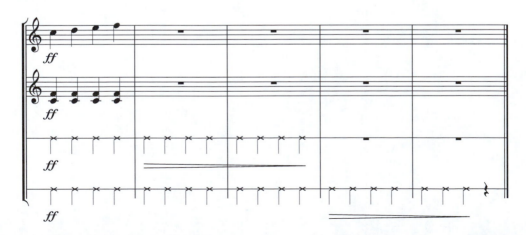

Musical Conversation

Figure 6.9 is a first experience in melodic improvisation. Students will use what they know about skips and steps, contour and direction, and duration to engage in melodic conversations with teacher and peers. This experience is an opportunity for students to use what they know to think in sound, organize those ideas, and produce an original product.

The musical selection was written for solo trombone. The trombone switches back and forth from playing with and without a mute. The music contains clear contrasts in pitch and playing technique, and displays an obvious character of conversation and dialogue with elements of questions and answers. The title is based on Lewis Carroll's poem "The Hunting of the Snark." The "snark" is a mystical fantasy animal.[9]

Figure 6.9: Lesson Plan: A Musical Conversation

Materials:
- Arne Norheim: "The Hunting of the Snark" (excerpt) (CD, Track 6).
- Six or seven barred instruments, each with two mallets.

Lesson assumes:
- Extensive experience singing melodies and analyzing those melodies for contour, direction, and duration characteristics.
- Sufficient experience playing barred instruments to be comfortable using them.

National Standards: 2, 3, 6, 7, 8, 9
Grade: 2 or 3 or as an introductory experience for students of any age

Organization:
Whole-group listening problem followed by a group improvisation experience.

Objective:
To provide an opportunity for students to expand their understanding of the use of dynamic change to generate a particular effect by using that understanding to create an original work that utilizes similar compositional strategies.

Connection to prior knowledge/experience:
- Talk with the children about melodies they know well and have analyzed during prior lessons. Talk about how these melodies sometimes contain phrases that seem to be musical questions and answers (e.g., "Paw Paw Patch," where a question is asked three times, on two different sets of pitches, and finally answered [resolved] in the fourth phrase of the melody).
- "Today we are going to do some work with questions and answers."

Pose problems: Students will:
- Listen to "The Hunting of the Snark" and theorize about what they think it is about. In the ensuing discussion, the teacher will focus attention on what the music does to "impersonate" a conversation.
- Try some improvised instrumental musical conversations with the teacher or peers, using barred instruments.
- Engage in improvised musical conversations with peers.

Students solve problems:
- Students listen and theorize about what is represented in the music.
- Students talk about how the music represents these ideas.
- Students take turns improvising a dialogue with the teacher and/or peers.

Groundwork that enables:
What the students already know about melody should enable them to analyze the listening example. The discussion of the listening example should enable them to engage in improvisational conversations with the teacher. The experience engaging in improvisational conversations with the teacher should enable them to engage in conversations with peers, without (or with less) teacher support.

Students share and discuss solutions:
Discussion occurs during the listening phases of the lesson. During the improvisation phase, students spontaneously sharing musical ideas throughout the experience. Verbal discussion is generally not needed during this phase. The understanding takes place through musical thought and interaction only.

Assessment:
Students will indicate their understanding of how the characteristics of melody can be organized to produce a musical conversation through their comments during the discussion of the listening example and through the musical ideas expressed during the improvisation phase of the lesson.

Extension:
- Older students might be asked to work with a partner to *compose* a musical conversation, differing from improvisation in that the pieces would be planned to the extent that students could replicate them on request.

Since this is the first improvisation experience presented, you may require some additional information in order to understand how to carry it out.

You can begin by saying, "I have a recording of some music that is supposed to sound like two people talking. Please listen to the music and see if you can figure out who these people might be and what they might be talking about."

During discussion of the listening experience, the teacher should ask focus questions like, "What did you hear in the music that made you think that?" "What is the music doing that makes it sound like that?"

To carry out the improvisation portion of the lesson, set six or seven barred instruments in a circle in the center of the room. Place two mallets on each instrument. Sit behind one instrument and invite volunteers to take places behind the remaining instruments. The rest of the class remains in their seats in the outer circle, where they can easily see and hear what is happening in the small group.

Suggest that the group try to have some conversations. Often, the students begin immediately (with little or no prompting) with one student making a statement on his or her instrument and someone else answering. If they seem to need more support than that, the teacher might suggest that they try some questions and answers. "I will ask a question. Who will answer me?" or "Linda, do you want to ask me a question or should I ask you a question?" This last way of working seems to set children at ease. The least threatening option seems to be the one in which they ask a question and wait, curiously, to see how the teacher will respond. It is actually a very effective way to begin because it helps establish a model for what is expected in the activity. Once they are at ease and feel comfortable with the process, the conversation generally takes off on its own with students interrupting and responding to one another quite eagerly.

Once this first group has finished saying what they want to say, a second group will take their place until eventually all students have had an opportunity to participate.

It is important to note that there is no intention that these questions and answers will resemble balanced phrase structure or cadences. There is no expectation that the answer will contain part of the question or a similar rhythm. These are to be spontaneous conversations, more similar in character to those portrayed in "The Hunting of the Snark." Someone might ask a very long question, and someone else might reply with a very short answer. Someone might "speak" for a while and someone else might respond with something that seems to be totally unrelated. With more experience, the students will begin to listen more carefully to one another, and the group improvisations will become more cohesive.

As the conversation in the circle becomes more comfortable, and more and more of the students in the small group are participating, the teacher should gradually withdraw from the conversation (gradually withdraw the scaffold) and allow the students to continue on their own.

How will you know when a conversation is over? In most cases, if all participants are "tuned in," it will be obvious. If the conversation seems to be wandering or continuing beyond the time allotted, the teacher can always "step in" and play something that pushes the conversation to a close.

The students in the outer circle—the audience—are generally very involved in the process in anticipation of the fact that they will soon be asked to take a turn. And they are curious about what their peers will do to solve the problem. It is an interesting process because some conversations are funny and some are quite serious. Each develops its own character, which is fascinating to all involved. When carried out with an air of acceptance and encouragement, this activity can be a most exciting one and not at all intimidating. The following is a transcription of an actual conversation between a teacher and a first-grade student who had never before engaged in such an activity.

Improvised Conversation

(BASED ON "THE HUNTING OF THE SNARK")

Student's motions were rhythmic. Student's pitches somewhat coincidental.

The sample lessons in this chapter were provided as models for what lessons for beginners might look like. They also serve as models of what teaching through problem solving looks like. As we move on to the lessons for more experienced students, keep in mind the ways in which the activities described in Chapter 7 build on understandings nurtured in the lessons in this chapter. You might try the activity in Box 6.6 with a partner or, if you feel ready, on your own.

BOX 6.6 (ACTIVITY)

Select some materials and try planning and carrying out some problem-solving lessons for young students and for older beginners. You might choose a teacher-directed lesson described in a school music text or journal and "turn it around" so that it becomes a musical problem for students to solve. Construct the lesson using the suggested lesson plan format.

ENDNOTES

1. For more information on singing with children, please see P. Bennett and D. Bartholomew, 1997, *Songworks I,* Belmont, Calif.: Wadsworth.
2. This idea comes from Mary Pautz.
3. These numbers refer to the nine U.S. National Standards for Music Education:

   1. Singing, alone and with others, a varied repertoire of music.
   2. Performing on instruments, alone and with others, a varied repertoire of music.
   3. Improvising melodies, variations, and accompaniments.
   4. Composing and arranging music within specific guidelines.
   5. Reading and notating music.
   6. Listening to, analyzing, and describing music.
   7. Evaluating music and music performance.
   8. Understanding relationships between music, the other arts, and disciplines outside the arts.
   9. Understanding music in relation to history and culture.

These National Standards are further described in:

The school music program: A new vision. 1995. Reston, Va.: MENC.
Performance standards for music: Grades preK–12. 1996. Reston, Va.: MENC.
National standards for arts education: What every young American should know and be able to do in the arts. 1994. Reston, Va.: MENC.

4. The piano-roll icons used in this chapter were developed by Eunice Boardman in her "Generative approach to music learning." (Bergethon, Boardman, and Montgomery, 1997.)
5. This lesson was inspired by one I learned from David Walker.
6. This lesson is based on a process I learned from Eunice Boardman.
7. As taught by Mark Stone and Amma Serwah, Oakland University.
8. These compositions were created by second graders who had previously worked with a Western skip/step song, not with "Lo Peter" or the Bewa song.
9. I was introduced to this piece by noted Norwegian music educator Magne Espeland. It appears in his book, *Musikk i bruk (Music in use),* Norway: Stord/Haugesund lærarhøgskule.

SELECTED RESOURCES

Andress, Barbara. 1998. *Music for young children.* Fort Worth, Tex., Harcourt Brace.

Beethoven, J., et al. 1995–present. *The music connection: Grades K–8.* Morristown, N.J.: Silver Burdett Ginn and Scott Foresman. *The Music Connection* is an entire curriculum comprised of a wide variety of resource materials including songbooks, textbooks, and CD collections. For complete information on *The Music Connection,* visit the Silver Burdett Ginn website at <www.sbgschool.com/sbgmusic/index.html>.

Bergethon, B., E. Boardman, and J. Montgomery. 1997. *Musical growth in the elementary school.* 6th ed. Fort Worth, Tex.: Harcourt Brace.

Bond, J., et al. 1995–present. *Share the music: Grades K–8.* New York: McGraw-Hill. *Share the Music* is an entire curriculum comprised of songbooks, CDs, videos, and other resources. For complete information on *Share the Music,* visit the McGraw-Hill website at <www.mmhschool.com/teach/music/sharethemusic/program/index.html>.

Seeger, R. C. 1948 *American folk songs for children.* New York: Doubleday.

Collections of music from around the world are published by World Music Press, P.O. Box 2565, Danbury, CT 06813. Browse the press's catalog at <www.worldmusicpress.com/>.

Chapter 7

DESIGNING MIDDLE-LEVEL MUSICAL PROBLEMS

Chapter 7 provides information about teaching middle- or upper-elementary children. It also includes examples of lesson plans for students with some prior experience working with musical ideas. The chapter also talks about designing units of instruction. Additional lesson plans can be found on the website at www.mhhe.com/wiggins.

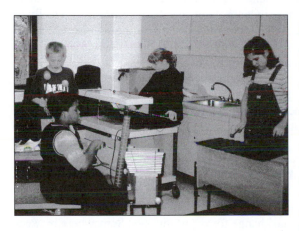

Once students understand the more basic musical elements and how they function in the songs, listening examples, and their own original products, they are ready to deal with broader, overarching musical issues in these same kinds of contexts. Students who have been engaged since kindergarten or first grade in a curriculum, such as the one presented here, probably will be ready to engage in the middle-level, problem-solving experiences suggested in this chapter by the third or fourth grade. In the case of older beginners, you would need to assess their understanding of the entry-level experiences in order to decide when it would be appropriate to move on to these more complex issues. For older beginners who might move rather quickly through the basic experiences, the use of these middle-level problems may be appropriate much earlier in the overall time frame.

As described in Chapter 6, broader issues that form the basis for middle-level problems might include investigation into the effects of tempo and dynamic change, more formalized work with form and texture, and more specific work with pitch and rhythm. At this point, students may have had enough experience with iconic representation of pitch and duration to begin to make a transition to standard notation. This is best accomplished by using both icons and standard symbols side-by-side for several months, giving students the option of reading either—or both—as they work. Eventually, individual students will no longer need the iconic version and will begin to prefer to use symbolic notation. Using both forms of notation side-by-side for an extended period of time enables individuals to make the transition when they are ready and allows students to take responsibility for accomplishing this on their own because they always have a reference point against which to check themselves. Students might continue to explore non-Western notation systems. An example, shared by Bryan Burton, can be found on the website *(www.mhhe.com/wiggins)*.

Students who have been solving musical problems since kindergarten or first grade, such as the ones described in Chapter 6, probably will be ready to make this transition sometime during their third-grade year. This is about the same time that many students become quite proficient at verbal reading and begin using their reading skills to enable them to do other kinds of investigation and learning. Their music experiences then parallel their language experiences because, as students become more conversant with standard notation, they become more able to use their new skills to investigate and learn more about music. Since in many schools instrumental instruction begins in fourth grade, it is helpful for students to have comfortably made the transition by the end of third grade. This also makes the third or fourth grade a good time to help students learn more about the specific instruments that make up the various families of orchestral and nonorchestral families. [However, rather than teaching an extended unit on identification of timbres with no musical context, it is preferable to teach students about specific instruments gradually as they have experience with them in listening, performing, and creating settings.] Students of this experience level might also enjoy exploring instrument timbres used by non-Western cultures. This can be accomplished easily, if such instruments are available in the classroom and can be augmented by exploration through CD-ROM resources.

At third or fourth grade, as children's dexterity and coordination mature, many general music teachers include experiences playing recorder and/or keyboard, which nicely parallel the transition to reading notation. [Early instrumental experiences should include opportunities for students to utilize iconic and symbolic notation side-by-side.] Third graders have often reached the musical maturity to be able to sing rounds and melodies with countermelodies, providing a link to choral singing, which in many schools begins in fourth grade as well. It is important for the skills learned in general music class to carry over into students' other musical experiences, both in school and out.

Third grade is also a time of social change for many students. Somewhere between the end of second and the beginning of third grade, many students become much more involved with peers, and peer interaction becomes one of the strongest centers of their lives. Through other classroom experiences and through experiences outside of school, such as scouts and sports teams, these children become better able to work with peers. As students become more autonomous in their social interactions, they begin to feel quite comfortable working with peers as partners or in small groups; and, in many cases, they seem to prefer this kind of instructional setting. They move away from dependence on adults and often seek peer advice in addition to, or instead of, that of adults. Therefore, at this point in their school lives, pair and small-group work can appropriately become a more prominent feature of the classroom experience.

Like the least experienced students, middle-level learners of all ages need to engage in singing, moving, playing, listening, and creating experiences; and they should be utilizing available technology in their classroom experiences. Middle-level learners are more capable of sustaining interest and enthusiasm during longer-term projects and units of study. Some of the lessons that follow are designed to be one-period music lessons, while others are a series of connected lessons forming a more extended unit of study. These lessons are intended for students in third, fourth, or even early fifth grade. The same lessons, if based on more sophisticated song material, would be appropriate for older students as well.

LESSON PLANS FOR MIDDLE-LEVEL STUDENTS

The Effects of Tempo Change

These first two experiences are designed to help students begin to understand tempo decisions that a composer or performer might make and the effects those decisions generate in a musical work.

To begin the lesson, the teacher might say something like, "You have known for a long time that some music moves very slowly and that some music moves very fast. What if you were going to make a piece that started out slow and then became fast or started fast and became slow? How would you do it? How might you get from a slow part to a fast part, for instance?" As students make suggestions, the teacher graphically represents their ideas on the board, in a way that indicates that it is the pace of the beat that is changing. One way to do this might be:

Suggestion A: | | | | | ||||||||||

Suggestion B: | | | | | (STOP) ||||||||||

Suggestion C: | | | | | | | | | | |||||||||||

The students will then listen and decide which diagram best represents what they hear in the recording (see Figure 7.1). You might tell the students they will hear a song that starts out in a slow tempo and changes to fast. Ask them to listen and keep the beat by patting their hands on their laps. When they feel the beat change speed, they should change the speed of their patting. They are to decide which of their suggestions, if any, was used by the composer. (This recording contains an accelerando.)

You might then ask, "Why do you think this composer decided to change speed?" [The singer is singing about someone being swallowed by a snake, is probably a bit nervous, and must finish the song before being gobbled up. Whatever their answers, they should recognize that the setting is appropriate to the text.]

The students might then perform their own version of the song. Because most children enjoy the humorous quality of this song, they generally ask to sing it several times. At this point, you might add instrument parts that play slowly at first and then accelerate at the appropriate point.

Figure 7.1 demonstrates how this lesson might be written in the lesson plan format suggested in Chapter 4.

Figure 7.1: Lesson Plan: The Effects of Tempo Change (Part I)[1]

Materials:

For Younger Students:
• Shel Silverstein: "Boa Constrictor," from the CD *Peter, Paul and Mommy*, 1969, Warner (#1785-2).

For Older Students:
• Cyril Scott (1879–1970): Pastoral Reel for Cello and Piano (CD, Track 7). 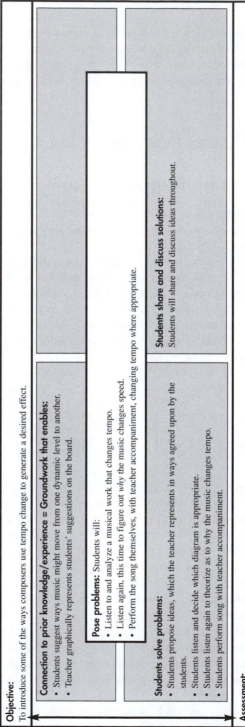 (Lesson is written for "Boa Constrictor" but can be adapted for Scott piece.)
• Chalkboard or whiteboard.

Lesson assumes:
• Experience finding and moving to beat.
• Familiarity with the idea that music can move in a variety of tempi.

National Standards[2]: 1, 6, 7, 8
Grade: 3 and up

Organization:
Whole-group analytical listening and performance problem.

Objective:
To introduce some of the ways composers use tempo change to generate a desired effect.

Connection to prior knowledge/experience = Groundwork that enables:
• Students suggest ways music might move from one dynamic level to another.
• Teacher graphically represents students' suggestions on the board.

Pose problems: Students will:
• Listen to and analyze a musical work that changes tempo.
• Listen again, this time to figure out *why* the music changes speed.
• Perform the song themselves, with teacher accompaniment, changing tempo where appropriate.

Students solve problems:
• Students propose ideas, which the teacher represents in ways agreed upon by the students.
• Students listen and decide which diagram is appropriate.
• Students listen again to theorize as to why the music changes tempo.
• Students perform song with teacher accompaniment.

Students share and discuss solutions:
Students will share and discuss ideas throughout.

Assessment:
Students will be able to describe what they have heard in the music through:
• Movement (patting motion).
• Iconic representation (discussion of diagrams on board).
• Verbal description.

Extension:
The small-group composition lesson that follows.

Depending on the length of the class session, there may be time during this first class to begin work on the composition project described in Figure 7.2. In a 30- to 40-minute class, there may be time for students to choose who they will work with and which instruments they want to play, which will save some time in the next class session.

It is very possible, particularly if there was time during the first class for students to form groups and start planning, that the students may enter the room already engaged in planning their compositions. If this is the case, it is best to stay out of their way and allow them to get to work with minimal teacher interference.

For the lesson in Figure 7.2, you might write the assignment on the board:

1. Find a group to work with (four, five, or six students in a group).
2. Choose instruments and a work area in the room.
3. Make up a slow section.
4. Decide whether the fast section will have the same music as the slow section or whether it will be a new idea.
5. Play the slow section. Play the fast section.
6. Create a connecting section that speeds up little by little.
7. Please be ready in 20 minutes (or more, if time allows).

While it is possible for students of this age to produce a work that satisfies these parameters in about 20 minutes, keep in mind that the more time they have to work, the more complex the music they will produce. It is possible for students to work on these pieces through two class sessions and share and discuss them during a third, creating a unit of lessons that takes place in four class sessions.

Figure 7.2: Lesson Plan: The Effects of Tempo Change (Part II)

Materials:
- Same as previous lesson (Part I).
- Assorted classroom xylophones, drums, and other percussion instruments, electronic instruments (preferably one for each student or enough for students to share).

Lesson assumes:
- Participation in the previous lesson.
- Prior experience playing classroom instruments.

National Standards: 2, 4, 7
Grade: 3 and up

Organization:
Small-group composition problem.

Objective:
To broaden students' understanding of the effect of tempo change on a work by providing an opportunity for them to develop their own original compositions utilizing tempo change.

Connection to prior knowledge/experience:
- Previous lesson's diagrams on board.
- Perhaps sing or listen to the song or piece one more time.

Groundwork that enables:
Last lesson's analytical listening/performing experiences.

Pose problem:
Students will work in small groups to create original compositions that use tempo change to generate a particular effect. They may use electronic or acoustic instruments or some combination of the two—whatever is available.

Students solve problem:
Students work with peers to select group members and instruments, develop thematic material, and set that material into a context that fits the prescribed tempo plan. Once they have developed their material, they will assemble the parts and practice the piece, making suggestions and corrections as they go, until they are satisfied with their work.

Students share and discuss solutions:
- Share finished products.
- Discuss decisions made by each group. Did they do what the assignment required? How did they choose to carry it out? How did they know when to change speed? Did they use some kind of signal or plan? What else did they change besides speed? How was one group's piece different from another's? What other kinds of decisions did they make?

Assessment:
Students' compositional processes and products will be reflective of:
- Their understanding of the function of tempo change in a musical work.
- Numerous other areas of their musical growth, including their concepts of simultaneity and ensemble, and understanding of the roles of texture, form, beat, meter, melodic contour, rhythmic motifs, dynamic change, and so forth.

Extension:
Explore the use of tempo change in other listening and performing experiences and consider the effects generated.

Sample of Student Work

Original Composition Based on "Boa Constrictor"
COMPOSED BY FIVE THIRD GRADERS IN JANUARY

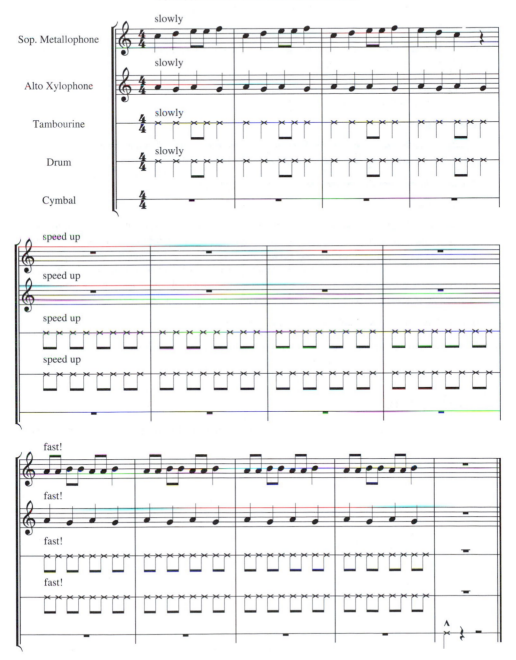

ASSESSMENT RUBRIC FOR TEMPO CHANGE PIECES

Below level:

Students exhibit simultaneity problems; there is no sense of underlying pulse or ensemble. Some group members might not understand where one section ends and the next begins.

Basic level:

1. Piece contains a slow section and a fast section, and an accelerando or some other way of connecting the two sections.

2. Group members stay together and maintain a common underlying pulse so that their tempo changes can be recognized by the listener.

Proficient level:

1. In addition to the basic-level criteria, the work contains recognizable thematic material—something more than all group members playing together on the beat.

2. The thematic material may be melodic or rhythmic in nature.

Advanced level:

1. In addition to the proficient-level criteria, there is some relationship between the thematic material and the tempo change. For example: The slow section may have one theme, the fast section another, and the accelerando or ritardando may contain some sort of connecting material (bridge or interlude). Or the slow and fast sections may contain the same thematic material with the only difference being the tempo change. In either case, it would be expected that the thematic material would make a complete statement of some kind, making the work sound like a unified entity.

2. The work is well-executed (well-rehearsed and performed) by the group.

3. The work might be sophisticated enough to evoke an affective response from the listener.

Tonal Center

The lesson described in Figure 7.3 suggests ways of introducing the idea of tonal center.

Figure 7.3: Lesson Plan: Tonal Center

National Standard: 1
Grade: 2 or 3, depending upon prior experience

Organization:
Whole-group performance problem.

Materials:

• Any song that is focused around the tonic, where the tonic falls on a strong beat and is repeated several times, such as "Head to Shoulders"[3] or "The Court of King Carraticus."[4]

Lesson assumes:

• Numerous prior experiences working with melodic contour.

Objective:
To help students begin to understand tonal center.

Connection to prior knowledge/experience = Groundwork that enables:

• "How can you tell when a song is over, even if you have never heard it before?" Explore some familiar and unfamiliar melodies, played two ways: with the final cadence unresolved (leaving them "hanging" on the dominant) and with the final cadence resolved.

• Encourage students to describe the way these two versions make them feel. Draw upon their descriptions of the closure that resolution generates.

• Identify the place to which the music returns as the "home tone."

Pose problem(s): Students will:

• Locate the home tones in a new melody, based on the opening activities and their life experience with harmonic resolution.

• Sing the melody, doubling all "home tones" on barred instruments.

Students solve problem(s):

• After the opening activity, students will learn the new song and try to locate the home tones. One way to accomplish this is to ask students to stand while listening and singing, and to sit whenever they think they hear the music "going home."

• Once they have identified all the home tones, ask some students to play only the home tones on barred instruments while everyone sings the song.

• In the case of "Head to Shoulders," students would then learn the handclap motions and enjoy the song in its cultural context.

Students share and discuss solutions:
Occurs throughout the experience.

Assessment:
Students will be able to describe the feeling generated by the concept of "home tone" and locate "home tones" in a simple song.

Extension:
Students who know how to play the recorder might try improvising or composing original melodies that focus around the tonic.

169

Head to Shoulders

African American Handclap Game   Collected and transcribed by Rosita Sands

Head to shoul-ders ba-by one   two three.   Head to shoul-ders ba-by

one   two three.   Head to shoul-ders, Head to shoul-ders, Head to shoul-ders, Head to

shoul-ders, Head to shoul-ders ba-by one   two   three.   Knee to an-kle ba-by

one   two   three.   Knee to an-kle ba-by one   two   three . . .

Knee to ankle baby one two three.
Milk the cow baby one two three.
Push the buggy baby one two three.
'Round the world baby one two three.
That's all baby one two three.
(Cumulative verses at the end)

Directions for handclap game on website.

Once the students have understood the idea of tonal center (home tone), they can work in pairs or independently to graph the contour of a melody, indicating the home tones. One way to do this is to use worksheets on which a line has been drawn to represent the home tone:

Home Tone Line

For the first attempts, choose songs that begin on the home tone and do not dip below, so that all of the lowest-sounding pitches will be home tones. After students have had several opportunities to hear a song in its entirety, sing it one line at a time and ask students to draw the contour they hear— making their line touch the "home tone line" whenever they think the music reaches the home tone. Students might then perform the song sitting down on all the home tones and standing for the rest of the song or playing all the home tones on a barred instrument as they sing. A song like the Dutch spinning song "Sarasponda" (below) works very well for this activity.[5]

Sarasponda

Dutch Spinning Song

Sa - ra - spon-da, sa - ra-spon-da, sa - ra - spon-da ret set set. Sa - ra -

spon-da, sa - ra-spon-da, sa - ra - spon-da ret set set. Ah do ray oh. Ah

do ray boom day oh. A do ray boom day ret set set, Ah say pa say oh.

Older beginners probably will be ready to engage in an activity like this shortly after they have been introduced to the idea of home tone as the place where familiar songs come to rest comfortably and sound as though they are finished. [Playing the first line of "America," ending on the penultimate dominant chord with the leading tone in the melody, works well to demonstrate this phenomenon.]

What Do You Hear?

It is helpful to structure some classroom experiences in ways that will enable you to learn more about how your students perceive and understand the music they hear. In particular, these kinds of experiences can help you to plan future instruction by helping you to iden- tify what students already know. One particularly useful tool is a music puzzle technique, an idea conceived by a Norwegian music educator, Magne Espeland.[6] For this lesson, the puzzle pieces in Figure 7.4 should be photocopied (enlarged, if possible) and cut apart. Each group will need 6–8 copies of the first puzzle piece and 3–4 copies of the others. Students should have more pieces than they will need to solve the puzzle.

FIGURE 7.4

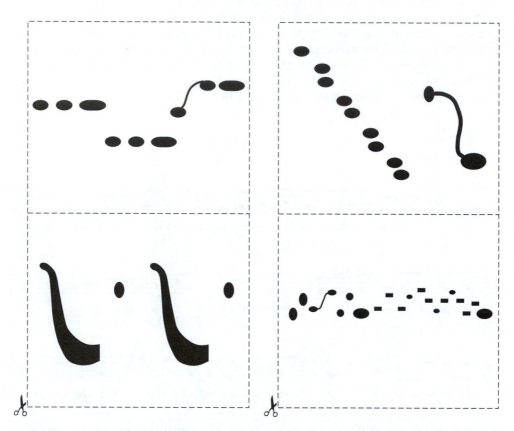

Whether or not students have prior experience with analysis of form will color the nature of their work in this lesson (Figure 7.5). The assignment can be an early experience with form or an expansion of prior experiences with form. Student responses will be more or less sophisticated, but the materials can be used in either case because they promote discussion on a variety of levels.

Figure 7.5: Lesson Plan: What Do You Hear?

Materials:

- Dimitri Kabalevsky (1904–1987): "March" from *The Comedians* (CD, Track 8).
- Puzzle pieces—a total of four different patterns illustrating different parts of the composition.
- Extra puzzle pieces of each of the four patterns.
- Blank paper cut to the same size as the puzzle pieces.
- Scissors and markers for each group.

Lesson assumes:

- Prior analytical listening experiences in which students have listened to identify and represent their understanding of generally obvious elements such as dynamics and steady beat.
- Prior experience with graphic representation of musical ideas.

National Standards: 6, 7, 8
Grade: 3 and up, depending upon prior experience

Organization:
Small-group analytical listening problem.

Objective:
To help students develop and demonstrate their understanding of a work by organizing a number of puzzle pieces. The pieces contain graphic representations of the different aspects of the music, such as the form, rhythm, and, in part, the dynamics of the piece. Arranging the puzzle pieces provides an ideal starting point for further dialogue concerning organization of thematic material to create form, melodic questions and answers, dynamics, contour and direction, rhythm, orchestration, etc.

Connection to prior knowledge/experience:	**Groundwork that enables:**
• Relate to prior experiences "tracking" graphic representations of music as they listened (e.g., "Ballet of the Unhatched Chicks"). Today the graphic representation has been "cut apart" like a puzzle which they will need to assemble in a way that fits what they hear in the music. **Pose problem:** Students will: • Listen to the music and arrange the puzzle cards according to what they hear in the music. • Think about and discuss the qualities in the music that influenced them to place the cards the way they did. • Compare their solutions to those of peers.	Prior experience with graphic representation of musical ideas.
Students solve problem:	**Students share and discuss solutions:**
• Small groups will listen to the music, study the puzzle pieces, and decide how to arrange them to best reflect what they hear. • Teacher needs to play the music as often as students need and request. • Students decide on a plan of action and arrange puzzle pieces. They may request additional pieces, or want to alter pieces with scissors or markers.	• When groups are ready, play music once again and ask one group to point to and actively follow along with their puzzle as the music plays. • Groups will then discuss the decisions made, explaining what they heard in the music that caused them to make particular decisions. • Encourage them to discuss the ways the piece is constructed.

Assessment:
Students will indicate the level and sophistication of their understanding of form, identification of thematic material, timbre, dynamics, and more through:

- Their discussions within their groups.
- Their decisions about the arrangement of the puzzle pieces.
- Their comments to the class during the sharing portion of the lesson.

173

Be aware that the puzzle cards in Figure 7.4 are not completely accurate representations of the thematic material for every section of the work. This is intentional. While the puzzle pieces are all identical, there are subtle differences among the sections of music. Students may choose to alter or redesign a puzzle piece or decide to place it slightly higher or lower in relation to the others. Some may use markers to thicken the lines to represent louder or thicker entrances of the theme. Some may make alterations that reflect timbral changes or additions.

As in many small-group, problem-solving lessons, much of the learning occurs during the times when the groups' ideas are shared with the larger group. To promote this, you need to think carefully about the questions you might ask students. For this lesson, you might ask:

> "What did you hear in the music that made you decide to put the puzzle together in just that way? Why have you (or have you not) lined up the cards right after one another?"
>
> "Did you decide to change or add anything to the cards? Why?"
>
> "Do you think the composition consists of different parts? If so, how many parts? Are the parts alike or different? Which instruments are playing the different parts?"

Espeland suggests an alternate approach to this same piece (or similar pieces): a movement problem in a small-group setting, carried out in a similar manner to the lesson based on "Saltarello Giorgio," described on pp. 56–57. "Listen to the piece and decide how your group will move (or walk) to reflect what you hear in the music."[7]

Puzzle cards can be made for any music that has a recognizable pattern. Here is an example of a lesson that uses puzzle cards to enable students to become immersed in the contour of a melody. The cards are to be used with a recording of the melody of "Uncle Sam," a Native American song (CD, Track 9). This particular version, collected by Bryan Burton, was learned from an elderly Seneca singer in western New York in 1989. The flute version that appears in the CD collection is from South Dakota. Burton writes extensively about the song and its cultural context in his *Moving within a Circle* (book with recorded examples, 1993, World Music Press). From this valuable resource, you can learn a traditional Iroquois dance that can be performed with this song. There are many other ways students might explore this melody within an appropriate cultural context. However, they must first be drawn into its beauty, which in this case I think can be best accomplished by learning to understand the elegance and purity of the melodic line.

The following puzzle cards might be used to accomplish this:

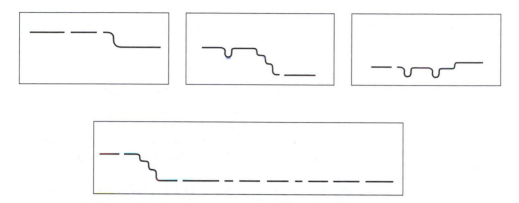

As with the Kabalevsky piece, students should have opportunities to listen to the melody repeatedly until they are able to agree on an arrangement of the cards that adequately reflects what they hear.

In solving the puzzle, students will become familiar with the melody. Once they are familiar, you might continue in one of several ways. You might connect the experience of the flute melody to an experience with the sung version that also appears in *Moving within a Circle*. This might be followed by an experience with the Iroquois dance described in that source.

A different way of continuing this lesson would be to encourage students who are familiar with soprano recorder to explore their recorders to try to play the melody or improvise a similar-sounding melody. If possible, you might purchase plastic Native American flutes that have been developed specifically for use by students in schools.[8] According to R. Carlos Nakai, the well-known Native American flute expert and performer,[9] it is a Native American viewpoint that the music that students create on such a flute will always be "authentic," since expertise is considered experience-related. The music of a novice is respected for that individual's level of experience in the same way as the music of an expert is respected for his or her level of experience. Novices are expected to make their own music in the style of what they hear. Young children who are familiar with the basic principles of recorder playing can easily improvise original flute melodies on school versions of Native American flutes.

DESIGNING EXTENDED UNITS OF INSTRUCTION

A unit of instruction generally consists of a series of interrelated lessons. In designing a unit, the teacher needs to think on an even broader level than when planning one lesson—considering all aspects of the element or principle that will form the basis for the unit and deciding which aspects will be addressed within this particular unit. Box 7.1 suggests a strategy for unit planning.

BOX 7.1

To plan a unit:

- Choose a musical concept or principle that students need to understand.
- Think about the various aspects of that concept or principle.
- Decide which aspects of the concept or principle this unit will address.
- Design a series of performing, creating, and listening experiences that have the potential to bring students to a higher level of understanding of the concept or principle.
- Check to see whether you have included multiple ways for students to work with the concept or principle and multiple ways through which both the teacher and students will be able to assess student understanding of the concept or principle.
- Check to see whether you have included a variety of instructional settings, including teacher-guided, whole-group instruction, small-group or pair work, and, if appropriate, independent work.

The result will be a unit of lessons designed around a series of musical problems for students to solve. The unit will consist of some combination of performance-based problems, listening-based problems, and creating-based problems. As students participate in these experiences and work together to solve these problems, they will reach progressively higher levels of understanding, and they will move closer and closer to being able to understand the higher-level concept that underlies the unit.

Planning a Unit on Texture

Consider some of the thought processes that might underlie the designing of a unit dealing with texture:

1. **Choose a musical concept or principle that students need to understand.**
   Through assessment of the products of several composition assignments, the teacher has determined that students are not using much textural variety in their work, indicating they may have limited knowledge of textural possibilities. Therefore, the teacher decides to plan a unit that will enable the students to explore various aspects of texture.

2. **Think about the various aspects of that concept or principle.** In dealing with texture, students need to develop an understanding of the various textural possibilities and the wide array of effects these different textural options can produce. They need to understand that music of all styles, genres, and cultural contexts has certain commonalities in its textural organization. If music is sound, moving through time and space, organized to express, then texture is one of the ways in which music (of all kinds) is organized.

3. **Decide which aspects of the concept or principle this unit will address.** What does one need to understand in order to understand textural possibilities? Within the unit, specific lesson plans will focus on one or more of the following ideas.

Within the concept of texture, students need to understand that:

- Music moves in layers (few or many).
- Some music is arranged in thicker layers than others (thick or thin).
- Some music has only one layer.
- Sometimes all the layers start and end together.
- Sometimes the layers start and end at different times.
- Some music has only one melody (monophony).
- Some music has more than one melody or one melody performed at different times within the work (polyphony).
- Some music moves in blocks or chunks of sound (homophony or chordal motion).
- Some music has a melody with an accompaniment (students tend to identify this as "background" or "chords").
- These possibilities can exist in all styles, genres, and music of all cultural contexts.

4. **Design a series of performing, creating, and listening experiences that have the potential to bring students to a higher level of understanding of the concept or principle.**

Sample Unit on Texture

LESSON 1: "I LOVE THE MOUNTAINS"

Perform and analyze:

Melody.

Melody and countermelody.

Melody and countermelody accompanied by a repeating bass line.

Melody and countermelody accompanied by a repeating bass line and chords.

Melody and countermelody accompanied by a repeating bass line and chords and additional countermelody.

Graphic representation of student performance.

LESSON 2: "ONE BOTTLE OF POP"

Perform and analyze:

Connect last week's experience to notation. With a partner, compare the page of music to last week's experience with a graphic score.

Can they figure out how the score indicates the song should be sung?

Can they describe the texture?

Perform the song.

LESSON 3: "RÍU, RÍU, CHÍU"

Listen and analyze:

Use understanding of score and graphic score to understand the texture of what they hear.

Listen and graph what they hear (in pairs or small groups).

LESSON 4: TEXTURE PIECES

Create/Perform:

Either realizing a texture chart provided by the teacher or developing their own—or developing charts
for one another—create pieces that use a variety of textures.

Perform their finished products for the class.

5. **Check to see whether you have included multiple ways for students to work with
   the concept and multiple ways through which both the teacher and students will
   be able to assess student understanding of the concept or principle.** In this unit,
   students both sing and play in a variety of textural settings, using both iconic and symbolic representation of textural ideas. They engage in analytical listening with an
   opportunity to demonstrate their understanding through graphic representation and a
   compositional experience based on what they learned throughout the unit.

6. **Check to see whether you have included a variety of instructional settings, including teacher-guided, whole-group instruction, small-group or pair work, and, if
   appropriate, independent work.** In this unit, students engage in teacher-guided,
   whole-group instruction followed by work in pairs, analytical listening in pairs or
   small groups followed by extended work in small groups, with a culminating whole-
   group activity.

UNIT: TEXTURE

Melody and Countermelody

The lesson described in Figure 7.6 introduces texture (melody/countermelody) as an
organizing tool.

Figure 7.6: Lesson Plan: Texture (Melody/Countermelody)

Organization:
Whole-group performance problem.

Materials:

- "I Love the Mountains."
- Chalkboard or whiteboard.
- Barred instruments (bass xylophones and/or metallophones, if available).
- Piano or keyboard.
- Bass line represented in icons (see below).

Lesson assumes:

- Extensive experience singing with peers and proficiency at singing a melody in tune, when other musical ideas (accompaniment patterns, etc.) are present.

Objective:
To introduce texture as an organizational tool.

Connection to prior knowledge/experience = Groundwork that enables [in this lesson]:

- You might relate this unit to the students' own composition experiences, talking about how when they make up their own pieces, some of the decisions they usually need to make are: how many parts there will be, whose part will be played alone, will there be a drum part or other "background" idea, and so on.
- The class might talk about decisions students have made in particularly memorable compositions. This unit will provide the students with a broader basis from which to make these decisions. They will learn about how professionals make textural decisions, and what some of the choices are.
- You might relate the number of layers and the thickness of the layers in a piece of music to fibers in clothing.

Pose problem: Students will:

- Learn to perform the melody of the song against the ostinato countermelody, and with a simple accompanying figure (the bass line).
- Perform the melody, countermelody, and bass line along with a chordal accompaniment.
- Perform the melody, countermelody, bass line, and chordal accompaniment along with an additional melody.
- Decide on a way of diagramming the texture of their performance.

Students solve problem:

- Challenge students to play the bass line while the teacher sings the ostinato, making it clear that each pitch lasts two beats. Once they feel comfortable with the ostinato, ask the students to sing it along with the bass line, while the teacher sings the melody. Once they are comfortable with both ostinato and melody, divide the class in half, and challenge them to sing the parts together, switching parts at the appropriate points.
- Find a student who knows how to play the chordal part of the piano duet based on "Heart and Soul." (There is always at least one!) Ask that student to add that part to the performance. You might ask the xylophones to play twice through the progression, add the piano part for two repeats of the progression, bring in the ostinato ("I Love the Mountains") to be sung twice through the progression, and then add the melody. Let everyone continue until the piece ends, and then all end simultaneously.
- Find a student who knows how to play the melody part of the piano duet based on "Heart and Soul" (or play it yourself). Let the students begin the arrangement as before, and at one point, add the "Heart and Soul" melody as well.
- Using suggestions from the group, create a score that graphically represents the texture they performed.

Students share and discuss solutions:

Sharing occurs throughout.

Assessment:
Students will show their understanding of the textural aspects of this work through their ability to perform and graph the arrangement.

BASS LINE FOR "I LOVE THE MOUNTAINS"

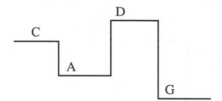

I Love the Mountains

English Folk Song

I love the moun-tains, I love the roll-ing hills, I love the flow-ers,

I love the daf - fo-dils, I love the fire - side When all the lights are low

Boom-di-a - da, boom-di-a - da, Boom-di-a - da, Boom-di-a - da, boom!

Song may be repeated many times with "Boom-di-a-da" sung as an introduction, ostinato, and coda. Singers switch parts on each repeat.

SAMPLE TEXTURE SCORE FOR "I LOVE THE MOUNTAINS"

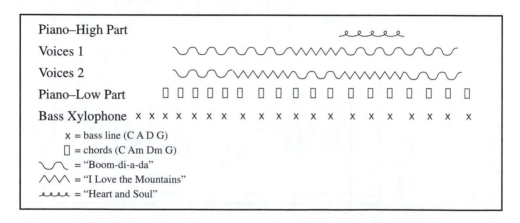

Notating Texture (Score-Reading)

The lesson presented in Figure 7.7 introduces score-reading.

Students can use their understanding of graphic scores to begin to understand how to interpret symbolic scores, such as "One Bottle of Pop." You might begin by asking, "What do you already know about what is written on this page? Can you tell who sings first, second, and third? Can you tell when the xylophones begin to play? Will all the performers finish at the same time? Does the music tell you anything about what the melodies might sound like?"

If students are familiar with this song from outside of school, it is best to use a different one of a similar nature. This lesson will not be effective if the students already know the song.

Figure 7.7: Lesson Plan: Notating Texture (Score-Reading)

National Standards: 1, 5
Grade: 4 and up, depending upon prior experience

Organization:
Performance problem/work in pairs.

Materials:

- "One Bottle of Pop," or other melody with countermelodies or three-part round, written out in score form (one score for each pair of students) with a fourth line of the score containing the notes of a bass line that supports the underlying harmony of the round (should be a song students do not already know).

Lesson assumes:

- Experience performing rounds and experience with graphic texture scores.

Objective:
To help students use what they know about a graphic texture score to understand the layout of a conventional musical score.

Connection to prior knowledge/experience:

- Relate this experience to the previous lesson's graphic score of the texture of "I Love the Mountains."

Pose problems: Students will:

- Try to make sense out of a symbolic score, drawing on prior experience with a graphic score.
- Use the information they are able to glean from the symbolic score to perform the round with accompaniment.

Students solve problems: Students will:

- Work with a partner to consider the musical score.
- Decode the different elements of the score and begin to perform the various parts as they interpret them. (Work from their speculations to develop a plan for how the song is supposed to sound.)
- Perform the song with accompaniment from the score.

Groundwork that enables:
Remind the students about some of the principles they used during the last class to create a texture score. Which voice is heard first? What does it mean when one line is written directly over another?

Students share and discuss solutions:
Occurs throughout (support from partner, sharing with whole group).

Assessment:
Students will be able to perform the arrangement successfully with minimal assistance from the teacher.

One Bottle of Pop

Traditional

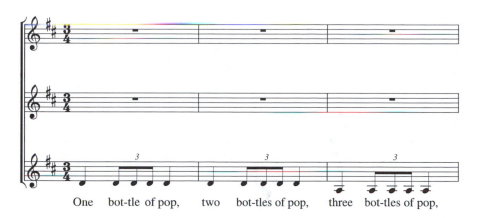

One bot-tle of pop, two bot-tles of pop, three bot-tles of pop,

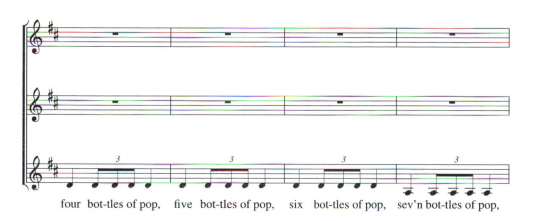

four bot-tles of pop, five bot-tles of pop, six bot-tles of pop, sev'n bot-tles of pop,

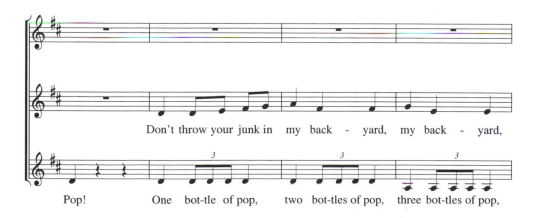

Don't throw your junk in my back - yard, my back - yard,

Pop! One bot-tle of pop, two bot-tles of pop, three bot-tles of pop,

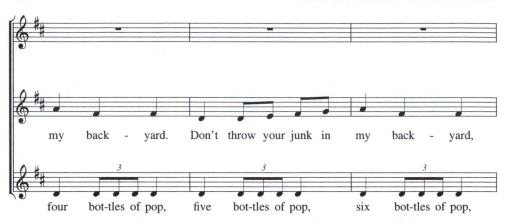

my   back - yard.   Don't throw your junk in   my   back - yard,

four   bot-tles of pop,   five   bot-tles of pop,   six   bot-tles of pop,

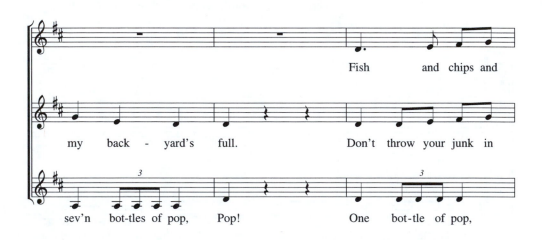

Fish   and chips and

my   back - yard's   full.   Don't throw your junk in

sev'n bot-tles of pop,   Pop!   One   bot-tle of pop,

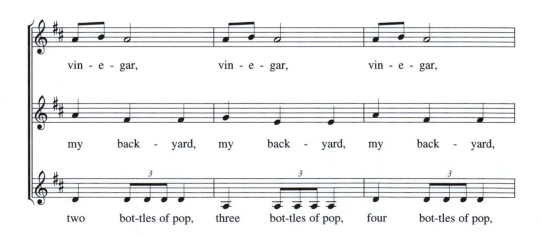

vin - e - gar,   vin - e - gar,   vin - e - gar,

my   back - yard,   my   back - yard,   my   back - yard,

two   bot-tles of pop,   three   bot-tles of pop,   four   bot-tles of pop,

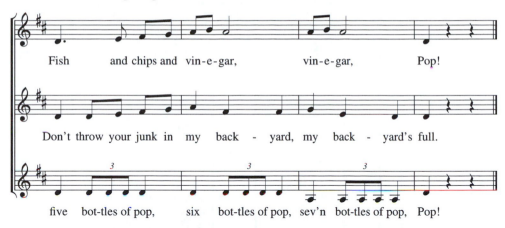

Students will probably notice the repeated notes, the rhythm, and the contour aspects of the top two lines of the score in particular. Depending on their prior experience, they may recognize skips and steps and might even be able to sight-read parts of the melodies (perhaps using numbers.)

Once they figure out the bass line and when it starts, ask some students to play that line. Generally, some students can figure out how the lowest vocal line fits with the bass line. Then, help them to remember what they already know that will enable them to figure out the remaining lines.

Solo and Ensemble

The lesson in Figure 7.8 asks students to use what they know to analyze the texture of a listening example (CD, Track 10). "Ríu, Ríu, Chíu" is a Spanish Christmas carol, an anonymous *villancico* (part song), which was published in a volume called *Cancionero de Upsala* in 1556.

Figure 7.8: Lesson Plan: Texture (Solo/Ensemble)

National Standard: 6
Grade: 4 and up, depending upon prior experience

Materials:

- "Riu, Riu, Chiu" (CD, Track 10).
- Texture chart on chalkboard and on handouts (one for each student).
- Pencils for each student.

Organization:

Independent analytical listening problem.

Lesson assumes:

- Prior experience graphing texture: representing more than one melody, an accompanying part, one voice singing, many voices singing, and so on.
- Prior analytical listening experience.

Objective:

To help students apply basic understandings of textural characteristics to analytical listening experience.

Connection to prior knowledge/experience:

During the next class, students will have an opportunity to work with a small group of peers to compose an original piece that explores changes in texture. Today they will analyze a recording to learn more about how professionals utilize textural variety in their pieces. (Connecting to future lessons is as important for older students as is connecting to prior experiences. The connection becomes the impetus for participating.)

Groundwork that enables:

The work done during the two prior classes and students' awareness of what they will need to do in the next class establish the groundwork for this experience.

Pose problem:

Students will graph the texture of the recording as they listen, based on prior experience graphing the texture of their own performance.

Students solve problem:

- Remind students of the ways the class has agreed upon to represent various textural elements.
- Each student will need a blank chart and a pencil. Some may prefer to use colored markers as well. The teacher will point to the numbers on the chart on the board, so the student will know when each new section begins. The students are to graph the texture they hear in each box.

Students share and discuss solutions:

Once all students are satisfied with their scores, encourage them to share what they have drawn, and produce a collaborative answer on the chalkboard (or on a piece of chart paper, if you want to save it for reference during the composition assignment).

Assessment:

Students will show their understanding of texture through their ability to graph what they hear and explain it to others during the large-group sharing at the end of the lesson.

Extension:

On your own, try to graph the texture of "Huagu Ge: Flower Drum Song" (CD, Track 11).

TEXTURE CHART FOR LESSON IN FIGURE 7.8

1	2	3	4	5	6	7	8

For this type of activity, it does not really matter what specific representations students decide to use as long as the group agrees upon their meaning. You might use different kinds of "squiggley" lines to represent more than one melody, thick dashes or lines to represent chords, slashes or dots or Xs to represent a percussion part, a "splat" for a cymbal crash, and so on.

In this particular work, because the texture is consistent throughout, the students will have many opportunities to perfect their graphic scores. They should end up with the same diagram for sections 1, 3, 5, and 7 and a different one for sections 2, 4, 6, and 8.

Charting the texture of a work is often a good "doorway in" to non-Western musics because many of them have more of a linear organization than a formal one. For example, students might use a texture chart to begin to understand "Huagu Ge: Flower Drum Song" (CD, Track 11), which appears in *The Lion's Roar,* a collection of Chinese Luogu Percussion music by Han Kuo-Huang and Patricia Shehan Campbell (book with recorded examples, 1992, World Music Press, pp. 48–53). By its construction, a texture chart that is organized in sections, such as the one suggested for "Ríu, Ríu, Chíu," suggests both form and texture. In the case of this example of Chinese percussion music, this format works well because the piece has a strong and obvious formal design as well as a consistent texture. The chart would require six sections. Some of the sections are repeated at different points in the work, which makes graphing the texture chart a less difficult process. For non-Western musics, where form is not a genuine organizing characteristic, students would need to construct a more free-form texture graph without numbered sections. This would make the process more challenging and would therefore make it more appropriate for students with greater experience.

Compose a Texture Piece

You might allow one or two class periods for this project (Figure 7.9), more if you have the time. As with most composition assignments, the complexity of the products will reflect the amount of time allotted for the work.

Figure 7.9: Lesson Plan: Compose a Texture Piece

National Standards: 2, 4, 5, 7
Grade: 4 and up, depending upon prior experience

Organization:
Small-group compositional problem.

Materials:
- Classroom instruments, as available.

Lesson assumes:
- Students have worked with texture in prior performing and analytical listening experiences.

Objective:
To help students apply their understanding of textural variety to a compositional activity. Using texture as a "doorway in," students will compose an original work.

Connection to prior knowledge/experience = Groundwork that enables (in this lesson):
Based on what they have learned during the past three class sessions, students will have an opportunity to explore texture on their own.

Pose problem:
Based on their prior experience with texture, students will work with a small group of peers to create an original work that shows textural variety.

Students solve problem:
There are many ways to approach this, all of which work well, so long as the focus remains on incorporating textural interest and variety into the work. Students might:
- Compose pieces and then share them with the group.
- Realize a texture score created by the teacher.
- Create an original texture chart and then realize it.
- Create texture charts and then "swap" charts, so that each group is working to realize another group's chart.

Students share and discuss solutions:
Students will share ideas with peers throughout the compositional process and will share and discuss their finished products in the final phase of the project.

Assessment:
Students will show the depth of their understanding of textural possibilities through:
- The pieces they create.
- Their comments during discussion of the project.

188

UNIT: MONOTHEMATIC WORKS

This next unit is a series of experiences designed to help students draw together their understandings of the choices composers have available to them when planning a work. They will have opportunities to use what they know about dynamics, tempo, texture, timbre, and register to analyze and then compose a work designed to produce a particular effect. In order to emphasize the use of compositional tools other than melodic characteristics, the students will work with pieces that have only one theme in which, throughout the work, the theme is repeated again and again while other elements are altered.

Expressive Qualities of a Work

Older and more experienced students need to work with the more basic concepts such as loud/soft, fast/slow, and high/low in context. It is not important that the music is loud or soft or fast or slow, but the effect these changes generate is significant. This unit deals with the kinds of effects that changes in dynamics, tempo, pitch, and texture can create in a musical work and in its effect on the listener.

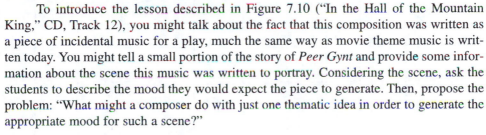

To introduce the lesson described in Figure 7.10 ("In the Hall of the Mountain King," CD, Track 12), you might talk about the fact that this composition was written as a piece of incidental music for a play, much the same way as movie theme music is written today. You might tell a small portion of the story of *Peer Gynt* and provide some information about the scene this music was written to portray. Considering the scene, ask the students to describe the mood they would expect the piece to generate. Then, propose the problem: "What might a composer do with just one thematic idea in order to generate the appropriate mood for such a scene?"

Figure 7.10: Lesson Plan: Expressive Qualities of a Work

National Standards: 6, 7, 9

Grade: 4 and up, depending upon prior experience

Materials:

- Edvard Grieg (1843–1907): "In the Hall of the Mountain King" from *Peer Gynt Suite No. 1* (CD, Track 12).
- Rhythm of the theme written on the chalkboard, in either icons or symbols, whichever is more appropriate for the students' level of experience with notation.

Organization:

Large-group analytical listening problem.

Lesson assumes:

- Prior experience working with dynamics, tempo, texture, timbre, and register in analytical listening, performing, and creating venues.

Objective:

To help students use what they know about dynamics, tempo, texture, timbre, and register to expand their palette of choices in compositional and listening experiences.

Connection to prior knowledge/experience:

"Suppose a composer decides to write a piece where the same melody will appear over and over again throughout the entire piece. How would you expect that piece to sound? What might the composer decide to do with that melody to make it more interesting, without changing the melody itself?"

Pose problem: Students will:

- Theorize about some of the choices a composer might make to generate interest and excitement in a monothematic work.
- Listen to the recording to see how many of their ideas were also used by the composer of this work.

Students solve problem: Students will:

- Generate a list of ways they think the composer might choose to manipulate the melody in order to generate a mood of excitement or anticipation, or whatever mood they expect they will hear.
- Listen to the piece to see how many of their theories are correct.
- Generate a more complete list of ways one can alter a theme to make a piece interesting, one that includes both Grieg's ideas and the students'. This list will be used as a basis for the composition project that follows.

Groundwork that enables:

Students will suggest ways a composer might make a monothematic piece more interesting and exciting.

Students share and discuss solutions:

Students share ideas throughout the lesson.

Assessment:

Students will show their understanding through their comments and suggestions throughout the lesson. The depth of their understanding will be assessed in the lessons that follow.

Here is the thematic idea that is used throughout this piece:

"IN THE HALL OF THE MOUNTAIN KING"—THEMATIC IDEA

During the listening portions of this lesson, it is helpful if you track the rhythm of the theme from time to time (which makes the accelerando more obvious) and draw students' attention to their theories written on the board. Are they right? Have they second-guessed the composer? Have they perhaps thought of some ideas the composer did not use? Has the composer thought of some things they overlooked?

As a follow-up lesson, students could work in small groups to generate an original work that has the following characteristics:

- The piece should be based on only one melodic idea.
- The piece should establish a mood through changes in elements other than the melody itself.
- Students may utilize techniques used by Grieg, their own ideas, or some combination of the two.

ASSESSMENT RUBRIC FOR MONOTHEMATIC COMPOSITIONS

Below level:

One has a sense that the students are "making it up as they go along" with no evidence of prior organization or plan.

Basic level:

1. Students use a variety of sound sources and means of sound production.
2. There is an attempt at establishing a particular mood and some sense of organization (prior planning) evident in the performance.

Proficient level:

1. The work succeeds in conveying a particular mood.
2. Sound sources are used effectively in contributing to the mood generated by the work.
3. Prior planning and intent are evident in the performance.
4. There is a sense of ensemble in that players share a sense of the intent and contribute appropriately to the overall work.

Advanced level:

1. In addition to the proficient-level criteria, the work is well-executed (well-rehearsed and performed) by the group.
2. The work is sophisticated enough to evoke an affective response from the listener.

Samples of Student Work

Based on "In the Hall of the Mountain King"
COMPOSED BY A FOURTH-GRADE STUDENT, FOR PIANO

This notated version represents only two repetitions of the theme. In his work, the student began by playing this theme on the very highest keys of the piano, very slowly and softly. The second repetition was played one octave lower (in the manner shown by the notation), a bit faster and a bit louder. He then continued to move down the piano, with each repetition sounding louder and faster than the preceding one, until he reached the very lowest keys.

Based on "In the Hall of the Mountain King"
FIVE FOURTH GRADERS

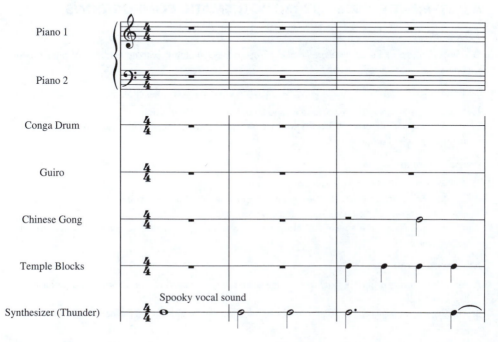

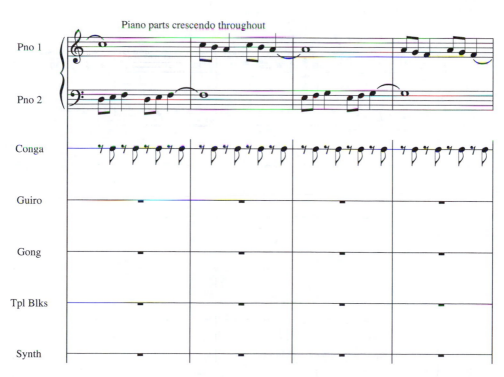

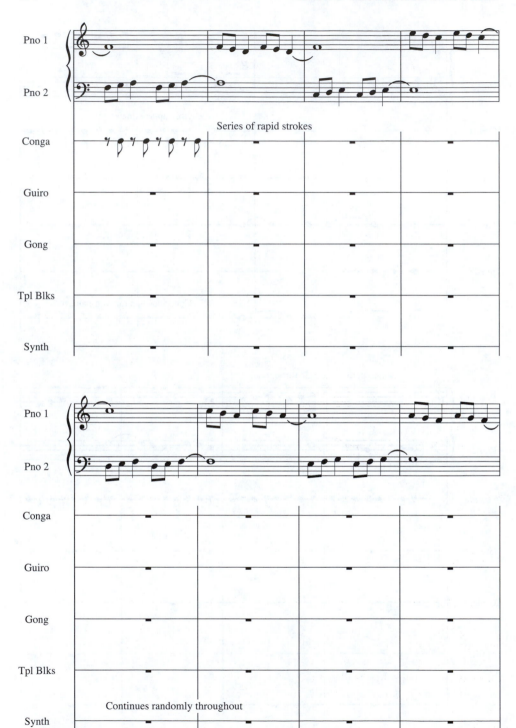

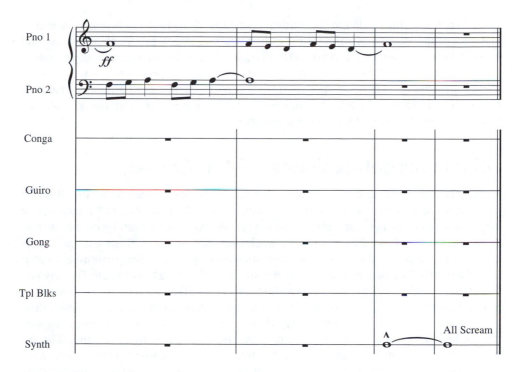

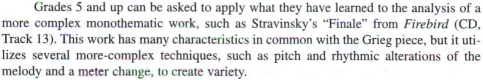

Grades 5 and up can be asked to apply what they have learned to the analysis of a more complex monothematic work, such as Stravinsky's "Finale" from *Firebird* (CD, Track 13). This work has many characteristics in common with the Grieg piece, but it utilizes several more-complex techniques, such as pitch and rhythmic alterations of the melody and a meter change, to create variety.

Students might also study "Fantasia on Dargason," from Gustav Holst's *Suite for Band,* No. 2, 4th movement, which contains many repetitions of the main theme until it is eventually paired with the melody of "Greensleeves."

RELATED ISSUES

Cultural and Historical Contexts

In designing lessons and units such as those found in Chapters 6, 7, and 8, it is often appropriate to make connections to the historical and cultural contexts of the works. In general, these connections will make much more sense to students if they are made *after* they have had opportunities to explore the music itself. For example, knowing that a piece was written during the American Revolution will be relatively meaningless to a student who does not know enough about the style of the piece to understand what makes it characteristic of eighteenth-century music.

When studying world musics, cultural context is often critical to formulating understanding of the music itself. Here it might be important to talk briefly about the cultural context *before* exploring the music. However, it is through experience with the music itself that students will formulate their understanding. One approach might be to set the stage for the music with some discussion of its context, then explore the music, and later return to contextual or historical issues once students have a better frame of reference based upon their understanding of the music itself.

Middle School Exploratory Mini-Courses

Units, such as those described in this chapter, can be easily adapted to the 10-week exploratory mini-courses so prevalent in middle schools. In designing such a course, one might plan to devote the first week or two to separate explorations into specific basic elements of music followed by a series of week-long unit projects. These extended units could easily be designed so that on Monday students engage in either performing or analytical listening experiences that will provide the basis for creative work. On Tuesday and Wednesday, students might work in small groups or at MIDI stations to create original works based on that initial experience. On Thursday, they might share and discuss their pieces; and, on Friday, they might engage in a follow-up listening or performing experience based on a work that utilizes the same technique in a more complex manner. The last two weeks of the course might be devoted to free composition, where students who have worked under specific guidelines and parameters all semester long are now free to create any kind of piece they wish (perhaps for in-school publication or performance).

Block Scheduling

While it is beyond the scope of this book to provide a detailed description of what it is like to work within block scheduling in secondary schools, it is worth mentioning that adopting the mindset and approach suggested in these pages offers one solution as to how music teachers might adapt to such situations. When performing ensembles suddenly begin meeting for 90-minute or 2-hour blocks of time, it becomes possible to begin to include more than just performing in students' experiences. This kind of scheduling permits marvelous opportunities to begin to incorporate listening and creating experiences into the curriculum. It also provides exciting opportunities for the integration of technology. Further, the curriculum becomes even more powerful when the performing, listening, and creating experiences (and experiences with technology) are carefully interwoven to connect to the concepts students need to understand to be able to perform their music more effectively. Ideas similar to those presented in Chapters 7 and 8 may work well in these kinds of extended classes.

BOX 7.2   THINK ABOUT THIS . . .

- Are there threads of similarity in the ways the lessons in Chapter 7 were conceived and constructed?
- What concepts are being taught? Around what elements or principles is the unit organized?
- In which processes do students engage?
- What musical problems are the students asked to solve?
- How does the teacher know whether or not the students have understood?

BOX 7.3 (ACTIVITY)

Use materials and ideas from the school music textbook series as a springboard for developing problem-solving lessons for middle-level students. Teach some of these lessons to your peers. If possible, teach some to schoolchildren at your field placement.

ENDNOTES

1. This lesson was previously published in S. L. Stauffer and J. Davidson, ed., 1996, *Strategies for teaching K–4 general music,* Reston, Va.: MENC (Music Educators National Conference), and is used by permission. The complete National Music Education Standards and additional materials related to the Standards are available from MENC—The National Association for Music Education, 1806 Robert Fulton Drive, Reston, VA 20191. The Standards (with commentary) can be downloaded from the MENC website at <www.menc.org/publication/books/prek12st.html>.
2. Please see the information regarding the National Standards in endnote 3 of Chapter 6, p. 159.
3. Collected in South Florida by Rosita Sands, Center for Black Music Research, Columbia College.
4. J. Bond, et al., 1995. *Share the music* (Grade 4, p. 263). New York: McGraw-Hill.
5. This idea and the idea behind the lesson in Figure 7.3 come from Eunice Boardman.
6. The lesson was originally published in M. Espeland, 1992, *Musikk i bruk (Music in use).* Norway: Stord/Haugesund lærhøgskule. It is used by permission.
7. Also an idea borrowed from Magne Espeland's *Music in Use.*
8. Plastic Native American flutes (PF Series), designed by flute maker Ken Light, can be ordered through the Amon Olorin Wood Flutes Catalog, available from Amon Olorin Flutes, 492 Lemlama Lane, Arlee, MT 59821. The catalog is also available online at <www.aoflutes.com/catalog_B.htm>.
9. R. Carlos Nakai shared his views with music teachers during a session at the Biennial National Inservice Conference of MENC in Phoenix, April 1998.

SELECTED RESOURCES

Beethoven, J., et al. 1995–present. *The music connection: Grades K–8.* Morristown, N.J.: Silver Burdett Ginn and Scott Foresman.

Bergethon, B., E. Boardman, and J. Montgomery. 1997. *Musical growth in the elementary school,* 6th ed. Fort Worth, Tex.: Harcourt Brace.

Bond, J., et al. 1995–present. *Share the music: Grades K–8.* New York: McGraw-Hill.

Collections of music from around the world are published by World Music Press, P.O. Box 2565, Danbury, CT 06813. Browse the press's catalog at <www.worldmusic-press.com/>.

Chapter 8

DESIGNING COMPLEX MUSICAL PROBLEMS

Chapter 8 provides information about teaching students who have considerable experience working with musical ideas. It also includes examples of lesson and unit plans for older students. Additional lesson plans can be found on the website at www.mhhe.com/wiggins.

The transition between middle-level and complex problems is much gentler and less obvious than the transition between entry-level and middle-level work. The problems presented in this section are very similar in format and assumptions to those suggested in the previous chapter. Highly experienced students still need to engage in singing, playing, listening, and creating experiences. They may have more opportunities to utilize technology available to them than less-experienced students. Students at this level of experience tend to utilize movement less frequently in formulating and sharing ideas because they have had much more experience expressing musical ideas through performance and verbal descriptions and labels.

Many students working on this level of proficiency are relatively comfortable with standard notation, but it is important to be sensitive to those who are not. It should not be problematic to continue to include both icons and symbols when music needs to be represented, even at this level. Insisting that everyone use symbols might exclude or alienate some students who have not quite mastered the system. Their ability to hear and understand music and to use that understanding to perform and create music is really more important than their ability to decode the notation system. By the time they have reached their upper-elementary, middle school, and high school years, those students who have opportunities for other experiences with musical notation, such as instrumental lessons or choral experiences, tend to become more conversant with the system more quickly. Those who choose not to perform or study privately, whose only experience with the system is in the general music classroom, will always be less proficient because they have less of a need to know. If the goal of the general music class is to nurture musical understanding such that students are better able to engage in and enjoy music once they have left school, we need to recognize that for many of our students that engagement will be as consumers of music. Educated consumers need to know how to listen to and make choices about the music that will be part of their lives—not how to read musical notation.

UNITS OF INSTRUCTION

Older students enjoy working on long, extended units. Most of the work they do in non-music classrooms is organized in this manner, so they are accustomed to working with particular ideas in depth over extended periods of time. Since they are quite capable of sustaining interest in a long-term project, it is best to organize instruction for upper-elementary and secondary students in units comprised of a series of interrelated lesson experiences. Within units of instruction, as more experienced students work with more complex ideas, one lesson plan may even take several class sessions to complete. Students engaged in solving complex problems will still need to work within a variety of instructional settings, including large-group, teacher-guided work, small-group, partner, and independent work. However, older students tend to prefer time spent working with peers over time in a whole-class setting. They are also much more capable of functioning without the teacher once they have achieved this level of expertise. Therefore, the bulk of these units are designed to capitalize on the students' ability to function within, and preference for, non-teacher-directed settings.

For the most part, the lessons in this chapter could be carried out using either traditional classroom instruments or MIDI stations. However, it is important to keep in mind that before students are able to work with a sequencer, "laying tracks" to the beat of a metronome, they need to have had numerous experiences playing music together with peers in "live" ensemble settings.

The lessons in this chapter should work well with upper-elementary and middle-school students. They can be easily adapted for high school students and adults. Again, readiness to engage in these lessons is more dependent on the prior experience than on the age of the learner.

UNIT: ARRANGING A ROUND

In this unit, students will learn a round, study its harmonic structure, and then use their understanding to develop arrangements of the round. In the lesson described in Figure 8.1, they first learn the round. In the lesson described in Figure 8.2, they arrange the round.

Learning the Round

Figure 8.1: UNIT: ARRANGING A ROUND
Lesson Plan: Learning the Round

National Standard[1]: 1
Grade: 5 and up, depending upon prior experience

Organization:
Large-group performance problem.

Materials:
- Joanne Hammil: "Mud"[2] (for older students: a round with more sophisticated lyrics).

Lesson assumes:
- Students have experience working with the relationship between melody and harmonic structure in simple folk and pop songs.
- Students have analyzed simple melodies for the chords they imply and have improvised melodies over chord progressions played by their peers.
- Students have had enough experience singing "in parts" to sing a five-part round and keep track of their own melodic line within the ensemble.

Objective:
To build on students' understanding of the relationship between melody and harmonic structure, extending that understanding to what makes a round "work."

Connection to prior knowledge/experience:
- Talk briefly with students about the process of arranging music and the differences between arranging and composing.
- Tell students they are going to try their own hand at some arranging, developing an arrangement of a simple round called "Mud." In order to be able to accomplish this, they first need to be very familiar with the round, since they will have to be able to both sing and play it without the teacher's assistance in order to do this project.

Pose problems: Students will:
- Match the visual representation of each phrase to the sound of the phrase, using what they know about either iconic or symbolic notation.
- Use what they have learned from these "matching" experiences to learn to sing the song.
- Learn to sing the round in two parts, and then in three, four, and five parts, against the repeating chord and bass line pattern.

Students solve problems:
- Students identify, from either icons or notation, the various lines of the round as the teacher sings them.
- Students sing the whole melody from the icons or notation with the melody to be able to sing it without the teacher, play the chord progression as an accompaniment and ask the class to try singing it as a two-part round.
- Students try the round in three parts.
- Students let the teacher know when they feel they are ready to try four parts and finally five.

Groundwork that enables:
Knowing the round well is essential to the students' success in this project. They all must be familiar enough with it to sing the melody accurately. It is not essential that everyone know how to play the entire round on an instrument, since there is nothing to say that the arrangements cannot be vocal. Adding the instrumental option, however, enhances the possibilities.

Students share and discuss solutions:
The performance of the round represents a sharing of understanding of the ideas.

Assessment:
Students' successful performance of the five-part round will represent a level of shared understanding of what it is to sing five different melodies against one another and against an accompanying chord progression.

Mud
A FIVE-PART ROUND

Joanne Olshansky Hammil   Joanne Olshansky Hammil

Arranging the Round

Figure 8.2: UNIT: ARRANGING A ROUND
Lesson Plan: Arranging the Round

National Standards: 1, 2, 4, 7
Grade: 5 and up, depending upon prior experience

Organization:
Small-group arranging problem.

Materials:
- Handout of "Mud" (or other round) printed in both iconic and symbolic notation.
- Classroom instruments, as available (acoustic/electronic/MIDI station).

Lesson assumes:
- Students know this five-part round well enough to work with the melody on their own.

Objective:
To enable students to apply their understanding of this round and its harmonic structure to the development of original arrangements of the round.

Connection to prior knowledge/experience:	**Groundwork that enables:**
• Review the five-part round and remind students that today they will work with their peers to develop their own arrangements of the round.	Previous class should provide sufficient background.

Pose problems: Students will:
- Work as a class to review the round.
- Work from the handout to learn to play any part or all of the round on a pitched instrument.
- Work in groups of five or six to develop an arrangement of the round.

Students solve problems: Students will:
- Sing the five-part round as a reminder of what they already know.
- Work alone or with a partner to learn to play at least part of the melody successfully.
- Work with peers to develop an original arrangement of the round.

Students share and discuss solutions:
- When ready, groups perform their arrangements for the class.
- As students share their final products, see if the listeners in the class are able to figure out the "master plan" as designed by the arrangers. Can they figure out the plan? Can they replicate it?

Assessment:
Students will show their understanding of the way rounds are "put together" through the arrangements they develop. Students will also make decisions about timbre, tempo, dynamics, form, texture, and possibly even style as they work to develop their arrangements.

Extensions:
- Students might develop arrangements that the whole class will perform. This adds an interesting twist, because it puts the onus of leadership on the students, who are then responsible for communicating their ideas, and for leading the group's performance of their ideas. Teaching their arrangement to the class sometimes enables individuals to see their work in a way they have not understood it before, and sometimes results in editing and refining of the work.
- Students might try making arrangements based on other rounds they know. This might be something they try on their own at home, bringing in their own plans and leading their peers in a performance of their own arrangement.
- Find two rounds that share a common underlying chord progression and ask the students to try mixing the phrases of the round into one complicated arrangement to be sung, played, or some combination of the two.

In order to carry out the arranging portion of this lesson, each student will need either a notated or iconic version of the song and a pitched instrument. Keyboards, chromatic resonator bells, or chromatic barred instruments are necessary to play the fourth phrase with the G-sharp. Students may also opt to sing the fourth phrase if the instrument situation poses a problem—or a different round could be used.

Students' work on the arrangements will be based on their understanding that, since all five of the lines fit with the same chord progression, any of the lines will fit with any other line in any order and at any time. They may opt to sing and/or play any of the five phrases of the round. Someone in the group may opt to play or sing the bass line or chords. Some may decide to use one of the phrases of the round as a repeating ostinato. There is no requirement that the entire round be present in the arrangement, although students usually do prefer to have it appear in its entirety at least once. Sometimes they develop complicated accompaniments to the melody, based on series of repeating ostinati, both sung and played. Some arrangements are purely vocal or instrumental. Some utilize, as an accompaniment, particular rhythm patterns derived from the melody but played on non-pitched instruments. The possibilities are endless, which is what makes the project so interesting to the students.

This project can easily take more than one class session. More time will enable students to produce more complex work.

You might use the following rubric in assessing student work on this project:

ASSESSMENT RUBRIC FOR "MUD" ARRANGEMENTS

Below level:

Students are not able to conceive of performing two ideas simultaneously or able to describe what they would need to do to be able to perform a round.

Basic level:

1. Students can sing the melody accurately.
2. Students can assemble the "pieces" of the melody into some sort of arrangement and perform it with some sense of accuracy, although not perfectly.

Example: One child sings the melody while others sing the last phrase of the melody repeatedly as an ostinato. A drummer accompanies by providing a steady beat in the background.

Proficient level:

1. In addition to the basic-level criteria, students can perform at least one section of the melody on an instrument and incorporate that part into the arrangement.
2. There is a sense of ensemble in that players share a sense of underlying pulse and show their understanding of the arrangement by playing or singing their parts in the appropriate time in relation to other group members' parts.

Advanced level:

1. In addition to the proficient-level criteria, there is a relationship among the parts that gives the listener the sense that they are part of one unified work or idea.
2. Additional material (intro, bridge, coda, accompanying part) enhances and sounds like a part of the overall work.
3. The arrangement is well-executed (well-rehearsed and performed) by the group.
4. The arrangement might be sophisticated enough to evoke an affective response from the listener.

Sample of Student Work

Arrangement of "Mud"

ARRANGED BY 5 FIFTH GRADERS IN OCTOBER

UNIT: BITHEMATIC FORMS

(VERSE AND REFRAIN, ABA FORM, ETC.)

(3–6 CLASS SESSIONS)

Hearing Bithematic Form

For the lesson described in Figure 8.3 (CD, Track 14), you will need a handout containing some version of a form chart, such as the one suggested below:

1	2	3	4	5	6	7	8	9	10

In making the transition from analysis of familiar songs to unfamiliar instrumental works, the most common misunderstandings seem to involve confusion with text, as when the verses have different words each time and the refrain does not. Since this lesson requires that students apply their understanding to instrumental music, they must understand that it is the change in the melody that is the key issue.

Students may complete worksheets in small groups, with partners, or independently. Draw a blank chart on the board and point to the numbers as each section begins so that students will understand where sections begin and end. They may need to hear the work more than once.

Figure 8.3: UNIT: BITHEMATIC FORMS

Lesson Plan: Hearing Bithematic Form (1 session)

National Standards: 1, 6

Grade: 4 and up, depending upon prior experience

Materials:

- Several familiar songs in binary form (familiar songs that utilize a verse-and-refrain format are good choices).
- Tchaikovsky: "Trepak" from *The Nutcracker* (CD, Track 14).
- Charts and pencils.

Lesson assumes:

- Basic understanding of melodic contour in order to be able to discriminate thematic changes.
- Some prior compositional experiences.

Organization:

Whole-group listening problem (could also be small group or partners).

Objective:

To help students develop an understanding of a composer's use of bithematic forms (binary and ternary).

Connection to prior knowledge/experience = Groundwork that enables:

- Working from familiar binary songs (verse and refrain) helps the students develop an understanding of the idea of binary form (A theme and B theme).
- Be sure they understand that the essential difference between sections is related to differences in melody.
- Using the song material, also discuss and identify introductions, bridges (transitions), and codas.

Pose problems: Students will:

- Listen to "Trepak" and complete the form chart (handout), working from their understanding of binary form in songs.
- Discuss possible ways of expressing the form in a "short-hand" way.

Students solve problem: Students will:

- Review familiar songs, singing through them and identifying A sections, B sections, introductions, bridges, and codas.
- Listen to and analyze "Trepak."
- Figure out a way to label the form of this piece without using so many letters and labels.

Students share and discuss solutions:

Where students propose solutions that differ, encourage discussion. "What did you hear in the music that made you fill in the chart that way? Let's listen one more time and perhaps you can tell us about what you were thinking."

Assessment:

Students will be able to describe the form of the music they have sung and apply that understanding to analysis of the orchestral work, indicated by successful completion of the chart and from their comments during discussion of the chart.

You might choose an alternative approach that creates more of a whole-class activity and provides opportunity for peer support. Distribute to the entire class cards labeled "A," "B," "Intro," "Bridge," or "Coda." Be sure there are more cards than sections (i.e., extra "A," "B," and "Bridge" cards). Students who are holding what they believe to be the correct label for each section run up to the front of the room and take a place to form a sort of "human form chart," similar to what they might have written on the worksheets. To prevent accidents, they will need to know who is to be the first A, second A, third A, first B, first bridge, and so on. With the human form chart, students help one another to know when to run up, providing more support than they might have completing worksheets with partners or independently.

With either the human or the paper form chart, students will need to know that there is no introduction and that the first music they hear will be A. This will enable them to have a point of comparison as they listen. They generally decide that ABA is a reasonable way to describe what they have heard—with one A representing all the repetitions of A in the opening section, one B representing the Bs, and introductions, bridges, and codas being a bit "less important" in the overall scheme of things.

The solution should eventually look something like this:

1	2	3	4	5	6	7	8	9	10
A	A	A	A	B	B	Bridge	A	A	Coda

Composing in Bithematic Form

Figure 8.4 describes a composition lesson that builds on the previous analytical listening experience. This lesson is not intended to be used as an introductory compositional experience. Success requires prior compositional experience.

Figure 8.4: UNIT: BITHEMATIC FORMS
Lesson Plan: Composing in Bithematic Form (3 or 4 sessions)

Materials:

- Tchaikovsky: "Trepak" from *The Nutcracker* (CD, Track 14).
- Assorted classroom instruments: barred instruments, drums, rhythm instruments, synthesizers—preferably one for each student or enough for students to share (or can be done at a MIDI station).

Lesson assumes:

- Reasonably secure understanding of what "ABA form" means.
- Understanding of introduction, bridge, and coda.
- Prior experience composing with peers in small groups.

Organization:
Small-group composition problem.

Objective:
To help students further their understanding of a composer's use of bithematic forms through the development of an original bithematic work.

Connection to prior knowledge/experience = Groundwork that enables:

- Briefly review the principles taught during the last class. Analysis of the songs and "Trepak" during the previous class session provides a basis for this assignment. If students seem unsure, take a barred instrument and model a very simple ABA piece.

Pose problem: Students will:

- Compose a piece in ABA form, with options of adding introduction, bridge, or coda.
- Rehearse their piece until it is ready to be performed for the class (or for a videotape or for a concert or sharing time).

Students solve problem:

- Students will develop an original work that moves in ABA form.
- Project may take two or three class sessions. Students should keep in mind that both A sections should have the same melodic material and that the B section should have contrasting melodic material.

Students share and discuss solutions:

When students are ready, share the finished products. Discuss the decisions made by each group, as evidenced by their performance of their piece.

Assessment:
Students will show their understanding of ternary form and bithematic music through their compositional processes and products. Their compositions will also reflect numerous other areas of their musical growth, including their concepts of simultaneity and ensemble, and understanding of the roles of texture, form, beat, meter, melodic contour, rhythmic motifs, dynamic change, and so forth. Videotape or audiotape recordings of compositional products can easily become part of a portfolio of student work that can be used for assessment and record-keeping purposes.

You might try making a video of this particular project, building on students' non-school experience with this medium. Dedicate one class session to videotaping the finished products—producing a videotape that contains compositions done by all members of a particular grade level. This videotape would then be shared with all students on that grade level. This allows time for evaluative comments and for students to grow in their conception of possibilities they might want to use in subsequent assignments. Such grade-level sharing often serves to model ideas for students, ideas that surface in later work, intentionally "borrowed" from their peers. ("We want to make a bass part like Jennifer's group made in their ABA piece. How did they do that?") Informing the students from the outset that they will have an opportunity to make their work public (through video or even a live performance) serves to focus their energies from the beginning of the project. It also serves as a kind of anticipatory set.

In discussing the finished products, you might ask questions such as:

- "Did they do what was required for the assignment?"
- "How did they choose to carry the assignment out?"
- "Did they develop two distinctly different thematic ideas?"
- "How did the performers know when it was time to begin a new section? Did they use some kind of signal or plan?"
- "How was this piece different from that one?"
- "What other kinds of decisions and choices are reflected in their work (other than decisions related to form, such as dynamic contrasts, tempo change, meter changes, use of melody and accompaniment, use of canon, use of percussion to accompany the melody, etc.)?"

Avoid critical or judgmental questions like, "Did you like this piece?" That is not the point of a lesson of this nature, although spontaneous applause and praise is always welcome. You might use the following rubric to assess student work.

ASSESSMENT RUBRIC FOR ABA PIECES

Below level:

The piece does not have three sections or does not contain two different thematic ideas. Some group members do not understand where one section ends and the next begins.

Basic level:

1. The piece is organized into three sections. The B section is in some way different from the A.
2. There is some attempt at melodic structure for each of the sections.

Proficient level:

1. In addition to the basic-level criteria, the work contains two distinct melodic ideas that are executed with relative accuracy by the performers.
2. There is a sense of ensemble, in that players share a sense of underlying pulse and show their understanding of the plan (form) by playing their parts in the appropriate time in relation to other group members' parts.

Advanced level:

1. In addition to the proficient-level criteria, there is a relationship between the two thematic ideas that gives the listener the sense that both are part of one unified work.
2. Additional material (intro, bridge, coda, accompanying part) enhances and sounds like a part of the overall work.
3. The work is well-executed (well-rehearsed and performed) by the group.
4. The work might be sophisticated enough to evoke an affective response from the listener.

Samples of Student Work

Piece in Ternary Form
COMPOSED BY 4 FOURTH GRADERS IN JANUARY

Piece in Ternary Form

COMPOSED BY 2 FOURTH GRADERS IN JANUARY

Piece in Ternary Form
COMPOSED BY 4 FIFTH GRADERS IN JANUARY

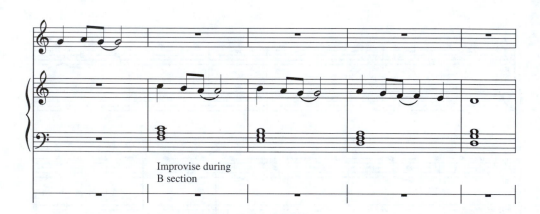

Improvise during
B section

Percussion Stop

Advanced Piece in Ternary Form
COMPOSED BY 5 FIFTH GRADERS IN FEBRUARY

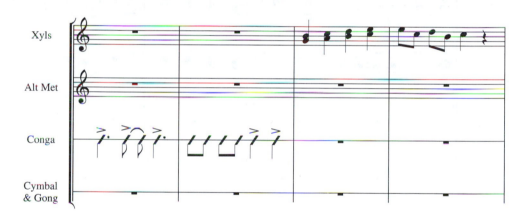

UNSUCCESSFUL TERNARY PIECE

Three students worked together. One played a wind chime, one a set of temple blocks, and one an alto xylophone. They understood that they needed to create two contrasting ideas and even developed a simple accompanying figure, but they did not understand the formal structure of the assignment.

One student began by playing a repeating rhythm pattern on the temple blocks:

Some time during her second repeat of the pattern, the wind chime began. The student playing the wind chime did not seem to sense the underlying pulse of the temple block rhythm, in spite of the fact that the rhythm was being played quite regularly. Watching the children move, one could see that they were not sensing a common pulse. Their bodies moved in completely different tempi.

Following two repetitions of the rhythm pattern and after the wind chime had begun, the xylophone player began her melody:

etc.

She played a third tempo, seeming to sense a third underlying pulse. They continued for a few repetitions (each independently repeating her own pattern) until suddenly the xylophone stopped. Almost immediately, the wind chime stopped (sort of midstream) and then the temple block player finished her pattern and stopped.

These students showed their ability to develop two independent thematic ideas (xylophone and temple blocks) and to conceive of a textural (or at least a procedural) organization (who plays first, second, third). However, they did not show an understanding of organizing those thematic ideas into ABA form. They also exhibited a rather naive understanding of principles of rhythmic simultaneity.

A More Extended Bithematic Work

Figure 8.5 (CD, Track 15) describes a lesson that can be used to follow up and extend student understanding developed during the previous listening and compositional experiences.

Figure 8.5: UNIT: BITHEMATIC FORMS
Lesson Plan: A More Extended Bithematic Work (1 or 2 sessions)

National Standards: 6, 7, 9
Grade: 4 and up, based upon prior experience

Materials:
- Bizet: "Farandole" from *L'arlésienne Suite No. 2* (CD, Track 15)
- Blank form chart with 14 blanks.
- Pencils.

Organization:
Independent work within the large-group listening experience. Small group later.

Lesson assumes:
- Extensive prior experience in performing, analytical listening, and composing of bithematic music.

Objective:
To provide an opportunity for students to apply and expand upon what they know about ABA form to understand a more complex bithematic work.

Connection to prior knowledge/experience = Groundwork that enables:
Relate today's lesson to the extended unit on ABA form that students have just completed. "Now that you are all experts on ABA form, let's see if you can figure out the form of a more complicated piece that uses an A theme and a B theme."

Pose problems: Students will:
- Listen to and analyze "Farandole" for form, completing a form chart in a way that reflects what they think they hear.
- Use their form charts to work with a small group of peers to develop a more extensive list of what they hear in the music in addition to the form.

Students solve problems: Students will:
- Complete a form chart as the teacher plays the recording and indicates sections by pointing to numbers (as with "Trepak").
- Listen and identify other elements they hear in addition to form.

Students share and discuss solutions:
- Students share their ideas about the form in order to agree upon one way of filling in the original form chart.
- Students share"what else they hear" in the work.

Assessment:
Students will show their understanding of form by their ability to analyze the music and fill in the form chart. Students will show their ability to set their understanding of form into a larger context by analyzing other characteristics of the music occurring within each formal section of the work.

Once students are satisfied with their own answers, the class should share their ideas and produce a version that reflects consensus. Remember to ask students with disparate answers what they heard in the music that made them think that their answers were correct. Try to get inside their heads to understand how they are thinking about and understanding the music. This will help you to know how to lend support when needed and how to design future instruction. The finished chart should look something like this:

1	2	3	4	5	6	7	8	9	10	11	12	13	14
A	A	Bridge	B	B	B	A	B	A	B	Bridge	A+B	A+B	Coda

Since it will probably take several listenings and some time to hear individual sections of the work, because it is so long, some students will probably finish with portions of the chart before others. After several listenings, you might suggest that students who have already figured out the form may want to start adding to their charts their own comments about orchestration, dynamics, tempo, articulation, texture, etc., in each section.

Once the class has agreed on an analysis of the thematic structure of the work, it is time for everyone to turn their attention to other details of the work. ("What else do you hear?") One way to accomplish this, which students generally enjoy, is to make it a contest (see Box 8.1).[3]

BOX 8.1

Divide the class into groups (teams) of five or six students. Each group should be seated on the floor (or at a table or large desk) around a sheet of chart paper. Across the top of each sheet print the letters that reflect the form of "Farandole." [You might want to do this ahead of time.] Each group will need two or three markers and may want to refer to notes they made on their individual charts during last week's lesson. The contest rules are as follows:

- Play the recording as many times as the students need to hear it.
- Groups write on charts things other than form that they hear.
- If a group lists an aspect of the work that no other group has found, that item will be worth 1,000 points.
- If two groups hear and identify the same item, each group gets 500 points.
- If three groups identify it, each gets 300 points.
- If four identify it, each gets 200 points.
- If everyone identifies it, all groups get 100 points (or however you decide to do this).

Using high values seems to encourage them to listen very carefully and makes the contest exciting.

Whether or not you decide to use a contest format, what is important is that the students try to hear as much as they can in the music and get to know the piece intimately through repeated listening that is highly analytical in nature. Whatever approach you decide to take should stimulate good discussion of the details of the music and the ways in which the music is put together to create the desired effect. The result is generally that students come to relish the piece and often ask to hear it played when they enter the music room.

UNIT: METER

(2–4 CLASS SESSIONS)

This unit assumes prior experience moving to and feeling music that moves in either "twos" or "threes." Students would have worked on the experiential level moving in ways that reflect the accent and ways that beats are grouped and organized. Meter is the feel that time signature represents.

Identifying Meter

(1 SESSION)

Consider some familiar songs and pieces, and analyze them for how the beats are organized into meter. You might ask students to pat their laps for the downbeats and clap for the weaker beats. They can use these motions to "test out" whether the various songs and pieces are moving:

1 2 1 2 1 2 1 2   or   1 2 3 1 2 3 1 2 3 1 2 3

Once the students have the idea, try a piece that has two or more sections that change meter from either "twos" to "threes" or from "threes" to "twos." Renaissance dance movements often do this quite clearly (for example, Robert Johnson's "The Satyr's Dance" [CD, Track 16].

This lesson is followed by a small-group composition project that is described in Figure 8.6.

Compose a Piece that Changes Meter

Figure 8.6: UNIT: METER

Lesson Plan: Compose a Piece that Changes Meter (1–3 sessions)

National Standards: 2, 4, 6, 7
Grade: 4 and up

Organization:
Small-group composition problem.

Materials:

- Classroom instruments.
- Recording, from the previous class, of the piece that changes meter.

Lesson assumes:

- Experience moving to and identifying meter in twos and threes.

Objective:

To help students expand their understanding of meter; to help them develop the ability to change back and forth from duple to triple.

Connection to prior knowledge/experience = Groundwork that enables:

- Relate the composition experience to the exploration and identification of duple and triple meter during the previous class.
- Play the piece that changes meter again, and ask students to pat and clap softly to be sure they remember the feel of the meter change.

Pose problem:

Students will compose an original piece that either moves in twos and then threes (and may return to twos) or the reverse. There must be at least one change in meter from duple to triple or triple to duple.

Students solve problem:

Students will work in small groups to develop first one section of music that moves in either twos or threes. They then have two options: (1) they might choose to set the same theme into the new meter or (2) they might choose to develop a second thematic idea in the new meter.

Students share and discuss solutions:

As each group shares its finished product, encourage the others to see if they can figure out where the change occurs and describe the plan the group formulated

Assessment:

Students will show their understanding of the concepts of meter and meter change by their ability to produce a composition that lies within the parameters of this assignment.

Extensions:

After the students share their pieces, challenge them to figure out the meter of some music that has twos and threes in combination, such Brubeck's "Take Five" (in $\frac{5}{4}$ time, which feels like 3 + 2) or his "Unsquare Dance" (in $\frac{7}{8}$, which feels like 2 + 2 + 3) or "I Like to Be in America," from *West Side Story* (which feels like 3 + 3 + 2 + 2 + 2). In such pieces, it is fun to try to walk around the room to the music, taking a step on only the strong beats (e.g., stepping on all the "ones" of a **1** 2 3 **1** 2 **1** 2 pattern). Students will need to move in some way in order to be able to learn to feel complex meters such as these.

As students work to solve this problem, you should be aware that shift in meter will be quite a challenge for them to accomplish, even though they may be able to "intellectualize" it. It is not uncommon for students to develop a theme in twos and then, thinking they are changing to threes, begin to play either the same idea or a new one in fours (1 2 3 ♪). Sometimes it helps to suggest that at least one student in the group play a strong 1 2 or 1 2 3 accompanying figure on a nonpitched percussion or low-pitched barred instrument while others play the theme along with the accompaniment. Sometimes the presence of a strong accompanying figure will enable the others to make the shift in feel.

When sharing the finished products, be sure to ask, "What else did they do besides changing meter?" This will encourage discussion of the different approaches: who used an accompanying figure and who did not, who used different thematic material when the meter changed and who maintained the same theme but shifted the feel of the theme, and so on. Changing meter was the "doorway in"; students would have had to make many other decisions as well, and those should not go unnoticed or uncelebrated.

In assessing student work, you might use a rubric such as the following:

SAMPLE ASSESSMENT RUBRIC FOR METER PIECE

Below level:

Students might have difficulty finding a common underlying pulse, making it difficult for the listener to perceive the organizational plan.

Basic level:

1. Students are able to establish a common underlying pulse.
2. There is an attempt at organizing the pulses into twos or threes and an attempt at making the shift.

Proficient level:

1. The students successfully perform material that can be perceived by the listener as moving in twos and threes.
2. Students effectively make the shift in meter.
3. There is a sense of ensemble in that players share a sense of underlying pulse and show their understanding of the relationship between their parts and those performed by the other group members.

Advanced level:

1. In addition to the criteria for "proficient," the work contains thematic material (melodic or rhythmic) that does more than represent grouped pulses. Students are able to combine some rhythmic complexities with the idea of metric organization.
2. The work is well-executed (well-rehearsed and performed) by the group.
3. The work is sophisticated enough to evoke an affective response from the listener.

UNIT: HARMONIC STRUCTURE

(4 SESSIONS)

Introduction to Tonic and Dominant Harmonies

The introductory lesson in this unit (Figure 8.7) is based on the lullaby "Hush Little Baby." Students will first learn to hear and identify tonic and dominant sonorities (I and V_7 chords).

Figure 8.7: UNIT: HARMONIC STRUCTURE
Lesson Plan: Introduction to Tonic and Dominant Harmonies (1 session)

National Standards: 1, 2, 5, 7
Grade: 4 and up

Materials:
- "Hush Little Baby" or other simple folk song that can be accompanied by only I and V_7 chords. (It is preferable that students be somewhat familiar with the song from previous experiences.)
- Resonator bells or other barred instruments.

Lesson assumes:
- Extensive experience with tonal center.
- Extensive experience singing scale numbers in connection with at least portions of melodies to help them identify characteristic passages within familiar melodies, such as 1–2–3–4–5, 5–4–3–2–1, 1–3–5, 5–3–1, and so on.

Organization:
Whole-group performance problem.

Objective:
To introduce the concept of tonic and dominant harmonies.

Connection to prior knowledge/experience:
- On a piano, play the opening phrase of "America" (or some other harmonized familiar song with a similar harmonic structure) stopping on the penultimate dominant chord, ending with the leading tone.
- Ask students to describe what you have done. Encourage them to describe the feeling of the incomplete cadence. Ask them to complete the cadence and encourage them to talk about how they knew what to do.

Groundwork that enables:
- Remind students about what they know about the home tone in Western music, and show them that musicians also use "home chords" to establish a sound of completeness.
- Play the sound of the home chord on the piano (in several inversions) and then play a dominant chord. Resolve it. Play several versions.
- Ask students to identify sonorities with hand signals, as described below.

Pose problem:
Students will use their ears to try to establish a chord progression that will work to accompany a simple folk song, based on their prior experience with home tone and on the opening experiences with home and away chords.

Students solve problem:
- Students play resonator bells, beginning with the home chord, and use their "collective" ears to determine when the chords change.
- Once they solve the problem, they will use their solution to accompany the song.

Students share and discuss solutions:
Students solve this problem by thinking together as a group. There may be some discussion of the solution, but if the song is simple enough, they generally agree on one solution through their communal performance of the chords.

Assessment:
Students will show their understanding of the sound and function of tonic and dominant harmonies by deciding upon and performing a chord progression that works for the song.

Hush Little Baby

American Folk Tune

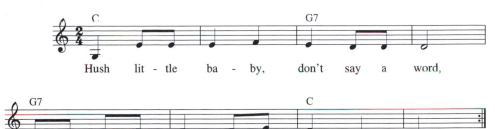

Hush lit - tle ba - by, don't say a word,

Ma - ma's gon - na buy you a mock - ing bird.

2. And if that mocking bird don't sing,
    Mama's gonna buy you a diamond ring.

3. If that diamond ring turns brass,
    Mama's gonna buy you a looking glass.

4. If that looking glass gets broke,
    Mama's gonna buy you a billy goat.

5. If that billy goat don't pull,
    Mam's gonna buy you a cart and bull.

6. If that cart and bull turn over.
    Mama's gonna buy you a dog named Rover.

7. If that dog named Rover don't bark.
    Mama's gonna buy you a pony cart.

8. If that pony cart falls down,
    You'll be the saddest little (boy/girl) in town.

In preparation for solving this performance problem, students need to learn to hear and identify tonic and dominant chords with hand signals. As you lay the groundwork for the problem, tell the students that the chords they are hearing are called tonic and dominant. But, for classroom purposes, you will call these chords "home" and "away" chords because "away" chords sound as though they are moving away from "home" and do not sound finished until they return "home."[4] In this classroom, the signal for the "home chord" will be clasped hands. The signal for the "away chord" sound will be hands open to the side (like an open clap).

Once they understand the hand signals, play some inversions on the piano and see if students can identify the two sonorities with the proper signals. Doing this as a whole-class activity enables students who need support to check their solutions against those of their neighbors with just a simple glance around the room. Eventually, individuals will become more secure and competent.

In this lesson, determining the underlying harmonic structure of the song is a whole-class activity.[5] Distribute one resonator bell and one mallet to each student (or as far as your instruments will go). Or ask each student to play one bar on a barred instrument (three or four can share one xylophone for this activity, if you have enough mallets). Students might be assigned any pitches in the tonic or dominant chords. This lesson is in C major, so you can distribute all the diatonic pitches except for the note "A."

On the chalkboard, indicate:

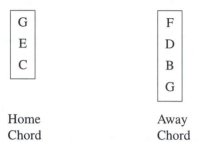

Home   Away
Chord   Chord

Ask the whole class to play their bells or bars in a gentle tremolo. Once they understand the technique, point to the box labeled "home chord" on the board and ask only players holding those pitches to play a sustained tremolo. Switch to the "away chord," and back. Once they have the idea, pose the problem.

Most simple songs both begin and end on the home chord. Therefore, in order to solve this problem, it would seem to make sense for the home chord players to begin. As they play their tremolo, the teacher will sing the song. ("Hush Little Baby" works well because it can be appropriately sung slowly and with a bit of *rubato,* making it easier for students to hear the chord changes.)

The students are to remain on the home chord until it no longer feels "comfortable." At that point, they should switch to the away chord and back, and so on, until they have determined a pattern with which they feel comfortable. (This song also works well because it has many stanzas. By the time the teacher has reached the fourth or fifth stanza, the class has usually agreed on a pattern of $I–V_7–V_7–I$ for each stanza.)

Using Tonic and Dominant Harmonies

The second lesson (Figure 8.8) in the unit builds on understandings developed in the first lesson but, this time, students work in small groups with less teacher support. This lesson is based on "A Ram Sam Sam," a song that American children have sung for many years. Some sources attribute its origins to Morocco. Even if its origins are Moroccan, it is likely that the harmonies and perhaps even the rhythmic and melodic design have been altered from the original to sound Western. This song should not be taught as an exemplar of Moroccan music. However, it is a useful and familiar round and one that children enjoy singing.

A Ram Sam Sam

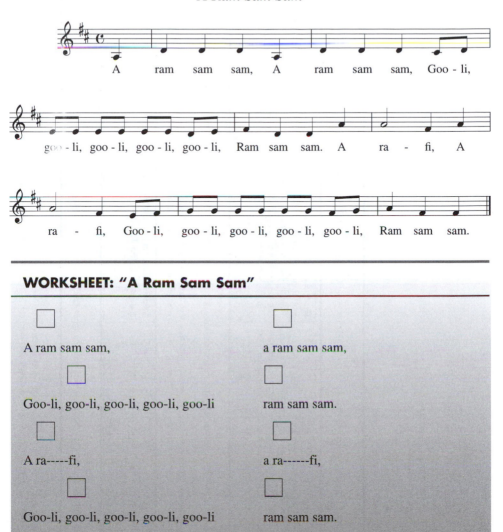

WORKSHEET: "A Ram Sam Sam"

☐   ☐

A ram sam sam,   a ram sam sam,

☐   ☐

Goo-li, goo-li, goo-li, goo-li, goo-li   ram sam sam.

☐   ☐

A ra-----fi,   a ra------fi,

☐   ☐

Goo-li, goo-li, goo-li, goo-li, goo-li   ram sam sam.

The lesson requires Autoharps or Omnichords. Guitars, keyboards, or other chording instruments may be used, but students may require more specific instruction before they are able to play chords.

This time, the students will work in the key of D major. They know that in the last class they played C–E–G as the home chord and G–B–D–F as the away chord when the home tone of the melody was C. Help them to discover that the home chord is built on the first note of the scale, and the away chord is built on the fifth.

Figure 8.8: UNIT: HARMONIC STRUCTURE
Lesson Plan: Using Tonic and Dominant Harmonies (1 session)

National Standards: 1, 2, 5, 7
Grade: 4 and up

Materials:
- "A Ram Sam Sam" or other $I - V_7$ song the students know well.
- One worksheet, pencil, and Autoharp pick for each instrument (and group).
- Four or five Autoharps or Omnichords (electronic Autoharps).

Lesson assumes:
- A basic knowledge of home tone, home chord, and away chord.
- Ability to sing the song independently (in this case, "A Ram Sam Sam").

Objective:
To help students use their basic understanding of tonic and dominant harmonies to figure out the harmonic structure of a simple folk song; this time, working in small groups, without teacher support.

Organization:
Small-group performance and listening problem.

Connection to prior knowledge/experience:
- Students enjoy opportunities to play Autoharps and Omnichords. The instruments themselves generally intrigue them. Today, they will have an opportunity to play these instruments on their own, without the teacher, and everyone will have a chance to play. Generally this is motivation enough to make them anxious to begin work.
- Connect today's experience to the problem they solved in the last class using "Hush Little Baby."

Pose problem:
- Try to figure out the chords for a new song, based on their prior experience determining the chords for "Hush Little Baby." This time, they will be playing in D major where D is the home tone.
- Take turns accompanying while their group sings the melody, once they have decided what chords they will play.
- Take turns accompanying while the whole class learns to sing the song as a round with the chordal accompaniment.

Students solve problem:
- Students strum "home" chord and sing the melody. When the accompaniment sounds wrong, they will change to the "away" chord.
- Once they solve the problem, they will use their solution to accompany the song.

Groundwork that enables:
- Working from what they learned in the last class, the group will determine what chords are the I and V_7 when the home tone is D.
- If D is the home tone, what, then, would be the home chord? Can they figure out what the away chord must be? Can they locate those buttons on the Autoharp or Omnichord?
- In the last class, they also learned that songs usually begin and end on the home chord. Does this help them know how to begin the worksheet?

Students share and discuss solutions:
Students will share ideas throughout the process.

Assessment:
Students will show what they know by their ability to figure out the chords and perform them appropriately to accompany the singing.

Extensions:
- Students might make a graphic score of the texture of their performance of the round with accompaniment.
- Students might try to figure out and play chords for other songs that can be accompanied with I and V_7, this time using keyboards and/or guitars.

In solving the problem, each group assembles around one instrument with their worksheet, pick, and pencil. Each group decides who will push the buttons and who will strum for that group as they solve the problem. The others will sing the song.

As the group sings, the "strummer" will strum a steady beat coinciding with the empty boxes on the worksheet—one strum for each box (boxes are placed on the downbeat of each measure in the song). The "button pusher" should begin with the home chord and continue strumming that chord until it does not sound right with the singing. When it does not sound correct, he or she should try the away chord.

As soon as there is some consensus within the group, students are to fill in the boxes on the worksheet with their solution. At this point, you may want to suggest that students raise their hands to get your attention. You may want to check each group's solution and help them with any discrepancies they may be experiencing. So long as the solution "works" and the group is satisfied with the sound, it should be considered correct. In this case, the most conventional solution is:

$$D \; D \; A_7 \; D$$
$$D \; D \; A_7 \; D$$

This is why it works as a two-part round.

Group members then take turns accompanying while the group sings the song. Depending on the amount of time remaining, they may opt to play as partners (one strummer and one button-pusher) or try to perform the accompaniment alone. This works well since not everyone will finish at the same time. Those who figure out the chords first will have more time to practice and will be able to try it alone. Those who have a bit of trouble can each still get a turn to play—but with partners.

Once everyone has solved the problem and practiced playing and singing, ask all four or five Autoharps in the room to play simultaneously while the whole class sings. Next, try the melody as a round several times, switching players until everyone has had a turn to accompany the round.

Sample of Student Work

A vignette that was part of a research study (Wiggins, 1992) captured fifth graders at work on this particular lesson (see Box 8.2).

BOX 8.2

Lynn was strumming while Louise was pushing the chord buttons, and all students in the group were singing. At one point, Lynn counted off the beats to get them started:

Lynn: "One, two, three, 'A ram sam sam, A ram sam sam, Goo-li, goo-li . . .' "

They had played three I chords in the key of D. Lynn stopped strumming immediately when she heard that the third one did not fit with what they were singing.

Louise: "It goes D and D here?"

Lynn: "No!"

Louise: "It's A?"

Lynn: "Listen! Listen to the sound! It goes [begins singing] 'A ram sam sam, A ram sam sam.' Ready? Go. [sings and strums] 'A ram sam sam, A ram sam sam' "

The group continues singing and strumming, but Louise is still pressing the "D" button for the third chord, which should be A_7.

Sheila: "Stop. That's A."

Lynn: "It's an A. Listen, listen, listen, listen, listen."

After the class was over, I asked Lynn how she and her group had worked to solve this particular problem. She replied, " You sing it out loud. Then you can hear yourself think. You can hear what you're thinking."

Hearing Tonic, Dominant, and Subdominant Harmonies

The lesson in Figure 8.9 extends students' understanding to include subdominant harmonies (IV chord) as well.

Figure 8.9: UNIT: HARMONIC STRUCTURE
Lesson Plan: Hearing Tonic, Dominant, and Subdominant Harmonies (1 session)

National Standards: 1, 2, 3, 5, 6, 7
Grade: 4 and up

Organization:
Whole-group performance and listening problem.

Materials:
- "Peace like a River."
- Autoharps, keyboards, guitars, Omnichords, or some combination of these instruments.
- Chart on chalkboard (see below).

Lesson assumes:
- Experience figuring out tonic and dominant chords for simple folk songs.

Objective:
To help students expand their understanding of harmonic structure to include subdominant harmonies.

Connection to prior knowledge/experience:
- Talk with the students about what they already know about home and away chords and how they are used to accompany melodies.
- Talk about the need for more chords for some songs.
- Introduce the IV chord (resting chord) as the next most commonly used in Western music.

Groundwork that enables:
- From the piano, play some I and V_7 chords, and then some I, IV, and V_7 chords, using the hand signals. Play some inversions as well. Playing single bass notes with chords in the right hand will help make identification a bit easier.
- Ask students to identify the chords using the hand signals.

Pose problems:
- Figure out chords for "Peace like a River," based on prior experience figuring out chords for songs, plus the new information about IV chords.
- Accompany the song playing the chords on available instruments.

Students solve problems:
- Class will listen as the teacher sings the song and plays the chords and will try to identify the chords using hand signals. A student "scribe" will record the class's answers on the chart. Eventually, there should be consensus.
- Once the progression has been agreed on, students will take turns playing it to accompany class singing.

Students share and discuss solutions:
Students share ideas throughout.

Assessment:
Students will be able to identify appropriate chords and perform the song with accompaniment.

Extensions:
Once students have become proficient at this kind of experience, whenever possible, they should be accompanying their own singing with chords and bass lines. Also, whenever possible, they should be figuring out what chords should be used to accompany, unless the chord progression is too complex for their level of experience.

235

Peace like a River

American

I've got peace like a riv-er, I've got peace like a riv-er, I've got

peace like a riv-er in my soul.   I've got peace like a riv-er, I've got

peace like a riv-er, I've got peace like a riv-er in my soul.

CHALKBOARD CHART FOR LESSON 8.9

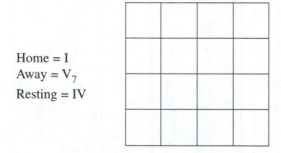

Home = I
Away = V$_7$
Resting = IV

You might begin this lesson by saying something like, "Not all songs can be accompanied by just those two sonorities. In most simple Western music, the tonic is the most prevalent harmony and the dominant, the second most common. The third most common chord is what we call the 'resting chord.' [Demonstrate the sound as you talk about the differences.] We will call it the resting chord because it is a comfortable place to rest, but it is not home. It does not push us home with quite the same force as the away chord does, but it is still not home. In our classroom, the signal for a resting chord will be crossing your arms across your chest, as in 'rest in peace.' The resting chord is built on the fourth note of the scale. Can you hear that in the bass as I play?"

As students work together to solve the problem, a student volunteer will fill in the chart on the chalkboard, following the hand signals suggested by the class. The volunteer will record in each box the chord that the majority of the class is showing at each point or record two chords if there seems to be discrepancy. This student may refer to the list to the left of the chart and use chord numerals instead of writing "home," "away," and "resting."

The teacher plays and sings the song, playing block chords with a single bass note, one for each empty box, and singing the melody without playing it. This will help the class to hear the chord changes more clearly. Sing through the song as many times as the students need to hear it in order to figure out the chords. If there is disagreement among the group, encourage them to work it out among themselves.

Once they agree on a way of harmonizing the melody, it is their turn to play. Help them to realize that knowing the numbers I, IV, and V is not enough information, that they also need to know what the home tone will be in order to know which chords to play. (If the students will play keyboards, perform the song in C major, because these chords will be the easiest for nonpianists to play. If they will play Autoharps and/or guitars, you might want to choose a different key.)

As the students figure out the chords in the key you play, create a parallel set of boxes that indicates chord letter names as opposed to numerals, for example:

C	C	F	C
C	C	G_7	G_7
C	C	F	C
C	G_7	C	C

If students do not know how to find chords on the keyboard, you might start by having them play the bass line only. Students who already know how to play chords can do so, paired with a bass line player at each keyboard. Some students might also double the bass line on low-pitched xylophones. It is best if everyone has a chance to play something, even if they need to take turns as the class sings the song several times through.

This is a new song for the class, but having heard you sing it many times as they figure out the chords, they are usually ready to sing it right away. If students are unsure of any parts of the melody, you might go over that first. Ask the students if they know the song well enough to sing it without practicing it. They will know.

Singing Chordal Harmonies

Up to this point in this unit, students have relied on instruments to create the harmonies to accompany their singing of melodies. With this background and prior experience, it is now time for them to try singing harmonies. Depending on their prior experience, fourth-grade students may not be ready to attempt this yet.

This lesson (Figure 8.10) is based on a South African protest song that is generally performed either unaccompanied or accompanied with body percussion sounds.

Figure 8.10: UNIT: HARMONIC STRUCTURE
Lesson Plan: Singing Chordal Harmonies (1 session)

National Standards: 1, 3, 5, 7, 9
Grade: 5 and up

Organization:
Whole-group performance problem.

Materials:

- "Freedom Is Coming."[6]
- Autoharps, keyboards, guitars, Omnichords, or some combination of these instruments.
- Chart on chalkboard (see below).

Lesson assumes:

- Considerable experience hearing and playing I, IV, and V_7 chords in an instrumental setting.
- Experience singing simple melodies by scale number.

Objective:
To help students extend their knowledge of chordal harmony to an *a cappella* singing experience.

Connection to prior knowledge/experience = Groundwork that enables:
Students have had many experiences playing chords. They will try to perform a piece that is traditionally sung without instruments playing the chords.

Pose problem:
Students will learn to sing a song with chordal harmonies, based on prior experience hearing and playing chords on instruments to accompany singing.

Students solve problem = Students share and discuss solutions:

- As a group, students try to figure out how the three different lines written on the chalkboard might sound.
- Divide the class into three groups. Each group should practice its part until comfortable.
- When everyone is ready, ask the students singing the lowest part to begin. Once they have sung their part through twice, add the middle line. After 2 more repetitions, add the top line.
- Once students are comfortable singing the parts with numbers, substitute the lyrics "Freedom Is Coming" for the numbers.
- Can they listen carefully to what they are singing and figure out when they are singing I, IV, and V_7? Can they identify then with hand signals?
- When students are secure in the chordal accompaniment, teach the melody line. Some students can sing the melody over the sung chords.
- When they are secure with melody and sung accompaniment, try improvising vocal lines over the sung chords. Add body percussion.

Assessment:
Students will show their understanding and proficiency by their ability to figure out and perform the song.

Extensions:

- Talk with the students about the roots of South African music and how its rhythmic aspects are from traditional African tribal music and its chordal aspects from European influence over the years.
- Talk about the role of music in political movements and the impact of protest songs sung in connection with various causes in the United States. Learn some protest songs in this manner. Students who have mastered this piece would also be able to sing three-part chordal backgrounds to other melodies. Songs with repeating chord progressions work best.
- Try singing other part songs in this manner. There are many that use a repeating pattern of I-vi-ii-V_7. Some students can sustain chordal harmonies while others sing the melody. This also makes a marvelous background against which some students might improvise melodies.

Freedom Is Coming

From South Africa

CHALKBOARD CHART FOR LESSON 8.10

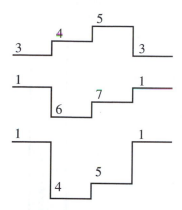

As students learn to perform this piece, you might want to visually and physically separate the three groups. Sometimes students are able to perform more accurately at first if you provide each group with a barred instrument or keyboard to use as a "crutch," when necessary. One student from the group can be responsible for providing pitches for the group if members are unsure at any point.

Eventually, once the class is secure singing the chordal harmony, the teacher can add the melody line. Once they understand how it all fits together, students can take over responsibility for the melody line too; but, with upper-elementary students, this may not take place until a later class session when students are extremely secure singing the harmony parts.

Eventually, when students are very comfortable with the song, you might add improvised melodies over the chordal harmonies and/or body percussion, both appropriate in this style.

UNIT: THE BLUES

(4–6 SESSIONS)

This is an extended unit on the blues. Depending on students' prior experience, the length of the class sessions, and how much time students choose to invest in each phase, classes may progress through the various phases of this unit at different rates. Therefore, the ideas are presented here in a logical sequence with the understanding that it might take four or five lessons to complete all of the stages. The stages are cumulative, meaning that once a part has been added to the performance, it remains as students move into the next stage.

This lesson (Figure 8.11) is based on a traditional blues song found in most elementary music textbooks, the "Joe Turner Blues."

Figure 8.11: UNIT: THE BLUES
Lesson Plan: Singing Chordal Harmonies (1 session)

National Standards: 1, 2, 3, 6, 7, 9
Grade: 5 and up

Organization:
Whole-group performance problem.

Materials:
• "Joe Turner Blues."[7]
• Keyboards.
• Barred instruments plus resonator bells (if available).
• A "swing-style" repeating drum track, if available, either a synthesizer "preset" pattern or created with a sequencer and keyboard.
• Chart on chalkboard.

Lesson assumes:
• Extensive experience singing, playing, and hearing I, IV and V_7 chords.
• Assumes students know how to play chords and bass lines to accompany their own singing.

Objective:
To help students use what they know about tonic, subdominant, and dominant harmonies to understand and perform a blues progression.

Connection to prior knowledge/experience = Groundwork that enables:
Previous work with chordal harmonies provides a basis for this unit. You might connect this experience to "Freedom Is Coming," if this lesson follows that experience. There are both musical and cultural connections. If students have not sung that song, connect this experience to others they have had accompanying with chords.

Pose problems: Students will
• Figure out by ear the chords of a standard blues progression.
• Learn to perform the bass line, and then to add the chords.
• Learn to improvise melodies based on chord tones.
• Learn to improvise melodies based on chord tones plus "blue" notes.
• Learn to sing a traditional blues song.
• Listen to and analyze some authentic blues songs.
• Compose original blues songs.

Students solve problems = Students share and discuss solutions:
Since this lesson requires a rather lengthy description, please read the text for details. In this lesson, the student shares ideas throughout.

Assessment:
Students will be able to successfully perform what is required at each stage of the unit.

Extensions:
• Once students are comfortable with this, they can use the same process to accompany other popular songs that have repeating chord progressions. Particularly with a I-vi-ii-V_7 progression, it is easy to set up bells for soloists, using 1 3 5 6 on one side and 2 4 5 7 on the other, or some other combination where one student is responsible for improvising during the I and vi chords and the other during the ii and V_7 chords. You can then intersperse class singing over the chords and bass line with student improvisations based on the chords of the song, much the way jazz musicians improvise around the "changes" of a pop song.
• You might also extend this idea of improvising a melody that is generated by chord tones to a study of ground bass (see the website at *www.mhhe.com/wiggins*).

Joe Turner Blues

American Blues

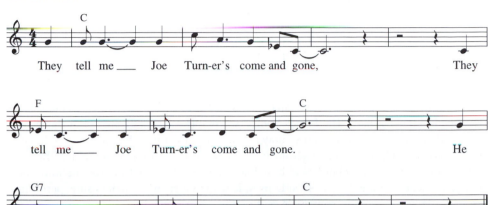

They tell me ___ Joe Turn-er's come and gone,   They

tell me ___ Joe Turn-er's come and gone.   He

left me here to sing this song.

> 2. He came here with forty links of chain,
>   He came here with forty links of chain.
>   He left me here to sing this song.
>
> 3. Joe Turner, he took my man away,
>   Joe Turner, he took my man away.
>   He left me here to sing this song.

CHALKBOARD CHART FOR LESSON 8.11

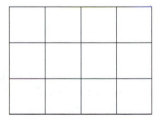

Ask a student to act as scribe (as in "Peace like a River") to record the chords in the empty chart as the class suggests. For each of the 12 chords, the teacher plays the block chords (with single bass note) of the blues progression, in the following pattern:

Play the blues in C major, to make it easier for nonpianists to play keyboards and to be able to use diatonic xylophones to play bass lines. By ear, the students should come up with:

$$
\begin{array}{llll}
C & C & C & C \\
F & F & C & C \\
G_7 & F & C & C
\end{array}
$$

Start the swing drum track. Students will perform the bass line in rotation, as described in the vignette "The Fifties Song" (see p. 44). Once they are comfortable with that, students who are ready to do so may add the chords. If possible, pair a chord player with a bass line player at each instrument as students move around the circle. This provides a solid sound with chords and bass lines played throughout the room and enables more experienced students to work side-by-side with players who are less sure, permitting stronger players to provide immediate scaffolding when needed.

Ask students which pitches should be placed in the center of the floor for improvising a melody over these chords. By now, they should be able to name the chord tones for the C, F, and G_7 chords. Place resonator bells or a glockenspiel with the pitches of the C chord on one side and the pitches of the F and G or G_7 (if you have enough bells) on the other.

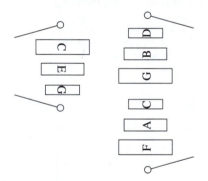

As students progress around the rotation, each pair will take at least one turn improvising, playing whatever bells they wish when their chord is being played. Since they only have chord tones available to them, they only need to listen to the progression, as it is played, and play when they hear that it is their turn (their chord). If you are playing with a swing drum track, the students will automatically "swing" the eighths of their solos.

At this point, it is appropriate to interject some of the historical and cultural significance of the blues. As part of this story, you might talk about blue notes and how and why that plaintive quality came to be in this music.

To the pitches for the solo, add the flatted third along with the major third (add E-flat to the C chord, A-flat to the F chord, and B-flat to the G chord). Invite students to play solos once again. Notice the shift in the quality of the sound.

On the chalkboard, write the lyrics to the "Joe Turner Blues." Invite students to read the lyrics of all of the stanzas, and to speculate as to who might be singing the song and what they might be singing about. Talk some more about the cultural and historical roots of the blues.

Start the drum machine, the bass line, and the chords, and invite the students to sing the "Joe Turner Blues" as they accompany. Intersperse instrumental solos (on resonator bells or glockenspiel—with blue notes added) between verses.

Play some examples of blues songs that follow this same format. (There are many variations on blues. Try to find an example that uses this basic progression and presents the text in this format.) Can the students hear the chord changes? What other characteristics do they note?

Notice that in the "Joe Turner Blues" each stanza has three lines of text (one that coincides with each line of the progression) and that, in each, the first two lines are identical. Talk about the fact that blues were often improvised on the spot and that people sang one line and repeated it as they tried to think of a second line to fit with it.

Students should realize that they can quite easily write their own blues song simply by thinking of two lines of text that will fit with the progression. Give the students 5 or 10 minutes to think of some lyrics. As groups think of lyrics, write them on the chalkboard.

Once you have accumulated a collection of lyrics, have the students begin to play the progression once again. Encourage groups to sing their own blues. Because of their familiarity with the style, students usually make up their own melodies on the spot, often without even realizing they are doing it. Combine the improvised stanzas with instrumental solos on the tone bells (glockenspiel).

For additional examples of units of complex problems designed for more experienced learners, please see the *Teaching for Musical Understanding* website at *www.mhhe.com/wiggins*. The questions and activities in Boxes 8.3 and 8.4 should help you assess your own understanding of lesson and unit planning processes.

BOX 8.3   THINK ABOUT THIS . . .

- Are there threads of similarity in the ways the units in Chapter 8 were conceived and constructed?
- What concepts are being taught? Around what elements or principles is each unit organized?
- In which processes do students engage?
- What musical problems are the students asked to solve?
- How does the teacher know whether or not the students have understood?

BOX 8.4 (ACTIVITY)

A good final project for a music methods course is to ask students to plan a unit of three to four lessons. The unit should be organized in a way that each lesson builds on the understandings and skills built in the lesson before. If possible, teach the unit, or at least one of the lessons, to children in a school setting. Assess your work using the assessment rubric on p. 82.

ENDNOTES

1. Please see the information regarding the National Standards in Endnote 1 of Chapter 6, p. 159.
2. "Mud," by Joanne Olshansky Hammil, is part of an excellent collection of original children's songs—*The pizza boogie songbook,* 1990 and 1995, Wayland, Mass.: JHO Music. Recordings of the songs are available on cassette or CD under the title *Pizza Boogie.* For ordering information, contact JHO Music at 800-557-7010. This song is reproduced here by permission.
3. This contest idea comes from Mary Pautz. She suggests that using large numbers for points makes the contest more exciting for students.
4. This way of labeling and signaling chords is from David Walker.
5. This idea is from Eunice Boardman, who has used it in many contexts.
6. Walton Music Corporation offers a choral arrangement of "Freedom Is Coming" (WW1174). Contact Walton Music online at <www.waltonmusic.com/index.html>.
7. See, for example, J. Beethoven, et al., 1995, *The music connection* (Grade 4, p. 13), Morristown, N.J.: Silver Burdett Ginn and Scott Foresman, and J. Bond, et al., 1995, *Share the music* (Grade 5, p. 291), New York: McGraw-Hill. This lesson is based on one that I learned from Lawrence Eisman.

SELECTED RESOURCES

Beethoven, J., et al. 1995–present. *The music connection: Grades K–8.* Morristown, N.J.: Silver Burdett Ginn and Scott Foresman.

Bergethon, B., E. Boardman, and J. Montgomery. 1997. *Musical growth in the elementary school.* 6th ed. Fort Worth, Tex.: Harcourt Brace.

Bond, J., et al. 1995–present. *Share the music: Grades K–8.* New York: McGraw-Hill.

Wiggins, J. 1991. *Synthesizers in the elementary music classroom: An integrated approach.* Reston, Va.: MENC (The National Association for Music Education).

Collections of music from around the world published by World Music Press, P.O. Box 2565, Danbury, CT 06813. Browse the press's catalog at <www.worldmusic-press.com/>.

PART 4
Your Classroom and Beyond

Part 4 is designed to help you form a more complete picture of what it is like to put *inquiry-based teaching into practice in your own school. Chapter 9 discusses issues related to the music classroom; Chapter 10, issues related to the experiences your students have in the classrooms of other teachers in the school.*

Chapter 9

AN INTERACTIVE MUSIC CLASSROOM

Chapter 9 deals with a variety of issues related to establishing an environment that will foster successful musical problem solving. These include a discussion of the physical makeup of the classroom and a more detailed look at the role of the teacher, the role of the student, and issues related to classroom management.

It may be helpful to think about teaching music in a musical cognitive apprenticeship as an interactive approach to teaching. The learning environment in which lesson and unit plans like those included in Chapters 6, 7, and 8 take place can be called an *interactive music classroom*. Throughout the text, the word *interaction* has appeared in several different contexts, all related to establishing effective music learning experiences. You have read about:

- The interactive nature of the structure of music itself—that music is a product of the *interaction* among its various structural elements.
- The idea that people develop understanding of musical ideas through a process in which new musical ideas interact with old—where schemas are built and transformed as a result of the *interaction* between new and prior knowledge.
- The development of musical expertise through direct *interaction* with the "substance" of music, through performance, listening, and creating experiences.
- The important role of social interaction in the process of learning music—*interaction* with both peers and teacher.

Overriding these processes is the impact of the emotional state of the learner, since emotion essentially pervades all other human actions and interactions (Goleman, 1995). Students' emotional sense of being affects their ability to function in both a social and a learning context, which impacts their willingness and ability to learn at a given time. Students also have an emotional response to the music itself, to the experience of engaging in the interactive processes of music, and to the experience of interacting with other people in the setting. One of the goals of interactive music learning is that the development of musical understanding and competency will provide students with opportunities to experience the emotional impact of the music itself and, therefore, find a place for it and value it in their lives. Thus, the role of emotion is pervasive throughout all aspects of the music teaching/learning process. *An interactive music classroom, then, is a learning environment that takes into account the interactive nature of the learning process, the interactive nature of music, the importance of interaction with music, and the importance of interaction among peers and teacher, and the impact of emotional interaction in the situation.*

Hopefully, exploring the lesson and unit plans in Chapters 6, 7, and 8 has helped you develop a better understanding of designing instruction within an interactive music learning environment. In this chapter, you will explore more about what is involved in carrying out this kind of instruction. Your own experience as a music student probably took place in predominantly teacher-directed, large-group, performance-based settings. As a result, you may have no model for what teaching in a student-centered, interactive classroom might be like. The ideas that follow should help establish a new role for music teachers, one in which they teach "from the sidelines" rather than from the "head of the class."

THE PHYSICAL MAKEUP OF THE CLASSROOM

Because of variation in circumstances from school to school, music teachers may not always have control over the physical nature of the space in which they teach. Sometimes music teachers are asked to teach music in someone else's classroom or in a corner of a gymnasium or on a stage. These conditions are far from ideal; however, teaching through problem solving is a way of conceiving, planning, and carrying out instruction, and the basic ideas can be adapted to just about any teaching setting. However, if your students are to have adequate opportunity to explore the "stuff" of music, they do need equipment and a place to work. The information provided in this section is designed to help you understand what a good music learning environment should look like. At the very least, it should provide a goal for the music teacher to work toward.

The physical makeup of the music classroom should reflect what will take place within its walls. If student chairs are set in rows, all facing the front of the classroom with a teacher desk or podium at the front of the room, it implies that students will be spending most of their time listening to a teacher who will be located at the head of the class. It also implies that it is not important for students to make eye contact with one another or to be able to see one another's actions. At the other end of the spectrum, there are music classrooms that have no student chairs at all. Here you might expect that students will be spending a good deal of their time actively moving around, but perhaps not much time sitting and listening, thinking and talking about music or musical ideas.

The arrangement of the furniture in a classroom tells a lot about what is apt to take place in the room. If you seat students in a circle or semicircle, so that they can easily see and hear one another, students are more likely to speak to and react to one another. A setup such as this tends to promote student/student interaction in both verbal and musical contexts. A wide-open space in the center of the circle can provide a convenient place to set up instruments, where instrumentalists can feel they are an integral part of the ensemble and where everyone can see what and how they are playing. Such a space implies that chairs can be easily moved into a series of smaller circles for small-group work or nearer to instruments or computers when necessary. Space also implies that at times movement might take place in the center of the circle. If the situation warrants, students might easily sit on the floor in the center of the circle. Setting classroom seating in a circle makes it easier for the teacher to see, at a quick glance, what and how students are doing during the various activities. This arrangement makes it easier for the teacher to stay "tuned in" to all of the students instead of losing contact with those who might choose to sit in the back of a classroom full of rows of chairs.

For some of the time, you may choose to sit as part of this circle as well. When a teacher sits on a student chair among the students, it carries great implications regarding whose ideas are important in the classroom. Schools and classrooms are full of power issues. The teacher can diffuse some of these issues by intentionally stepping down from the "pedestal" of the teacher's chair, desk, or podium. Of course, during teacher-guided, whole-group instruction, there will be times when the teacher will need to stand in a place where everyone can see what he or she is doing. There *are* times when you will need to teach from the "front of the room." However, it is also important to remember to step down from this position of power when it is not needed and to look intentionally for opportunities for students to take over that role instead.

As mentioned earlier, some general music teachers are not fortunate enough to have a music classroom; instead, they travel with carts from room to room, or they work in the corner of a gymnasium or cafeteria or auditorium. These situations will never be ideal, but thinking about what is important in your teaching can help you make some decisions about how you will deal with such circumstances. Even under these extreme circumstances, it still might be possible to have some say about how students are seated to learn. If you travel with a cart, you might ask classroom teachers to reset their furniture before you arrive, moving desks out of the way and resetting the chairs in a circle with plenty of room for music making. If it is important to you that students have the necessary equipment available to them, even if you do not have a classroom, then travel the halls with several carts instead of one. (It is possible that eventually your insistence on a proper teaching/learning environment for music may result in someone finding you a room rather than disrupting everyone else's.) If you have a place to teach but it is not a regular classroom, try to set up the space in a way that will be most conducive to the kind of teaching you want to be able to do.

However you decide to set up your furniture, you need to build into the setup a certain amount of flexibility so that students can easily move from whole-group to small-group, pair, and independent work. Student desks often inhibit such flexibility, making it preferable to use only chairs. Also, instruments will need to be readily accessible—stored in a place where students can easily take them out and carry them to the place they have chosen to work. Students should be encouraged to feel that the classroom instruments belong to them so they will come to value, respect, and care for them. Synthesizers generally will be more secure when placed on long tables as opposed to keyboard stands, which tend to be less stable in an active classroom. Tables also provide a place for headsets and small individual amplifiers as well as a place to rest a pencil and paper when writing during composing activities. The floor underneath long tables can provide convenient storage space for larger barred and percussion instruments, when they are not in use. If the room is large enough to accommodate it, you might place a synthesizer table as part of your circle of chairs so that, when synthesizers are used in ensemble playing, the players will feel a part of the group. Computers and MIDI stations are usually best placed around the perimeter of the classroom, out of the way of other activities and offering a bit of privacy for groups who are making use of them. An example of one such setup appears below:[1]

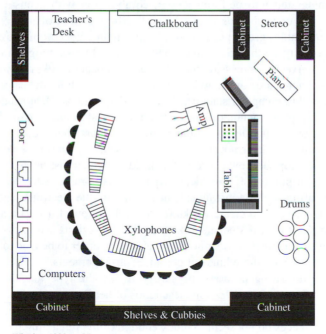

Wiggins, 1993, p. 27.

Kinds of Equipment

A classroom for teaching music ideally should contain as broad a selection of options for students as possible. Composing and improvising require a certain amount of classroom instrumentation. Of course, the larger and more diverse the instrument collection, the more options the students will have. At this point in time, it is almost imperative that a music classroom contain some electronic instruments. With the prevalence of this medium in the "real" music world, it needs to become an essential part of "school" music as well. Using the tools of the students' own musical culture can markedly increase the credibility of the curriculum in their eyes. In addition, inclusion of instruments representing a variety of world music cultures also enhances interest and possibilities for student learning.

In making decisions about purchasing both acoustic and electronic instruments, one should always consider the quality of the sounds produced by the instruments. It is important that the choices you provide for students be of the highest quality. When your budget is limited, it is sometimes preferable to buy a smaller number of better quality instruments, as opposed to buying a greater number of lesser quality. Variety is also an important factor. For example, for a class of 25 students, it is better to buy 5 professional-caliber synthesizers than 25 smaller, inexpensive nonprofessional keyboards. Five high-quality synthesizers can easily accommodate five groups of five for small-group work and can be easily integrated into performances in combination with acoustic instruments. Further, a room full of keyboards implies a very different kind of music class experience—one that resembles group piano lessons rather than a general music class. A small number of high-quality synthesizers can enhance a general music program without being so pervasive as to give the impression that the class has become a keyboard class or that the acoustic instruments are somehow less important. In addition, the same five synthesizers can be moved to computer stations, to create MIDI setups when needed.

An interesting phenomenon occurs when a music classroom contains both acoustic and electronic instruments. Despite some musicians' fears that electronic music will replace acoustic music, when students are presented with both options side-by-side, they actually tend to develop their own criteria for deciding which instrument is more appropriate for a particular purpose. If possible, set up the classroom in such a way that students would be able to bring acoustic instruments near to where the electronic ones are located because they often choose to create works for a combination of acoustic and electronic sounds. Keep in mind that, if students at keyboards are working with headsets, acoustic players in the group will need to wear headsets as well in order to be able to hear the keyboards when working with these kinds of combined arrangements.

If you are purchasing headsets, be sure you buy the type that blocks a certain amount of room noise. Students wearing these kinds of headsets seem to have no problem hearing acoustic instruments that are placed near the synthesizers. The kind of headsets that have foam earpieces do not seem to block enough of the remaining room noise when 25 people are composing at the same time, and students using them often have difficulty hearing their own synthesizers. While most synthesizers can accommodate only one headset, you can purchase "splitter boxes" that plug into the synthesizer and then accept six to eight headset jacks. There are also special headsets available for hearing-impaired students. Otherwise, students who wear hearing aids may prefer to use small amplifiers since headsets are not always compatible with their hearing aids.

Generally speaking, it is the lowest-quality instruments that have built-in sound systems. A professional-caliber synthesizer requires a separate sound system. There are various options for sound systems for classroom use. It is possible to purchase a small desktop combination amplifier/speaker for each synthesizer. This is a viable option because the small systems available today offer a high caliber of sound quality. However, if you also intend to use the synthesizers for performance in a large space, such as an auditorium or gymnasium, you might want to purchase a larger sound system that will also serve classroom use. It is possible to buy an amplifier or amplifier/mixer combination that will accept more than one synthesizer (maybe even all five). You might also consider some combination of the two options.

It is important to consider the number and location of electrical power sources in the classroom. Electronic instruments and sound systems do not consume very much electrical power. It is possible to run five synthesizers and a sound system from one electrical outlet. You will need to consider where electrical wires will be placed and try to avoid a situation in which students may trip over wires or cables. One solution is to install a "power pole" in the classroom,[2] which will enable you to run an extension cord up through the ceiling and over to a wall outlet. The keyboards and sound system can then be plugged into the "power pole," which can be placed out of the path of room traffic (ideally, very close to the table that holds the instruments).

A music classroom should have a high-quality sound system for playing recorded music, preferably with capabilities for playing compact discs, audiocassettes, and even records. It is essential that the music played for listening lessons be presented in its best light. The classroom will need an adequate supply of a wide variety of recordings, most of which will be accumulated over time and with experience. If possible, it is also helpful to have a number of listening stations available in the classroom for small groups or individuals to listen to a piece one more time during small-group work. Computers with CD-ROM capabilities can serve this purpose since they can also play CD recordings. If you intend to record student performances and original compositions for sharing and assessment purposes, you will need a reasonably good microphone for your sound system. (Not all audio systems accept an external microphone. Some will accept two, making stereo recording a possibility. This is something to keep in mind when purchasing a sound system.) It will soon become commonplace to record to compact discs and computer disks. As technology grows, recording and storing student work may become a very simple process for music teachers.

Suggested Equipment List for an Interactive Music Classroom

4 or 5 synthesizers (preferably professional caliber)

1 amplifier that will accept 4–5 inputs (or mixer and amplifier)

20–25 headsets

4–5 headset splitter boxes (4–6 headsets can be plugged into each)

tables to accommodate synthesizers, splitter boxes, headsets

2 (or more) bass xylophones (or 1 xylophone and 1 metallophone)

2 (or more) tenor xylophones (or 1 xylophone and 1 metallophone)

2 (or more) alto xylophones (or 1 xylophone and 1 metallophone)

2 (or more) soprano xylophones (or 1 xylophone and 1 metallophone)

2 (or more) glockenspiels

Assortment of drums of a variety of sizes and timbres

Assortment of classroom percussion (tambourines, maracas, claves, woodblocks, triangles, guiros, plus as
   many other interesting choices as you can find, including rain sticks, gongs, wind chimes, temple
   blocks, agogo bells, cabasas, a shekere or other kinds of rattles, slit drum, etc.)

1 or 2 sets of resonator bells

4–5 Autoharps or Omnichords (electronic Autoharps)

Shelves and/or closets to accommodate instruments

Piano

Guitar

Stereo (with excellent sound quality)

Metal-based chalkboard or white board for placement of magnetic icons

4–5 computers, if possible

BOX 9.1 (ACTIVITY)

With a group of peers, look through some catalogs of music equipment and materials. Given a particular budget for your program, decide which equipment you might order and prioritize your list.

THE ROLE OF THE TEACHER

In an interactive music classroom, the teacher will need expertise in some of the traditional roles of teachers but will also need to adopt newer ways of working.

Establishing an Environment for Classroom Discourse

Traditionally, teachers pose questions and act as a resource, providing answers to student questions. However, in an interactive learning environment, teachers endeavor to ask open-ended questions that promote higher-level thinking on the part of the students. Teachers in this setting are not seeking one-word, identification-type answers as much as they are asking students to analyze, synthesize, and evaluate musical ideas. Teachers are not only answering student questions, they are using their questions to learn more about their perspective and level of understanding. They are helping students to know how to seek their own answers to questions. Therefore, in this environment, classroom dialogue goes way beyond teacher questions and student answers.

Monitoring Student Progress and Understanding

In an interactive music classroom, teachers monitor student progress on an ongoing basis throughout their teaching. They are constantly providing opportunities for student input in an effort to assess the nature and depth of their understanding. Teachers in this environment are facilitators, working to enable students to figure out things for themselves. They sometimes clarify directions or information for students who are confused and spend a great deal of time encouraging and reassuring students—almost like a coach or cheerleader from the sidelines.

Focusing Student Energy

When necessary, teachers may need to direct or redirect student energies, particularly when individuals become unfocused or lose sight of the goal for a particular activity. The vignette in Box 9.2 shows how a teacher helped inexperienced composers focus on an early composition assignment.[3]

BOX 9.2 (VIGNETTE)

A third-grade class was working on a composition assignment in small groups (a piece that changes tempo, based on prior experience with "Boa Constrictor," Chapter 7, p. 162). One of the groups seemed to be accomplishing much less than the others because of disagreements within the group. The teacher had spoken with members of that group on several occasions during the class and eventually decided to ask for everyone's attention. "Now, we have one group that is almost ready, and one group that is well on its way. What the rest of you need to do is really focus on the assignment. In your group, think about these questions: Who's going to start? Who's going to do what? What's the assignment? How are you going to complete the assignment? OK?" The period ended shortly afterward.

The following class session, in an effort to prevent the same situation from recurring, the teacher began the class by asking the whole group, "What were some of the problems you were running into when you were trying to compose last time?" One of the students from the group that was having difficulty raised his hand.

Matt: "Like when you were supposed to do it slow and then get faster—that was kinda hard to figure out—how to do that."

Teacher: "So what do you think you will do today to maybe help that situation along? Was the problem that you had too many melodies in your group?"

Matt: "No, we didn't have too many melodies. We were just sort of arguing—about when to start or . . ."

Teacher: "Rhythms and that sort of thing? OK. Well, that's what we can work on today, then. David?

David: "I know another thing that can be hard. Trying to keep all the music in the same beat and when it gets faster, sometimes you can't follow it."

> **Teacher:** "Sometimes it kinda falls apart, doesn't it, because not everybody can play all at the same time? Is that what you're saying? Well, that would be something to work on too."
>
> After a few other student comments about problems with simultaneity and organization, the teacher said, "Well, it sounds like you're on the right path, so let's get started. Who can tell us exactly what the assignment was? What are you supposed to be doing?" As a result of these efforts to focus attention on the essential issues of the assignment, all groups were successful during the second class session.

Encouraging Expression of Musical Ideas

Teachers need to encourage students to express their understanding of musical ideas in ways that make sense to the students and then gently help them to become familiar with appropriate terminology. The vignette in Box 9.3 took place in a third-grade general music classroom where students were considering an iconic representation of the round "Scotland's Burning." In this excerpt, the teacher interprets what the students are saying and artfully guides them toward a deeper understanding and the ability to label appropriately. Notice, in particular, how she makes use of the students' own ways of describing the music.

BOX 9.3 (VIGNETTE)

Teacher: Can you describe what you see?

Tommy: It has jumps and leaps.

Teacher: It has jumps and leaps! Do you want to show us a spot where it does that?

Jennifer (while Tommy is walking up to the board): What about falls?

Teacher: We have falls. We could call it falls. Sure.

Tommy (at the board): A jump is here and a leap is here.

Teacher: OK. There's a great big leap or—we call these little ones a . . .

Maria: Skip.

Teacher: Skip. Good. What else besides that [pauses, giving students time to think] that shows us how the music might move? Lisa?

Lisa: Steps.

Teacher: Steps! Do you remember what steps look like?

The teacher points out some of the steps in the song. Billy then asks to go to the board to show some other examples of steps in the song.

Teacher: There's one more thing. What happens when we have a long row like that? [Pauses.] Who remembers? Oh, I want to see some different hands up. [Pauses.] Someone who hasn't told me anything yet.

Her efforts to encourage more students to answer have worked. At this point, almost all hands are raised.

Teacher: Kevin?

Kevin: It's sort of like little steps.

Teacher: Well I can see how you would think they were steps but they're not going up like when we go up steps—or going down, are they? They're all across in the same row. So what do you think?

Joseph: I think it would be a kind of musical sidewalk or something.

Teacher: OK. And what would a musical sidewalk be? What would be a musical way of talking about it? Who remembers, when I play (C C C C C C C C on piano), what is that?

Jason: Same notes?

Teacher: It's the same note. So think of a musical sidewalk as walking on the sidewalk and that's a repeated note. Good for you!

Providing Scaffolding for Learning

Within this learning environment, your primary role as teacher is to provide scaffolding for learners, enabling them to operate within the zone of proximal development,[4] resulting in their achieving a higher level of understanding and competence in music. In an interactive learning environment, the relationship between teacher and students might best be described as an apprenticeship. In apprenticeship learning, an expert and a novice work side-by-side: the apprentice performs those portions of the task in which he or she is competent, and the expert fills in and provides support or scaffolding where necessary. Effective teaching includes providing scaffolding where it is needed and stepping back when it is not. Teachers and students determine where support is needed through their constant interaction as they work together to complete a given task. Student/teacher interaction occurs on both formal and informal levels—that is, from the front of the classroom as well as in informal, personal conversations—and learning occurs in both settings.

The classroom excerpt in Box 9.4 is a transcription of student/teacher interaction in a whole-group setting. It is included as an example of the kinds of scaffolding teachers and peers provide that enable individuals to make sense out of new musical ideas. The students were engaged in filling out a form chart for Bizet's "Farandole" from *L'Arlésienne Suite* (see Chapter 8, pp. 221–224).

BOX 9.4 (VIGNETTE)

Students often mistake the second presentation of the "A" theme in this piece for the "B" section. This is probably because the orchestration and *tessitura* both change and the theme is played in canon. In this case, the teacher attempted to clarify the problem for the students:

Teacher: Please listen to number 2 and see if you can figure out why some people are unsure about whether it is "A" or "B." There is something unusual about the "A" theme in box number 2 that makes a lot of people not know it is "A." Do you know what it is?

Sam: It's the same thing, but it's in a different . . . pitch. [I believe he was trying to describe the difference in tessitura.]

Teacher: Is it a different pitch?

Someone: It's a different sound.

Teacher: It *is* a different sound.

Someone: A different chord.

Someone else: A different instrument.

Teacher: It's *not* a different chord. It *is* different instruments, but that's not what confuses people.

Sam: It's the same notes. [Because of his next statement, I believe he meant the same melody, and therefore it was still the "A" theme, which is what he had written on his own chart.]

Teacher: It *is* the same notes.

Sam: And that's how I knew it was "A!"

Matt: It was higher *and* lower.

Kenny: It's octaves!

Teacher: Very good! There is a place that's in octaves, but there's something else that you haven't found yet.

Later, after the class had listened to the whole work several times trying to get the complete formal structure on paper, the teacher asked whether or not anyone knew at this point what had happened in box number 2. Sam announced, "It's a round! There's a round!"

The teacher's focusing attention on that particular section of the work, coupled with the collective comments of the students and repeated listenings to the work, eventually enabled Sam to identify the canon as "a round!" The canon is actually at the octave, which was noted by both Matt and Kenny, although, at that point, neither identified what they were hearing as canonic. It was the collective expertise and experience of the group, with teacher support, that eventually enabled them to solve the problem. Note that, while the teacher commented throughout the interaction, she did not at any point give the answer to the students.

Providing a Model of Musicianship

One of the roles of a music teacher is to provide a model of what it is to be a musician. In a very traditional role, the teacher needs to model good vocal quality when singing, with excellent pitch accuracy and rhythmic accuracy, especially if students will be solving problems through listening as the teacher sings a song. However, in this apprenticeship setting, the teacher also needs to model musical thinking and thought processes, sharing with students the way she, herself, figures out the solutions to musical problems. The teacher should share with the students how she knows how to figure out the form or textural design of a work or how she knows when something is out of tune—and what that means—and how she goes about correcting the problem. How does a musician know when people are not playing or singing together, and what does that mean and how does one fix the problem? How does a musician know what chord fits with what part of a melody, and how does he figure it out? How does a musician know how to shape a phrase or make a decision about a tempo or dynamic change? What forms the bases for making these kinds of judgments and decisions? The teacher needs to share the strategies she uses to think things through musically and help the students understand the thought processes a musician uses to solve musical problems and to figure out musical ideas. The teacher also needs to draw attention to student strategies that work well for individuals and might work for others as well. Further, she needs to be able to model the processes in which musicians engage, everything from expertise in performing to ability to hear and notate melodies that children sing (when composing with children).

THE ROLE OF THE STUDENT

Interaction among peers occurs on a formal level when students make statements to peers or react to peers in a formal, large-group setting. It occurs on an informal level when peers work in small groups or comment quietly to one another during large-group instruction. As students work together to solve problems, their conversations include comments, questions, clarification, and interpretation of teacher instructions, suggestions, negotiations, evaluations, corrections, criticisms, and encouragement of one another. One of the most important roles they adopt is that of peer coach.

Box 9.5 is an excerpt from an actual conversation that occurred during a small-group composition project in a fifth-grade classroom. It is an excellent example of peer coaching, where one student clarified an idea for another and provided the support necessary for him to continue working on the project.

BOX 9.5 (VIGNETTE)

A group of fifth-grade students was working on an original piece that was to demonstrate a change of meter either from duple to triple or triple to duple (see Chapter 8, pp. 224–226).

Alex: I think this is two. Count for me. Keep going "1, 2, 1, 2" while I play.

He then proceeded to play the following melody on his xylophone:

Jim: No, that's eight!

Alex: It's not eight, Jim! Eight is the same thing as two! It doesn't matter how many notes you play, it's how much . . ."

Jim [interrupting]: "Oh! you mean it goes . . ." [He begins to play Alex's melody on his own xylophone, counting "1, 2, 1, 2" as he plays.]

Box 9.6 is an example of peer coaching in a non-teacher-directed setting (Ogonowski, 1998).

BOX 9.6 (VIGNETTE)

The students in this fourth-grade class are working in pairs. Each has a recorder, and students are about to begin a project in which they will develop a melodic conversation between two recorder players, using the four pitches they know how to play. As a first step in the process, the teacher asks the pairs to take turns making up melodies and then echoing what one another has played.

Jenny: You echo me first.

[Cindy has difficulty echoing her.]

Jenny: Try again. Just do it. Keep going. Don't lift your fingers up so high. You're kind of going like that when they come down [missing the holes she is trying to cover].

Cindy: Oh. But what was your melody?

Jenny: Here. [She plays it again, the same way.]

Cindy [still having difficulty]: For some reason mine isn't in tune.

Jenny: You're not covering the back [i.e., the thumb hole]!

Cindy [showing her how she is covering the holes]: Better?
Jenny: Put your fingers down. Your back one too. Cover it. All right? Good.
Cindy then plays the melody successfully.
Jenny: See? That was better!
Cindy: *That* is better!
Jenny: Yeah! Yay!
Cindy: Now I'll do one. [She plays a melody that Jenny successfully echoes.]

Peer coaching also occurs throughout whole-group activity, although often in more subtle ways. Boxes 9.7 and 9.8 are examples that occurred during a whole-group performance activity.

BOX 9.7 (VIGNETTE)

A fifth-grade class had just completed the small-group portion of the harmony lesson based on "A Ram Sam Sam" (Chapter 8, p. 230–234). The whole group was now performing the song while one member of each group strummed the chords on an Autoharp. In one of the groups, when it was Lindsey's turn to strum, she was unsure about when and how to play. Without a word, Lynn leaned over and pointed to the chords on their worksheet—pointing to each one deliberately on the downbeat of each measure—and began singing the chord names to Lindsey within her singing of the melody with the group. Her support enabled Lindsey to execute the accompaniment successfully.

BOX 9.8 (VIGNETTE)

A fifth-grade class was working in pairs and independently to practice playing a chordal accompaniment for "Peace like a River" (Chapter 8, p. 234–237). Ellen, who was practicing playing the chords on a keyboard, became aware that Kathy, who was working nearby, was singing the melody in one key and trying to play the bass line in another. Ellen immediately lent unsolicited support by joining Kathy's singing midstream and helping her to move to the correct key. Once Kathy found the key, Ellen continued her own practicing, without a word passing between them.

Since peer coaching plays such an essential role in both small- and large-group instructional settings, it would seem that teachers need to be aware that it is taking place and allow it to take its natural course.

MANAGING THE WHOLE GROUP

Classroom management is a broad topic, and it is not the intention of this section to address all the relevant issues. Such information is available from other sources (such as Glasser, 1986; Kohn, 1996; Seeman, 1994; Wolfgang and Glickman, 1986). The intent here is to discuss some of the factors that can influence students' ability and willingness to take initiative and participate in ways that enable them to think, share what they think, and learn from others.

Managing Whole-Group Discussion

In managing whole-group discussions, it is important to establish a setting in which the teacher does not always need to intervene in conversations among students. While an environment in which everyone tries to speak at once is not conducive to learning, one in which the teacher controls all conversation can be just as damaging. In general, asking students to raise hands to be recognized to speak in a large-group setting is helpful and appropriate, but it is also important to know when to relax such rules and allow interaction to run its natural course. If things begin to get too complicated, the teacher can always remind students that everyone has the right to speak and that perhaps the group needs to return to hand raising or some other way of ensuring that everyone has an opportunity. Students need to feel that they have the right to respond to their peers' ideas and genuinely discuss issues without the teacher's opinion becoming pervasive.

When working with the whole group, it is important to provide time for students to think before they answer questions. There will always be students whose hands fly into the air, sometimes before the teacher's question is even fully formed. While it is important to acknowledge enthusiasm, it is also important to allow time for others in the class to have an opportunity to think and respond. Some students need more time to think, and some answers require more thought. In addition, for some students, it is culturally inappropriate to respond to an adult so quickly. Some have been taught to wait a respectful amount of time before replying to an adult's question.

Teachers sometimes inadvertently call on students seated nearer to them or those they expect might misbehave. Studies of classroom interaction have revealed that, in some cases, teachers seem to favor certain groups of students over others, sometimes ignoring female and minority students (Rist, 1970; Rosenthal and Jacobson, 1968; Sadker and Sadker, 1993). While their actions may not be intentional, the effect is the same. It is important to organize large-group discussion in ways that allow and encourage all students to participate comfortably and eagerly.

Teachers need to allow time for students to complete their thoughts when they are speaking to the group. Teachers need to be careful not to assume they already know what students are trying to say and, therefore, move on before they are finished speaking. If teachers are not sure about what a student means, it is better to ask questions to find out rather than to make assumptions. Students become reluctant to participate in situations where they fear they will be misinterpreted, rushed, or ignored. Everyone wants his ideas valued.

It is important to create opportunities for students to be able to "test" answers before sharing them with the group. This creates a safer environment, and often encourages more reluctant participants to get involved. Madeline Hunter (1982) suggests techniques that many teachers use successfully:

- "If you think you know, tell your neighbor" (before ideas are shared with the group as a whole).
- "If you think you know, raise your hand. I will come over and you can whisper it to me." (Again, say this before the group shares ideas, which allows the teacher to learn more about how individuals within the group are thinking.)
- "Think about it for a minute. Talk it over with the people around you. When you are ready, we'll hear what everyone has to say."

Managing Classroom Noise

Because music is an aural art, it becomes necessary for a music classroom to have some agreed-upon rules about noise, particularly when working in a whole-class setting. The simplest way to deal with the situation is to ask students to agree to a classroom rule that no one (including the teacher) should talk while music is being made in the large-group setting. It makes sense to students that, when music is being played, others are trying to listen to it and classroom noise interferes with their ability to do so. They easily understand that it is a matter of respect for one another and of enabling everyone to accomplish their work. When the rule is applied to situations in which the class is listening to a recording, it ensures that everyone will be able to hear. When applied to class performance settings, it enables everyone in the ensemble to hear as they perform. When applied to times when groups are sharing original work with the class, it enables everyone to hear the compositions.

However, it is important to realize that students often need to hum or sing to themselves in order to figure out the answers to musical questions or problems. The teacher needs to develop the ability to recognize which classroom noise is constructive and necessary and which is disruptive and problematic. Since less-experienced musicians often need to enact musical ideas (physically carry them out) in order to work with them, a silent music classroom may actually be one in which there is little musical thinking going on. Further, in small-group work, students generally need to talk quietly among themselves—even while music is being made—in order to be able to solve performance, listening, and creating problems. Students can easily understand that large-group and small-group work operate under different circumstances and can easily adapt to following two sets of rules in these different settings.

Managing Disruptive Behavior

Despite your best intentions, planning, and efforts, there will be times when you will have to deal with individual students' disruptive behaviors. It is important to remember that understanding what constitutes appropriate and inappropriate behavior in a classroom setting is *learned* through the same kinds of processes as those through which content is learned. Learning appropriate behavior is contextual and requires understanding of the situation. Therefore, behavior modification techniques, such as rewards and punishments, are generally far less effective than engaging in a process that helps students understand what it is they need to be doing in class.

The work of William Glasser provides an excellent approach to classroom management. The approach he suggests has been described under several names through the years, including Reality Therapy, Responsibility Training, Control Theory, and most recently, Choice Theory. Glasser's approach begins with classroom meetings during which the teacher and students together establish goals for both the classroom and each individual student. When disruptive behaviors occur, Glasser suggests that teachers deal with the problem by helping the student better understand the situation and his or her role in it. Glasser's approach encourages students to *choose* to function properly instead of being coerced into complying with teachers' rules. For example, if one student is bothering another and preventing him or her from working, a teacher might approach the offending student and ask:

- "What are you doing?" (Do not ask *why* are you doing it, which can lead to excuses and rationalization and, in some cases, even a justification for the disruptive behavior in the mind of the student.)
- "Is that helping [you figure out the chords for this song, etc.]?" (The student will have to answer "No," indicating recognition that that particular behavior at that particular time does not help reach the goals.)
- "Can you make a plan for how you can resolve this so we can get back to work?" (Places the onus on the student to solve the behavioral problem.)
- "Thank you."

For more specific information about managing a classroom, please see the suggested resources list at the end of this chapter.

Meeting the Needs of All Students

Within the whole group it is important to be sensitive to individual needs of all students, including those with language differences and disabilities. Part of succeeding with the large group is getting to know all students as individuals. Small-group work permits a great deal of time and opportunity for this to occur. Working with individuals in the small-group setting can enable the teacher to learn more about how to provide appropriate support for those students during large-group instruction. Each situation is different, but you can turn most situations into positive ones by remembering that all students have ideas and that all students respond well to having those ideas valued. Large groups of students are just that—large groups of individuals. The key to managing large groups is knowing and respecting the students as individuals.

It is important to understand that when a learner is identified as having special needs, a problem area has been identified in the context of a continuum. For example, many students have visual problems and wear corrective lenses. If we consider the broad range of possibilities that might lie along a continuum that characterizes the qualities of vision, we would come to a point at which an individual is classified as legally blind. It is not a black-and-white situation, however. Some students may not be legally blind, but their vision may be only slightly better than that classification indicates. Students in your class may fall anywhere along that continuum. The same may be true for any other kind of special-needs classification. Not everyone who experiences reversals or has trouble differentiating left from right is identified as dyslexic. Not everyone who has moments of difficulty in differentiating foreground and background (visually or auditorally) is considered learning impaired.

Throughout your teaching, you need to be aware that a room of 25 students may indeed be perceiving the lesson in 25 different ways. The key is in thinking about it more as an extension of multiple perspective than as a concern for special learners. You will need to be continually sensitive to a wide range of possibilities and assume that you have students whose ways of learning lie throughout the continuum. When providing explanations, classroom instructions, answers to student questions, and so on, you should be aware that you probably need to say the same thing in several different ways. You will need to be sure that you share important ideas visually, aurally, and kinesthetically. As was discussed in Chapter 1 (p. 14), it is important to construct a learning environment in which it is possible for individuals to function on different levels simultaneously. Most important, if your classroom is a place where everyone's ideas are encouraged and welcomed, learners who do fall closer to the extremes of the various continua of classification will feel as much a part of the group as everyone else.

The focus of this book on multiple perspective as a means of addressing individual differences does not preclude the need to study special education issues more completely. A number of books address this issue for teachers in general and for music teachers specifically (e.g., Atterbury, 1990). Further, if your teacher preparation program does not already require you to take a course in working with special learners, it is advisable to take such a course as an elective.

MANAGING SMALL GROUPS

Organizing Small Groups

The first issue in small-group work is determining the makeup of the groups. Whose task should that be? Some teachers prefer to assign students to groups, sometimes asking that they work with the same group of peers all semester. This can aid in assessment, enabling the teacher to record classwork from consistent groups of students. However, working in this way can also set limitations on what students are able to accomplish over the semester. Students in most settings know one another much better than the teacher knows them. They are often the best ones to decide who will work well with whom. Particularly in creative activities, students know very well who brings to the situation a similar viewpoint to theirs, a similar way of working, or prior musical experience. The most successful groups are often those selected by the students themselves.

At times, it may seem appropriate to intentionally pair stronger students with those who need some support. When left to their own devices, students often do this on their own. Weaker students intentionally seek out partners who they know will help them to succeed. Stronger students easily adopt the role of peer coach, even without the teacher's orchestrating the pairing.

Allowing students to choose their own groups can elevate the status of individual students, sometimes students who are not necessarily the "stars" in other school settings. Good lyricists are always valued, and students quickly learn who they are.[5] Students who study instruments privately are also valued by their peers when choosing groups. Students also value peers whose sole music education experience is the music class itself but who happen to be very good at creating, listening, or performing. Sometimes particular students are valued because of something they did during a previous lesson ("Can you be in our group and show us how you did that great bass part last time?").

On the other hand, students who do not work well with others sometimes find themselves on the outside when students are given the right to choose their own group members. Rejection by peers can be the most powerful tool in reforming unacceptable behaviors. When the time comes and a student is either not sought out or refused entry into a group, he or she learns quickly that negative participation is not valued by peers and often makes an effort to participate differently this time.

Teachers are often concerned about what will happen to students who have social problems that leave them on the perimeter when groups are chosen. There is no easy answer, but an assortment of factors can influence such a situation. In schools where group work is the norm, students are often accustomed to dealing with this situation and are often able to work things out on their own. Where group work is not the norm outside of the music room, the music teacher has several options. At first, the student could be permitted to work alone or with a partner instead of with a group, but it would not be healthy to permit this arrangement for all subsequent projects. In subsequent assignments, if the student is still reluctant to join a group, it is possible to use the parameters of the assignment to coax acceptance. (For example: "In order to make a piece that follows this texture chart, you need a group of at least four people. Johnny cannot do this assignment alone. He needs three other people. Is there a group that could use another person?") Putting the focus on the musical problem rather than on the social situation can help a reluctant student ease into a less-than-comfortable situation. Students who do not get along with their peers generally need teacher support in order to learn social skills. Part of the teacher's job is to help such students learn to work in collaboration with peers. It is a necessary life skill and one that experiences in the music classroom can help nurture.

Managing the Classroom during Small-Group Work

Once the groups have been established and work on an assignment has begun, the teacher needs to be available to students who need assistance, support, or clarification. It is also important to stay out of the way when not needed. Be sure that students know you are available for any help they might need but that you will not bother them unless they seek help. This is particularly important in creative projects where teacher interruptions can cause students to lose their train of thought.

When organizing and managing small-group work, it is preferable to utilize a visual signal when seeking the students' attention. When everyone is working at an instrument, flashing or turning off the lights will get their attention much faster than an auditory signal will. Be sure that the students understand what the signal means and that they may also use the signal if, for example, there is a call on the P.A. system that the teacher does not hear because of the noise level of the classroom work.

The potential for noise is an important consideration. Group work in music can generate more noise than those in the classroom—and those next door—can handle. It is important for students to understand what constitutes necessary noise and what they could probably do without. Utilizing electronic instruments with headsets can greatly reduce classroom noise during small-group work, even if they are used in combination with acoustic instruments. Generally, the worst offenders seem to be large, low-pitched drums, whose sound seems to go right through classroom walls. This problem can be alleviated by asking students to substitute smaller hand drums during the bulk of their work and then to switch to larger drums for a "dress rehearsal" and final performance of their work.

AN INTERACTIVE MUSIC CLASSROOM

Let us reconsider the essential elements of an interactive learning environment. The environment should include a curriculum designed to promote understanding of the structural elements of music through carefully designed units of study in which students and teacher together engage in problem solving through analytical listening, creating, and performing activities. The students must be given the opportunity to understand the relationships among the various activities in which they participate. In this way, the activities become self-motivating. The teacher must be willing to adopt a variety of roles and often "coach from the sidelines" while the students "run with the ball" on their own. Teachers must understand how to design instruction and work within that design in ways that will not inhibit students or alter student work to fit their own vision of a "right" answer.

Teachers must know how to establish and operate within an open-ended learning environment that will encourage students to take initiative in their own learning. The physical setup of the classroom must reflect and promote the kind of atmosphere necessary for this kind of work as well. Equipment for music teaching and learning should be "real" and of high quality, reflecting music in the "real world," and motivating students to become actively involved in their own music learning. Teachers must also understand how to monitor student understanding and progress and how to adapt instruction as a result of what they learn. They need to get to know and meet the needs of each individual within the group, ensuring each student an opportunity to participate and learn. Teachers need to know how to focus student energy to help students become more productive. They need to know how to encourage and respond to student expression of musical ideas. They need to model what it is to be a musician and to know how to use their own musicianship to mediate learning by providing scaffolding that will enable students to grow in their musical competence and understanding. Students must also have opportunities to provide scaffolding and support for one another as they work together to learn. Teachers need to know how to manage a variety of instructional settings and how to help their students function within these different settings.

It must be recognized that students need to create their own music in addition to listening to and performing music of others. This important "third branch" of musical experience is so often neglected in the general music classroom. However, when used effectively as a teaching tool, creating can become a motivating force behind the entire curriculum. It gives students a personal reason for learning to become better listeners and performers.

Students are motivated to pursue what they perceive to be relevant to their lives. An interactive learning environment such as the one described here is perceived by students as a relevant learning environment because it is so closely aligned with their immediate needs. The nature of the assignments and the structure of the class necessitates the immediate application of newly acquired skills and understandings. Students take great pride in their original compositions and improvisations and are eager to improve their competence and musicianship in order to produce more impressive works. Permitting students the opportunity to create their own musical ideas, within the context of a learning environment such as the one described here, can result in an exciting and relevant music program in which they learn to value music as an important part of their lives. Providing students with opportunities to become personally involved with music is the key to a successful music education program.

ENDNOTES

1. From: J. Wiggins, 1993, "Elementary music with synthesizers," Special Focus Issue on Keyboards in the Classroom, *Music Educators Journal* 79(9):25–30. Used with permission.

2. The power poles that I have seen are made of lightweight aluminum. The pole is a four-sided unit, running floor-to-ceiling, with each of the four sides being about 3 inches wide. The pole is hollow, allowing an extension cord to be run from the synthesizer area to the ceiling. The cord is then encased in a plastic runner that is attached to the ceiling and runs down the wall to an electrical outlet. The system simply allows an extension cord to travel up and over the place where the children need to walk.

3. Thanks to Lori Cleland, Farmington Public Schools, Michigan, for the vignettes in Boxes 9.2 and 9.3.

4. See Chapter 1, pp. 13–16.
5. Many of the best lyricists that I have taught are students who have learning disabilities related to language skills. Many students who have been unsuccessful in writing under other circumstances seem to be able to generate outstanding song lyrics. For these students, music class might be the only place where their verbal ideas are successful and are valued by peers.

SELECTED RESOURCES

Atterbury, B. W. 1990. *Mainstreaming exceptional learners in music.* Englewood Cliffs, N.J.: Prentice-Hall.

Espeland, M. 1987. Music in use: Responsive music listening in the primary school. *British Journal of Music Education* 4(3):283–97.

Glasser, W. 1986. *Control theory in the classroom.* New York: Perennial Library.

———. 1990. *The quality school.* New York: Perennial Library.

Goleman, D. 1995. *Emotional intelligence.* New York: Bantam Books.

Hogg, N. 1993. *Identifying and resolving the dilemmas of music teaching: A study of junior secondary classrooms.* Ph.D. diss. Monash University, Australia.

———. 1994. Strategies to facilitate student composing. *Research Studies in Music Education* 2:15–24.

———. 1995. Identifying and resolving the dilemmas of music teaching. Paper presented at the American Educational Research Association Conference, San Francisco (April 22, 1995).

Kohn, A. 1996. *Beyond discipline: From compliance to community.* Alexandria, Va.: Association for Supervision and Curriculum Development.

Managing the disruptive classroom. 1994. Produced by Phi Delta Kappa, 60 min. Videocassette. Available from Phi Delta Kappa at the organization's website <www.pdkintl.org>.

Rist, R. 1970. Student social class and teacher expectations: The self-fulfilling prophecy in ghetto education. *Harvard Educational Review* 40:411–51.

Rosenthal, R., and L. Jacobson. 1968. *Pygmalion in the classroom: Teacher expectation and pupils' intellectual development.* New York: Holt, Rinehart and Winston.

Sadker, M., and D. Sadker. 1993. *Failing at fairness: How American schools cheat girls.* New York: Charles Scribner's Sons.

Seeman, H. 1994. *Preventing classroom discipline problems.* Lancaster, Pa.: Technomic.

Wiggins, J. 1993. Elementary music with synthesizers. *Music Educators Journal* 79(9):25–30.

———. 1999. Teacher control and creativity. *Music Educators Journal* 85(5):30–35.

Wolfgang, C. H., and C. D. Glickman. 1986. *Solving discipline problems: Strategies for classroom teachers.* 2d ed. Boston: Allyn and Bacon.

Chapter 10

MAKING CONNECTIONS TO OTHER WAYS OF UNDERSTANDING

(Coauthored by Robert A. Wiggins)

As a music teacher, you will be only one teacher in your students' lives. Throughout their day, they will interact with many other teachers and deal with many other school subjects in addition to music. Chapter 10 is designed to help you better understand what constitutes appropriate and beneficial ways of making connections to subject areas outside of music.

Hopefully, at this point, you have begun to formulate a solid understanding of the processes involved in thinking about and planning musical experiences in an interactive learning environment utilizing problem solving in an apprenticeship model. Most likely, you have also become aware that this vision of instruction stems from a clearly defined music curriculum that addresses goals and objectives built around concepts that real musicians understand and utilize continuously.

However, as a music teacher, you will sometimes be asked to augment or alter your curricular plans to align your work with that of classroom teachers or teachers of other subject areas. It is not unusual for classroom teachers to request your assistance in providing music for classroom plays, teaching music of a particular culture to enhance a social studies unit, or teaching songs designed to help students remember facts or steps in a process (singing the alphabet song, setting math facts to music, singing songs about personal safety). Where you have time in your schedule and/or your curriculum, accommodating these requests can be helpful and beneficial to your colleagues. However, you need to be alert to the possibility that these outside lessons may not further your curricular goals as a music teacher. Because they may interfere with your curricular goals, you need to be able to stand firm and defend the integrity of your program. This is just one more reason why it is so important that your teaching be based around students' learning of important musical concepts. If it appears to your colleagues that the songs you sing and the activities in which you engage are little more than entertainment, they will not hesitate to substitute their curricular goals for yours.

A related issue you may face as a music professional is the move toward an *integrated curriculum.* In elementary school, this might take the form of themed units that incorporate the teaching of more than one subject. At the middle level, more and more schools are being structured to allow teams of teachers from different disciplines to work with the same students in an integrated fashion. At the high school level, there has been a move toward humanities courses and integrated math/science courses. In some cases, these efforts include arts teachers, and in some they do not. In an ideal situation, the arts should be on an equal footing with other subjects; yet, this is not always the case.

Despite the presence of arts professionals in the schools, some teachers and administrators still see the arts as something outside the curriculum—something almost akin to an extracurricular activity. In those schools, the arts may not be thought important enough to be part of an integrated curriculum. Consider, for example, that the arts were not even included in the first version of the national education proposal *Goals 2000,* introduced during the Reagan administration. In some states, arts are still not part of the core curriculum. In some schools, arts are an extracurricular activity. Even when arts classes are included in the school day, they often meet only once a week or for just a portion of the school year.

Artistic thinking is equally marginalized in schools. Not only is an artist's world view often seen as less valid than the worldview taught in other disciplines, artistic thinking is generally undervalued in its own right in that it is often not assessed, graded, or reported to parents. Parents and arts educators alike too often see artistic achievement as stemming from an innate talent rather than thoughtful study. Some schools see the value of having arts experiences integrated with other disciplines, but they do so for the wrong reasons. They relegate artistic work to the role of entertaining performances or colorful decorations rather than a serious expression of the human condition. Some arts educators contribute to this misconception by establishing arts programs that are elitist, that ignore the popular culture in favor of high culture, that consist of "school" art and "school" music rather than real art and real music, or that place an emphasis on performance and competition over learning and conceptual understanding.

Considering this, it would seem like a positive step to have arts experiences integrated into themed units or entire courses. However, there is the danger that, in doing so, important objectives of arts curricula will get lost in the process.

Arts educators must be willing to stand firm to ensure that their programs are not compromised and must have the background to support that stance based on sound learning theory and knowledge of curriculum design. This chapter introduces some issues and ideas that may help you make a case for the integrity of music as a distinct discipline. First, you will read about ways experts in the field have described an integrated curriculum. You will learn about some typical approaches to integration and their impact on music curricula. Then, in contrast to the traditional approaches, you will have an opportunity to explore a more holistic vision of integration. The final section of this chapter shares vignettes from an actual elementary school that has adopted this more holistic approach.

DEFINING INTEGRATION

For most teachers the idea of an *integrated curriculum* refers to teaching more than one subject as part of the same lesson or unit. Yet, there are those who would argue that we will not really integrate the curriculum until we do away with subject distinctions completely (Beane, 1997). In this way of thinking, schooling should reflect real life. It is based on the idea that, since real world problems are not divided into separate subjects, teaching should not be either. According to Beane, as long as we continue to have separate subjects, the best we can do is to create a *multidisciplinary curriculum.*

However, the idea of a multidisciplinary curriculum is not troubling to some. Howard Gardner and his colleagues feel that it is important to recognize the concepts and procedures that make each discipline unique. In their way of thinking, distinct disciplines have developed because there is a need to look at problems from different perspectives (Gardner and Boix-Mansilla, 1994b). Even when the problem is the same, different individuals will ask different questions and seek different answers depending on their area of interest.

Teaching that recognizes this distinction can take the form of an *interdisciplinary curriculum,* based on themed units or cross-disciplinary courses (such as math/science classes). Working in this way can bring different subjects together while still maintaining their separate identities. It can help students see connections between subjects that heighten their understanding of each subject. However, an interdisciplinary curriculum is not a panacea and will not substitute for quality teaching within each discipline. Gardner and Boix-Mansilla (1994b) point out that it is not possible to engage in interdisciplinary work without some basic knowledge and skills of the separate disciplines involved.

Further, the problem that occurs when schools attempt an interdisciplinary curriculum is that it too often becomes little more than separate subjects taught in close proximity or one content area juxtaposed with another to strengthen the first without giving due regard to the second. There are two ways to prevent these problems from occurring. First, we need to protect and maintain the integrity of individual disciplines by giving sufficient attention to the curricular goals and basic concepts of each content area. Second, we need to focus our attention on how students understand the concepts and processes that connect the disciplines. As is explained more fully in the sections that follow, the way thought processes occur across disciplines is a far more important issue than the factual or chronological similarities between disciplines. Gardner and Boix-Mansilla put it this way:

> An individual interested in the Renaissance who approaches this era first as a historian, then as a scientist, then as an artist, is employing a multiplicity of disciplines. And yet, so long as no attempt is made at synthesis, the whole will not be greater than the parts. . . . An individual who not only applies more than one discipline but actually strives to combine or synthesize these stances is engaging in that rare but precious practice called interdisciplinary work (1994a, 208).

When an interdisciplinary curriculum reflects a multiplicity of disciplines, it opens the possibility of multiple worldviews and deeper understanding for students.

BOX 10.1 THINK ABOUT THIS. . .

The next section describes the ways curricular integration is currently practiced in the schools. As you read it, try to determine whether each practice represents integrated instruction, multidisciplinary work, or an interdisciplinary approach.

CURRENT PRACTICE

The authors' work with schools (R. A. Wiggins, 1997, 2000; and J. Wiggins and R. A. Wiggins, 1997) along with an examination of publications about curricular integration suggest there are five ways teachers and school systems engage in curricular integration:

- Teaching Tool Connections
- Topic Connections
- Thematic or Content Connections
- Conceptual Connections
- Process Connections

Each is identified here as a "connection"—the emphasis being on how the disciplines are connected and the resulting relationship that is created in the learner's mind. The first three levels of integration are those presently in use in schools. The last two represent a new vision of what integration could be, ideas that the authors have field-tested at one elementary school over a period of several years.

Level 1: Teaching Tool Connections

"Teaching tool" connections are included here because they are common practice in many schools. However, they probably should not be considered integration because they do not teach more than one discipline. Instead, in this case, one discipline serves another by providing a vehicle through which factual information can be more efficiently remembered. Some examples are singing the alphabet, multiplication facts, or a "big book"; drawing or decorating a picture of a number three; and using a song to memorize the state capitals or historical events. These activities do not teach music or art—or the "connected" subjects either. They may help students memorize what they are told, but they do not help them understand the concepts of any of the disciplines. While memorization may be a useful tool that allows students to function automatically and with less effort, it should not be thought of as teaching or learning. What is more of an issue is that, when a teacher utilizes this type of teaching tool, one discipline is considered less important and is relegated to a subservient position. At best, these activities could be thought of as mnemonic devices and, as such, should not be considered integration.[1]

Level 2: Topic Connections

A second vision of integration uses topic as a connection. In this case, two subjects are brought together because a characteristic of one enriches the students' understanding of the other. For example, knowledge of the politics of an era might help students understand the literature that was written during the period. Viewing artwork from a particular country might give students a better sense of the culture and history of that nation.

In most cases, these connections are helpful. However, you need to keep in mind that the connection often benefits one discipline more than the other. Once again, it is a possibility that one discipline will simply perform a service for another. For example, reading a play about Abraham Lincoln in history class may enrich the study of Lincoln but does not necessarily increase the students' understanding of drama as an art form. Likewise, reading the fact-based *Diary of Anne Frank* may not, in and of itself, teach anything about literature even though it may greatly help the student understand the human side of World War II.

Yet, if we take this connection a bit further, it is possible for topic connections to benefit both disciplines. If the teacher takes the time to address the way the playwright or the author used the art form to express the human condition, it becomes an example of curricular integration in which concepts and goals from both disciplines are addressed. Teachers can think of this kind of connection as a way to enhance instruction. The connection is usually momentary and the topic need not be the focus of an entire unit or even the entire lesson. Although the connection might be limited to a date, time, place, or idea that the two subjects have in common, the teacher is acknowledging that there are relationships between the two subjects and recognizing the importance of what is taught in other disciplines.

This is different from the next category, thematic connections. In this case, rather than merely enhancing student understanding, the theme becomes the basis for lesson planning. In some instances, themed units are used to determine the instructional goals and organization for the entire school.

Level 3: Thematic or Content Connections

One of the most common forms of integration in the schools is the thematic connection. In recent years, a flurry of books, videotapes, and in-service workshops have appeared that are designed to show teachers how to construct integrated thematic units. It is possible that thematic units are popular because they provide a way to incorporate a number of the current trends in teaching methodology. Thematic units typically involve group work, so they fit well in a constructivist classroom shaped around Vygotsky's principles (described in Chapter 1). Because of this group work, thematic units allow teachers to incorporate principles of cooperative learning and individualized instruction. The variety of activities across multiple disciplines allows the teacher to take into account students' varied learning styles and incorporate Gardner's theory of multiple intelligences.

While some thematic units may be generated from genuine problems that require students to use knowledge and skills from a variety of disciplines, others simply rely on choosing a topic that will be of interest to the students. This turns the process on its head. A theme *must* be chosen because it is connected to the concepts and principles that are important in each of the subjects. Concepts and principles must provide the basis for instructional goals. The process must begin with these ideas in mind.

In that same vein, you need to be wary of thematic units based on providing opportunities for children who possess a so-called "talent" in the arts to use that talent in their learning. When this occurs, a thematic connection becomes more like a teaching tool (Level 1) in which one discipline is in service to another. Basing the arts component of a thematic unit on "talent" is usually tied to an assumption that talent is something inborn rather than something that is developed through greater awareness of the disciplinary concepts and principles. Musical intelligence (or spatial, or bodily kinesthetic) does not refer to talent. Gardner says, "I don't think there's a principled way of saying language is intelligence and music is a mere talent" (1998, 27). Gardner has often defined intelligence as "the ability to solve problems, or make things that are valued in at least one community" (1998, 25; see also 1983). Simply providing an outlet for student "talent" is, at best, an example of multidisciplinary instruction and not interdisciplinary instruction based on the multiplicity of disciplines. If that is so, then the role of the arts in a thematic unit must include genuine problems that require knowledge of the concepts and principles of the discipline.

So, to develop a meaningful thematic unit, we need to start with questions that are meaningful to students and reflect issues of social importance. If we do this, student interest will stem from the nature of the problem rather than from the title of the unit.

> If a society values the question "What are human beings made of?" the student in that society should observe basic scientists attempting to answer the question; and to the extent that meaningful approaches to this question are being pursued by artists, technologists, spiritual leaders, or philosophers, these perspectives should be on ready display as well. . . . (S)tudents have the opportunity of acquiring literacies and disciplines not as unmotivated ends in themselves, but rather as part of an effort to gain leverage on questions with which thoughtful persons have long wrestled (Gardner & Boix-Mansilla, 1994a, 205).

The acid test of legitimacy becomes the question of whether or not the topic selected has any connection to *all* of the disciplines included in the unit. For example, a theme like "penguins" may provide a basis for legitimate integration in some disciplines, such as language arts and science, but can become "one discipline in service to another" where music and mathematics are concerned. Singing songs about penguins (snow, ice, etc.) does little to foster the goals of the music classroom. Likewise, counting, graphing, or including penguins in a mathematics word problem does not create a legitimate connection to a mathematics concept.

More legitimate connections for thematic units involve those that stem from a historical/cultural context. This approach is used more often at the middle or high school levels and can help students develop a more global view through interconnections among art, literature, music, science, or politics within a particular historical or cultural context. In a sense, this allows students to see how experts from a variety of disciplines would answer the question "What are human beings made of?" However, there are pitfalls to watch out for when an arts educator gets involved in such a project. It is easy for an integrated unit of this type to take a chronological focus that overemphasizes history at the expense of other disciplines. In addition, insufficient prior experience in the various disciplines can result in an artificial understanding of the connections. This is one reason that it is so important for students to have a solid grounding in the concepts and principles that make up each discipline. Without that solid grounding, it is doubtful that students will understand the connections. Therefore, the most valuable type of integration results from identifying and emphasizing the conceptual and process connections that exist naturally across disciplines.

A MORE HOLISTIC APPROACH TO INTEGRATION

Integration through enhancement and thematic association are routinely practiced by many good teachers. However, it is teaching through conceptual and process connections that can provide opportunities for students to experience the world through a variety of perspectives, strengthening their capacity for cognitive development and enhancing the quality of their lives. This more holistic vision of integration is rooted in the belief and understanding that individuals have many ways of perceiving the world, that one way of thinking is not necessarily better than another, that who we are is determined by our ability to understand the world from a variety of perspectives, and that thinking and understanding transcend subject area distinctions.

Level 4: Conceptual Connections

A fourth type of integration is through *conceptual connections*. In this case, the concept is the focus. Regardless of the topic, a concept or parallel concepts can be experienced through various disciplines. For example, one concept that is important in the study of the Civil War era is conflict and resolution. Whether students study the role of conflict and resolution in dramatic or literary representations, through harmonic resolution in music, or *denouement* in dance, it would seem sensible that they would better internalize the content of each individual subject through a larger understanding of the overarching concept that transcends the different fields of study. When students internalize these concepts as parallel ideas extending across disciplines, the concepts become constructs that have more universal application. Here, a construct is defined as an idea or a belief that guides action or explains an occurrence. Boxes 10.2 and 10.3 provide some examples might make this clearer.

BOX 10.2 FINDING RELATIONSHIPS AMONG BASIC CONCEPTS

When students understand about a basic concept in one discipline, it allows them to reason about the possible implications of a related concept in another. For example, there are similarities among:

- Estimating in math.
- Predicting in reading.
- Hypothesizing in science.
- Speculating about solutions to artistic problems.

BOX 10.3 USING RELATIONSHIPS TO EXPAND UNDERSTANDING

Examining concepts across individual disciplines allows the student to develop a schema for understanding common ideas. For example, a construct such as *conflict* is expressed in different yet related ways in various fields of study:

- History: conflict and its resolution.
- Science: opposing forces.
- Language Arts: conflict among characters, between characters and situations, etc.
- Music: dissonance, consonance, and harmonic resolution.

In addition, an understanding of constructs across disciplines can lead to more in-depth thought within any one discipline—in this case music (see Box 10.4).

BOX 10.4

A thorough understanding of the construct of *freedom* allows the student to think more deeply about the numerous (and sometimes less obvious) forms of human expression. For example:

- Consider the ways different composers have expressed views of political freedom (with a focus on the ways the composers manipulated musical elements to achieve their desired effects).
- Consider the ways some composers have sought freedom from the rules imposed by traditional Western systems of harmony.
- Study compositions created within different tonal and compositional systems. Compare them to those created in the absence of a system.
- Consider twentieth-century works that attempt to obscure organizational systems, and the ways in which we, as listeners, tend to impose our own organization on this "free" music.
- Consider connections between freedom and improvisatory music making.

In this example, the common construct is the broad way of thinking that crosses the various disciplines while, at the same time, it is a legitimate concept operating within the content of each discipline. You can also look at thought processes in a more abstract form.

Level 5: Process Connections

A fifth type of integration is through *process connections*. In this case, the process through which students engage with the subject matter is the focus, for example, classifying, predicting, connecting, sequencing, visualizing, organizing, reflecting, interpreting, symbolizing. Regardless of the topic, these processes are common among the various disciplines, and being aware of how they function in one discipline can enhance students' understanding of how they function in another. Box 10.5 provides examples of process connections.

BOX 10.5 CONNECTING THOUGHT PROCESSES (RATHER THAN CONTENT)

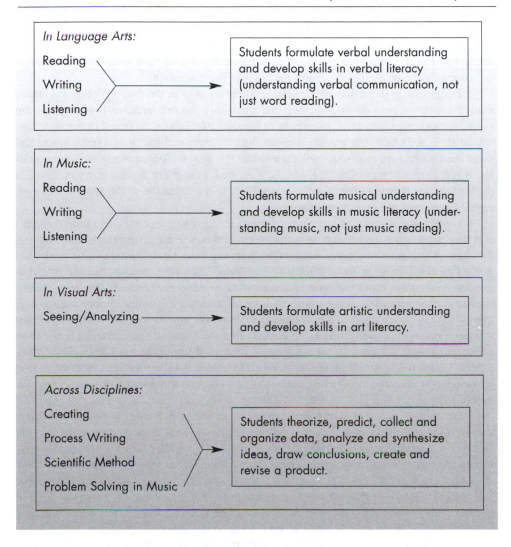

In all four examples in Box 10.5, the mind engages in similar processes, but the fields of knowledge are different and distinct. Each maintains its own integrity. The connection is based on the ways in which people process information and come to understand the various disciplines. The premise is that the processes for making intellectual decisions (cognitive decisions) are similar across disciplines. How the mind functions becomes the common denominator.

It may be difficult to imagine yourself applying Levels 4 and 5 to curriculum integration. Describing integration in this way does not provide a convenient model for applying it in the classroom. The intent of this chapter is not to provide a template for integrated lesson planning or to describe a specific set of topics that are most appropriate for thematic instruction. This type of integration depends more on an awareness of how the accomplished musician thinks about music and the ways in which that thinking parallels the thinking of a scientist, graphic artist, historian, mathematician, or expert in any other discipline. For this reason, it is vital that the music teacher be well versed in the underlying concepts and principles that form the basis of the discipline.

Integration is more than recognizing content overlap in the state syllabus. It is more than a matter of proximity—whether that proximity occurs because two subjects are taught in the same room at the same time or because two events happened in the same historical time and place. Integration is about the way people think; it is a recognition that there are multiple ways to view and understand the world. Consequently, it is not a matter of teaching students to think this way. Your task is to point out these connections in thought so that they are clear, timely, and subject to modification as the student's knowledge of concepts and principles matures.

Despite the absence of clear prescriptions for how to proceed, integrating concepts and processes is not as difficult as it may seem and has some distinct advantages. First, this type of integration is more a matter of changing your (and ultimately, the students') way of thinking about music and musical problems. Therefore, it does not require elaborate materials, large blocks of time, or a dramatically redesigned curriculum. What it does require is that activities in the music classroom stem from genuine, important musical questions. This is what will prompt students to think like and function as musicians. From this perspective, it should come as no surprise that this approach to curricular integration is consistent with the view of teaching music professed throughout this book. What does a person need to know to function as a musician? How does someone communicate that knowledge to someone else? How does someone use that knowledge to resolve musical problems?

In addition, when students are engaged in activities that involve genuine problem solving they will likely make many cross-disciplinary connections on their own. It is not so much a matter of teaching students how to think this way but rather a matter of recognizing and promoting this thought when it occurs. This means you will want to encourage students to look at the bigger picture, and you will want to avoid isolationist teaching that categorizes ideas in predetermined compartments. For example, an understanding of rhythm goes beyond knowledge of note values and time signatures. It should include a sense of the organization of sounds as they occur in the world; it should include a sense of movement. Beyond that, it should enhance the student's recognition of the rhythmic flow of words in a work of literature, the pacing of a play or an athletic contest, the unfolding of a geological event, or even the stages of emotional development in an argument that becomes heated. An awareness of the rhythmic nature of any of these will help a student understand musical expression. In short, concepts and thought processes are the "stuff" of real life. You have to work hard to avoid their integration. Letting them take center stage is inevitable.

Another advantage of this form of integration is that it maintains the integrity of the individual disciplines. While it is true that school subjects only partially represent the entire breadth and depth of the disciplines they are named for, there is value in that partial representation. While we cannot hope to adequately encompass all there is to the field of biological science, there is validity in asking a student, "How would a biologist think about this problem?"

There are questions and methodologies that are distinct to the different disciplines. As we have said before, individuals have different world views. These world views have not developed serendipitously; the commonality of thinking within a discipline serves a purpose. It is not advantageous to pretend that all students (or, for that matter, all professionals in a given field) would benefit from something of a "Leonardo DaVinci approach" to the world—that is, a Renaissance man sense of global "knowing" that somehow encompasses all disciplines without being specific to any one. There are defined parameters to each subject that make sense within that field of study. There are universal questions that apply equally to all fields. Once you get past issues of basic survival and interpersonal relations, the practical and philosophical questions that intrigue a musician are not the same as those that might intrigue an economist (except that a musician can also function as an economist, and vice versa). Once again, it is the connections between concepts and thought processes that are important, much more so than connections of content. Throughout the more traditional approaches to curricular integration, there is always the danger that each discipline will lose its identity. Music teachers need to be particularly alert to this possibility.

Finally, because this approach to integration is so tied to how teachers and students conceptualize information, it can be accomplished by the music teacher alone. While it would be preferable if all teachers recognized the importance of allowing and encouraging students to think across disciplinary lines, you need not wait for a schoolwide curriculum reform to begin. In fact it is probably better not to refer to this approach as integration at all. Some teachers have seen curricular integration as an opportunity to secure the place of music education in the core curriculum either through a service to other subjects or an enhancement approach (see Barry, 1996). Yet this seems misguided; music is secure enough to stand on its own. The key, then, is to assist students in recognizing the connection that musical thinking has to all other aspects of their lives. This is something far more encompassing than curricular integration. Because of this all-encompassing role of the arts in our lives, the term *arts infusion* more accurately describes the role of the arts in the school curriculum. The remainder of this chapter explores how a group of teachers in one elementary school revised their thinking about how the connections among disciplines could be brought to the fore.

A DIFFERENT CURRICULAR APPROACH

In 1996, the authors of this chapter began working as consultants to Stadium Drive Elementary School of the Arts in Lake Orion, Michigan. The faculty of Stadium Drive had previously opted to be an "arts" elementary school in a district in which each school was asked to develop a defining quality of their school. To support the arts emphasis in this school of 400 students, the principal received funding to hire a full-time drama teacher and full-time dance teacher, in addition to the visual arts, music, and physical education teachers who were already on faculty.

Early on, the teachers at Stadium Drive decided that they did not want to be a magnet school for artistically talented students. Instead, they wanted to devise a way for the arts to play a more significant role in the education of all students and throughout the curriculum. What follows is a blending of the ideas that became part of the "Mission Statement and Conceptual Framework" that guides this school as well as actual incidents that serve to illustrate students' awareness of arts concepts in all aspects of their learning. Long hours of discussion with the faculty and staff of this school helped shape this conception of *arts infusion*.

Arts Infusion

Arts infusion means enabling students to engage in all of the kinds of artistic thinking so that they develop to their fullest potential, develop a valid sense of self, and both recognize and celebrate their own strengths. But strengthening their thinking processes in these areas will also impact their thinking in other disciplines, such as language arts, mathematics, science, social studies, and physical education.

The theory behind arts infusion is that, since the various ways of thinking and knowing all occur within the same mind, they must be interconnected in some way. A curriculum can be designed to work from the premise that strengthening one way of thinking will impact others. Children working to solve problems in one discipline should be able to transfer some of what they have learned about problem solving in general to their work in other disciplines. The ability to analyze and synthesize in one discipline will impact the children's ability to engage in the same processes in another discipline.

In the traditional groupings of disciplines within schools, language arts, which really is an art form, is grouped with the nonarts (mathematics, science, social studies). Physical education, which is not really an art form, is often grouped with arts because of its status in public school curricula. Conceiving of the various ways of thinking in terms of the traditional curricular groupings present in American public schools may not fit our purposes.

In thinking about the conceptual aspects of the various disciplines, it is easier and perhaps more valid to think of the various disciplines through their intrinsic characteristics and not through traditional groupings. Dance, drama, music, visual art, and language arts have a great deal in common because they are all ways of *expressing* the human experience. Other disciplines, such a mathematics, science, social studies, and physical education, may have some aspects in common with the arts, but they do not have as many commonalities because they are not vehicles for expression. Mathematicians, scientists, historians, and athletes certainly express ideas, but their disciplines do not represent vehicles for expression of the human condition as do the arts. Mathematicians, scientists, historians, and athletes express more literal ideas about the world. Artists express both literal and nonliteral ideas about the world.

Understandings in nonarts subject areas certainly impact understanding in the arts and vice versa. However, all ways of thinking need to be recognized as having their own value. Students are not making music or art *in order to* learn language arts, although knowing about music and art can certainly influence the ways teachers teach and students learn language arts. Each discipline must be taught with integrity, focusing on the characteristics, concepts, and principles that make it unique. Making connections among the disciplines and among the ways of thinking about the disciplines is a natural outcome—one that has the capacity to greatly impact the overall learning of students engaged in such a curriculum.

In arts infusion, the various forms of artistic thinking are so intrinsically connected to other forms of thinking that they move beyond the kinds of integration found in most school settings. Finding conceptual and process connections among the ways of thinking and knowing is where the strength of such a program lies. Working with process and conceptual connections affords students opportunities to use what they have learned in one discipline to strengthen their thinking in another.

LEARNING THROUGH AN ARTS-INFUSED CURRICULUM

Descriptions of actual learning situations may help to clarify what it is to be a student learning through an arts-infused curricular approach. The following vignettes are drawn from numerous examples of actual experiences that took place at Stadium Drive Elementary School of the Arts.

Early in our work, we and the teachers realized that their ability to enable students to make concept and process connections across disciplines was partially dependent on their own awareness of what and how their colleagues teach. What emerged from our work was an understanding that teachers need to spend a great deal of time talking with one another about the concepts and processes specific to the disciplines they teach. Mutual awareness of one another's teaching enables teachers to help students make connections through formally designed lessons and through informal references to other learning experiences. In addition, we became aware that students often make such connections on their own.

Formal Connections Made by Teachers

Sometimes at Stadium Drive, teachers who work in different disciplines intentionally work together and plan to utilize conceptual and process connections to enhance the students' understanding in more than one subject area. Teachers only do this when the connection is legitimate and when the concept or process being connected is a legitimate component of each of the disciplines involved.

Pathways

One example of such a connection was planned by the dance teacher and the second-grade teachers who were teaching cursive writing. Since the classroom teachers generally attend the dance classes, the second-grade teachers were aware that one of the elements of dance that students learn about is "pathway." In dance, movement occurs along pathways. The dance teacher had asked the students to create dance studies that had only one pathway. Later, they were asked to create dance studies with two and three pathways. The second-grade teachers realized that both handwriting and dance are physical activities and that there were similarities between these activities. In teaching cursive writing, they began utilizing the dance terminology and concept of pathway, realizing that certain letters had only one pathway (uppercase "L") while others had two (uppercase "X") and others had three (uppercase "F"). They asked the students to create cursive letters in space before writing them on paper, saying "How many pathways will we use? Where will you start? Where will you end?" Each time the students needed to lift the pencil from the paper, they were to consider it a new pathway. Students formed letters using their whole bodies and then their arms before putting them on paper. Participating in the dance activity empowered the students' ability in the writing activity.

The connection was intentional on the part of the teachers, a connection that promoted and furthered understanding in both curricular areas. The infused concept that enabled the children to make the connection is the notion of pathway. An infused process that was important here was visualizing. The benefit to the students was that making this connection across disciplines enabled them to be more successful in both areas.

Characterization

Another example of a formal, planned connection occurred in the music classroom. The music teacher was aware that the students had learned about characterization through both language arts and drama experiences. He chose to connect the idea to the characteristics of thematic material of a musical work. He began by asking the students, "In a story or a play, what makes each character different?" Building on that knowledge, he began to develop the idea that composers utilize similar processes in developing the character of a musical theme but that musicians need to be able to do this without using words. "If a musician wants to develop a musical theme that has a particular mood or effect, what are some of the tools he or she can use? How does a musician establish the character of a musical idea?" The students drew upon their prior knowledge of the use of tempo, dynamics, duration, timbre, articulation, and so on, to solve this problem. Students were then asked to use what they knew about playing the recorder (which at this point in the semester involved just three notes) to compose a musical idea that suggested a particular character, mood, or effect. Each student then shared his or her melody with the class and spoke about what his/her intention had been. The group was then asked to comment on what the individual had done with the music in an attempt to portray the particular character, mood, or effect. (Since musical ideas are not literal, it would have been inappropriate for the teacher to ask the students to "guess" what was being portrayed by each individual. Therefore, the teacher chose to have the students discuss the musical tools used to carry out the idea instead.)

In this case, the connection was legitimate (again, an important distinction between a genuine, infused concept connection and forced, contrived, subservient integration).

Writers, actors, and musicians all establish character in their work. However, character is not established in the same ways in all three disciplines. By using the concept of characterization as a basis for conceptual connection among the three disciplines, the music teacher was able to maintain the integrity of each discipline while enhancing the students' understanding of the broader concept.

The benefit to the students was that making this connection across disciplines enabled them to have a heightened understanding and to be more successful in all three areas.

Point of View

Connections between theater concepts and language arts concepts are relatively easy to find because of the roles of language in both disciplines. A fifth-grade teacher worked with the theater teacher to develop a collaborative unit based on "point of view." The students in this class were preparing a theatrical presentation of "The Pied Piper of Hamlin." In preparation, the students read a version of the original story. From their knowledge of the story, they worked to develop a script. In the fifth-grade classroom, the students considered the ways dialogue is constructed and written in an expository story and in a script. They looked at format and style, and they considered how point of view is established and conveyed in each context. In the drama class, each student was asked to develop a character in the story that he/she wanted to play. For example, each rat was to have a distinctive personality, history, occupation, age, and so on. In order to accomplish this, the students needed to understand the essence of character, what is involved in creating a character, and how one finds similarities between one's own character and the one being played.

The students were first asked to draw a picture of the characters they wanted to portray. They then worked in pairs to develop dialogue for their characters. They were encouraged to write through the eyes of the character, developing their character so that, when portraying the character, they would be able to have what actors call "a life on stage." They were asked to consider, "What do you do in life? How do others see you?" Participating in this activity enabled the students to make conceptual connections and better understand what it is to view a situation from a particular point of view.

Infused concepts and processes addressed in this unit include: perspective, characterization, interpreting, and relationship.[2] In carrying out the project in the theater arts class, students needed to listen carefully to what their partners were saying, exchange ideas, compare, clarify, and defend ideas. They had to change their personae in order to accomplish this writing task. Changing persona is a theater activity which, in this case, empowered their writing. The experience is one that will help these students in future writing as well. Speaking dialogue helps the writer to know what it will sound like to a reader. Participating in this project enabled students to clarify their thinking in both language arts and drama. They were also able to learn the benefits of collaborative thinking. The theater experiences made the writing process more enjoyable, rewarding, and purposeful. The activity provided a vehicle that allowed for visualizing, reflecting, and editing. The teachers noted the high level of student confidence as they expressed their vision of their own characters. Also, there may have been students who were able to understand concepts of characterization during these activities where pencil and paper formats had not nurtured such understanding in the past.

Stories and Illustrations

The art teacher noted a similar connection in describing a link between visual art and language arts. In the previous theater/language arts connection, there may have been students for whom the opportunity to think as an actor or playwright may have enabled a higher level of understanding and creative product than the writing process alone might have produced. The art teacher had given some thought to what happens when children draw illustrations for their own stories. If a child writes a story and then draws an accompanying illustration, it is a form of integration, a rather low-level form. However, if a child writes a story, draws a picture, adds details to the picture that are not in the original story, and then *goes back* and embellishes the story with the details from the picture, a higher level of process integration has occurred. In the second scenario, the child is using visual thinking to further his or her verbal thinking. The child may be able to think of something visually that he or she was unable to think of verbally. In this second case, both artistic and verbal thinking have contributed to the creative product.

Informal Connections Made by Teachers

Because of their awareness of what and how their colleagues teach, teachers sometimes make connections on a less-formal level as a means of explaining or establishing a context for student understanding. In other words, the connection is not the main focus of the lesson. In such cases, teachers may call the children's attention to a particular commonality while "setting the stage" for a lesson, although that particular commonality may not be the main focus of the lesson.

Egyptian Art

For example, the art teacher, in teaching about Egyptian art, felt that, in order to understand the art, the children needed to know more about the cultural context in which it resided. Therefore, her lessons on Egyptian art involved more information about the cultural and historical setting of the work than it did actual art making. Knowing the students had had this experience, a fourth-grade teacher used the experience as a starting point for a social studies/language arts lesson dealing with Native American culture. She began her lesson by saying, "We have studied Native Americans, and we have learned that they told stories through their art. Do you remember what you learned in art class about Egyptians and their art? Do you remember what was important in what you learned about Egyptians and their art? Do you think those things are important in looking at Native American art as well?" In this way, the teacher was able to draw on understandings developed in the art classroom to enhance and extend the students' experience in understanding both cultural and literary (storytelling) aspects of the Native American perspective. Egyptian art was not the focus of the classroom lesson. The prior experiences of the students in the art class enabled them to better understand the social studies/language arts lesson. The success of this lesson hinged on the fact that the fourth-grade teacher had taken the time to learn about what the children had been doing in art class.

Historical Novels

There are many examples of this type of integration, where teachers establish informal links to other disciplines as an anticipatory set for a particular lesson or unit. For example, one of the purposes of reading a novel set in a particular time and place is for one to develop empathy for what it was like to live in that time and place. In such a case, one cannot appreciate the novel without understanding its context. In the same way, one cannot appreciate some art, music, dance, or theater without understanding the context in which it occurred. In these cases, contextual understanding enhances the art or literary experience as the art or literary experience enhances the contextual understanding. However, success of this kind of integration hinges on the students having sufficient knowledge within the particular field to be able to understand the work of art. If a student does not know enough about the particular elements of a work of art to be able to understand why it is representative of a particular time and place, connections like these are more in the teacher's mind than in the student's.

Role of the Individual within a Group

Having a personal concept of one's role within a group is essential to making music as part of an ensemble, acting within a theatrical ensemble, dancing within a dance ensemble, or playing a team sport. Students need to understand that the role of the individual within the group can vary and can even shift during a particular experience. They also need to understand the impact of the individual on others in the group. A trumpet player may have the melody in one part of a piece, the harmony in another, and will have to adjust his or her playing accordingly. A dancer or actor may be a lead or soloist—or part of a group. An athletic team member may switch from defensive to offensive or have a specific position to play. He or she may shift from being the central figure in a particular play to being a supportive player, assisting the teammate who has the ball. In each of these cases, the qualities of the actions of the individual will directly impact the success of the group. Students in classrooms adopt many different roles within the group as well. The qualities of their actions within the group will similarly impact the learning that takes place in that classroom.

Understanding how to function in these different settings is much more than a traditional vision of "teamwork." It involves high levels of self-awareness and of the connections between one's own actions and those of others—in time, in space—toward a common goal, purpose, or intent. Because the students at Stadium Drive frequently reflect on how they are thinking and connecting the various modes of thinking, the teachers have noted that their sensitivity to their own role within the various groups in which they engage has been greatly heightened.

Wood Sculptures

Sometimes it is a teacher's way of talking about process that establishes a connection. For example, the art teacher talks with children about the fact that there are many starting points when solving a visual art problem. First-grade students were working in art class to create wood sculptures. This particular project had many steps. First the students looked at the various pieces of wood and considered: What might go well together? What might create variety? Why? This process involved visualization. The next step in the project was to assemble the pieces of wood in a way that they would balance without glue. At this stage, some children commented about what their sculpture looked like: "That looks like a car (or a house or a horse)." The pieces were then glued together. During the second lesson, the children painted the work. The main shape was painted first and then they made decisions about the remainder. At this point, the art teacher helped the children decide a basis for selecting colors. Would the color be representational or just a color that they like? Would they place two colors next to each other because they like the way that looks? She talked with the children about what they were thinking when they were working, leaving the decisions open-ended and intriguing. One person might have been thinking about how the paint would go on and another about what color would look really good—both approaches are "correct" and appropriate. Students also looked at some professional work to try to figure out what they thought was important to that artist in making that work. "What do you think this artist was thinking about when he or she decided to make the work look like this?" During the third lesson, the children were given the option of gluing a variety of interesting things onto the painted work (feathers, and so on).

There are many parallels between this way of working and process writing. Talking about writing processes, learning to think like an author, thinking about what authors really do, all empower and motivate young writers. Teachers need to help students find meaning in their own creative processes. Finding meaning generates a purpose for engaging in the process and for producing a product. It also gives students ownership.

Composing original music and creating original dramas incorporate the same elements. In all cases, it becomes important to study what professionals do to accomplish their goals, and the professional work becomes a model for the students' creative process. There are also parallels to a more contemporary vision of the scientific method in which one revises and edits an experiment as it progresses, reflecting what has been learned along the way. In all cases, the issues that the students need to think about are basically the same as those professionals think about; the students are engaging in genuine creative experiences, and the processes are the same as those used by professionals.

Balance

Balance is a concept that is part of all art forms. The teachers at Stadium Drive noticed that drawing on students' experiences with balance from a physical perspective in physical education class and dance class enables them to have a much better understanding of balance in visual art and music. The music teacher, in rehearsing for an evening performance, noticed a group of reticent participants standing together on the risers. Rather than calling attention to those students, he began talking about balance—noting that there seemed to be a "hole" in the sound in that particular section. As the students worked to balance their sound, the reluctant singers had no choice but to assume their responsibility for the problem and to rectify the situation by singing out as strongly as the others. The students' prior experiences with balance in different disciplinary settings enhanced their understanding of its importance in this situation, which gave them a reason to care and a desire to solve the problem.

Connections Made by Students

These moments of conceptual and process connection seem to occur even when the connections are not necessarily the focus of a particular lesson. Most often, what occurs is that a teacher or student is able to make use of a perspective or understanding gained from a prior experience in another discipline to help better explain or understand a new experience in a different discipline. More often, it is a brief excursion that establishes a mindset or clarifies a confusion or misconception. Our first case illustrates this type of connection.

Daffodils

Two first-grade teachers were working together in teaching a unit that had been part of their curriculum before the advent of the arts-infusion curriculum. It was an interdisciplinary unit on daffodils, which took place within the first-grade classroom and did not involve special area teachers. The unit integrated science and language arts at the enhancement and thematic levels. Students studied the nature and needs of living things by learning about daffodils from a scientific perspective. Students also learned about cycles in nature, such as spring and the seasons. This aspect of the unit was used as the basis for a language arts writing assignment in which students wrote about what happens when seasons change. Students made daffodils in an arts and crafts project, using paper, paint, a small cup, scissors, and glue. During this project, they also used mathematics skills, in that they needed to cut particular paper shapes and needed to be sure they had the correct number of pieces to construct the flower. While this is certainly an integrated unit, the teachers carrying out this unit were not thinking of it in terms of arts infusion.[3] However, after their involvement with arts infusion, as the students were carrying out the arts and crafts project, some of them made a spontaneous connection that enabled all the students to carry out the project much more successfully and easily than students had in past years.

One teacher was describing what the students needed to do with the paper to make the leaves and stem of the daffodil: "After the paper is folded, the leaves need to be pulled out," she said. This step in the project tends to be a confusing one, because it is difficult for students to visualize how they will get from one point to the next, but this time, as the teacher explained it, several students said, "Oh, this is just like what we learned in dance! It's step-touch!" From the students' comments, the rest of the class immediately understood, and the children in these two first-grade classes were able to carry out this portion of the project without teacher help. In past years, these two teachers had had to walk around and help many individuals accomplish this step. This year, a few brief statements from a few individuals enabled everyone to function without teacher help. Obviously, the connection that occurred here was not planned by the teachers. It happened because of the richness of the learning environment at Stadium Drive and because of the increased emphasis on making connections that pervaded the curriculum and the children's thinking.

Success in this arts and crafts activity was dependent on the students' ability to visualize relationships and on their awareness of space and of how they operate within that space. In this case, the students were able to make a perceptual connection between the ways they perceived the two processes—the process of unfolding the paper (fine motor) and the process of the dance motions (gross motor). The dance experience enhanced and enabled their success in the classroom experience. In this case, the infused processes that enabled the children to make the connection are: visualizing, recalling, and connecting. The benefit to the students was that making the connection enabled them to be more successful with greater ease and independence.

Right and Left

A first-grade teacher noted that her students seemed to have far less difficulty differentiating right from left because of their experiences mirroring motion in both dance and theater classes and because they knew about stage right and stage left.

Symmetry

When the dance teacher talked about symmetrical and asymmetrical shape in dance, she related the concept to what the students had learned in mathematics. However, the students informed her, "Oh, we know that from art."

Sequence

A kindergarten teacher noted that her students were able to provide a label for a concept she was teaching (even before she told them what it was) as a result of their experiences in another class. While the concept of sequence pervades the kindergarten curriculum, teachers do not always label the concept with the label "sequence." Instead, they tend to concern themselves more with the concept of what a sequence is, which is more appropriate with young children. However, in both music and dance classes, the students had studied the concept of sequence and had learned to apply the label to the concept, so, to them, the connection was quite clear.

SOME CLOSING THOUGHTS

One of the goals of the approach to teaching music advocated throughout this book is that music teaching and music learning rise above simplistic involvement with subject matter.

Classrooms become laboratories in which students can function as real musicians and not simply as consumers of musical knowledge. Along with this goal should be the goal of helping students see the connections among concepts that influence their "musical view of the world" and related concepts in other disciplines. However, to reach this goal, the music teacher must be able to analyze the nature of any activities or experiences to be certain they do, indeed, promote understanding of legitimate, authentic musical concepts.

The music teacher who has created an authentic problem-solving activity is likely to be addressing questions of importance that stem from the curiosity of his or her students about how the world works. These curiosities do not end at the music classroom door but are equally important to the students when they are framed in terms that are more common in the math classroom, the language arts classroom, the science classroom, or in any other broad field of inquiry. Our efforts to help students understand the connections among the disciplines consist of providing opportunities for them to understand concepts deeply and see commonalities in other worldviews.

ENDNOTES

1. Perhaps playing music in the background while the class works could be included in this category. This practice stems from the learning-styles research and is used to create a comfortable atmosphere in the classroom. However, if a teacher believes this constitutes a means of "exposing" students to music, it represents even a further devaluing of the music curriculum.

2. At another time, such a unit could connect to a concept of perspective in social studies, where students could consider how it might feel to live during a particular time or to be faced with a particular decision.

3. The arts and crafts project is not a visual arts project because the intent is to construct a model of a daffodil. There is no aspect of this project in which the students are using the art materials to express what they feel or think. Using art materials for a nonartistic purpose, while certainly valid and important to children's learning, is not visual art making and does not constitute an art lesson.

SELECTED RESOURCES

Barrett, J. R., C. W. McCoy, and K. K. Veblin. 1997. *Sound ways of knowing: Music in the interdisciplinary curriculum.* New York: Schirmer Books.

Barry, N. 1996. Integrating music into the curriculum. *General Music Today* 9(2):9–13.

Wiggins, J. H., and R. A. Wiggins. 1997. Integrating through conceptual connections. *Music Educators Journal* 83(4):38–41.

Wiggins, R. A. 1997. Integrating music *into* the curriculum is the wrong mind set: A response to Barry. *General Music Today* 10(1):5–9.

Wiggins, R. A. 2001. Interdisciplinary curriculum: Stakeholder concerns. *Music Educators Journal.* (In press).

Chapter 11

EPILOGUE

"Go away, Mrs. Wiggins. We don't need you." It was said politely, but firmly. The group of fifth-grade girls was working on an original song they had decided to write and perform at an assembly program where a Holocaust survivor was to be the guest speaker. Because the piece was being written for a public performance and because the topic they had chosen was such a sensitive one, I was very curious about what they were doing. I did not want to find myself in a position of having to tell them that any part of the song was perhaps inappropriate or offensive, especially after all the time and effort that was going into the project. I only wanted a glimpse to reassure myself that they were in "safe" territory and that we could, indeed, include their song on the program. But they did not need me. They knew they did not need my help. They knew that they had learned enough to be able to tackle this project on their own—and they wanted to surprise me with their finished product.

They left me no choice but to trust them. On the day the song was ready, they invited me to hear it. Not only was the composition now complete, but they had developed an arrangement and had practiced it on their own. It was now ready for performance. I was astonished when I heard the piece for the first time. The lyrics and melody were incredibly sophisticated. For the most part, the lyrics had been written by a group member who had severe verbal-learning disabilities. The bulk of the harmonic structure and accompaniment had been developed by a different group member who had studied piano privately since first grade. The lyricist, the pianist, and a third group member had assumed most of the responsibility for creating the song. They then invited two other peers to join the group because the arrangement required five singers. They taught the newcomers the song and incorporated some of their suggestions as well.

A copy of the song appears below. The students' attempt at notating their melody had come close to what they wanted. The notated version that appears below was prepared by the teacher, by watching and listening to a videotaped recording of the students' performance.

A Dream within a Nightmare

3 FIFTH GRADERS

(one speaker) Millions of people died during the Holocaust.

(second speaker) and nothing can make up for the people who

died (third speaker) This song is dedicated to all those people who died and survived.

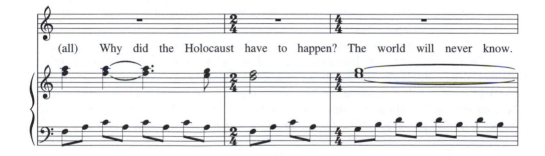

(all) Why did the Holocaust have to happen? The world will never know.

If you decide that the overriding goal of your music curriculum will be to nurture musical independence in your students, you will need to expect that the time will come when they will truly not need your help. Effective music educators should hear statements like "We don't need you" and "We can do this by ourselves" all the time. Is the music education profession ready to take the necessary steps to enable students to work toward and achieve musical independence?

What will your music classroom be like? What will it be like to be a student in your class? What will you teach? How will you teach it? Who will be responsible for making musical decisions? How will they be carried out? Ultimately, your own answers to questions like these will determine the kind of teacher you will be—and how effective a teacher you will be. I hope the ideas shared in this book have set you thinking about these issues and have provided a basis for you to begin to make professional decisions.

In this process, the role of the teacher as knowledgeable educator and musician cannot be underestimated. To be an effective music teacher, you need to understand music and how it operates within a variety of styles, genres, and historical and cultural settings. An effective music teacher is a knowledgeable and accomplished musician.

To be an effective music teacher, you also need to understand teaching and learning processes, know how to design instruction that has the capacity to inspire students to learn, and know how to enable students to be successful in learning. You need to know the importance of listening to and understanding students and making instructional decisions based on what you learn from such interactions. You need to know how to lead from the sidelines and manage instruction without controlling what occurs in your classroom.

To be an effective music teacher, you need to engage students in real-life, problem-solving situations that require them to use what they know and understand about music to perform, create, analyze, and respond to music. The challenges you create for students should be genuine and authentic—the same challenges that "real" musicians face. The questions you ask should be real questions—the same questions that "real" musicians seek to answer. Further, students need to be able to perceive the curriculum and content with which they are engaged as genuine and relevant to their lives. Students need to have a sense that the answers they are seeking are not "predetermined and fully predictable" (Perrone, 1994, 12). They need to feel that the ideas they bring to the classroom are welcome—important to and valued by everyone in the classroom.

Finally, to be an effective music educator you need to be able to look at your own and your students' successes and mistakes and learn from them. Studying the teaching and learning that take place in your own classroom is a powerful tool for empowering your own understanding of these processes. Taking time to reflect on your own decisions as a teacher and their impact on your students' learning is the beginning of the path to effective music teaching.

How effective a music educator will you choose to be? Music educators who enter the profession as well-prepared teachers and musicians have the capacity to transform music education such that it will effectively touch the lives of all students and become a vital and integral part of every child's life and ways of thinking. Designing music instruction to nurture musical understanding in all students has the potential to create a population that values music, uses music as a means of personal expression, and chooses to engage in lifelong experience with music.

REFERENCES

Anderson, R. C., et al. 1978. Schemata as scaffolding for the representation of information in connected discourse. *American Educational Research Journal* 15(3):433–40.

Anderson, R. C., and P. D. Pearson. 1984. A schema-theoretic view of basic processes in reading comprehension. In *Handbook of research on reading,* ed. P. D. Pearson, 255–91. New York: Longman.

Anderson, R. C., R. E. Reynolds, D. L. Schallert, and E. T. Goetz. 1977. Frameworks for comprehending discourse. *American Educational Research Journal* 14:367–82.

Atterbury, B. W. 1990. *Mainstreaming exceptional learners in music.* Englewood Cliffs, N.J.: Prentice-Hall.

Ausubel, D. P. 1968. *Educational psychology: A cognitive view.* New York: Holt Rinehart & Winston.

Bamberger, J. 1991. *The mind behind the musical ear: How children develop musical intelligence.* Cambridge: Harvard University Press.

Barrett, J. R., C. W. McCoy, and K. K. Veblin. 1997. *Sound ways of knowing: Music in the interdisciplinary curriculum.* New York: Schirmer Books.

Barry, N. 1996. Integrating music into the curriculum. *General Music Today* 9(2):9–13.

Bartlett, F. C. 1932. *Remembering: A study in experimental and social psychology.* Cambridge: Cambridge University Press.

Beane, J. 1997. *Curriculum integration: Designing the core of democratic education.* New York: Teachers College Press.

Beethoven, J., et al. 1995. *The music connection: Grades K–8.* Morristown, N.J.: Silver Burdett Ginn and Scott Foresman.

Bergethon, B., E. Boardman, and J. Montgomery. 1997. *Musical growth in the elementary school.* 6th ed. Fort Worth, Tex.: Harcourt Brace.

Boardman, E. L. 1988. The generative theory of musical learning (Part II). *General Music Today* 2(2):3–6, 28–31. Reston, Va: MENC (Music Educators National Conference).

Bond, J., et al. 1995 to present. *Share the music: Grades K–8.* New York: McGraw-Hill.

Bruner, J. 1960. *The process of education.* Cambridge: Harvard University Press.

———. 1971. *Toward a theory of instruction.* Cambridge: Harvard University Press.

Campbell, P. S. 1998. *Songs in their heads: Music and its meaning in children's lives.* New York: Oxford.

Darling-Hammond, L. 1998. Teachers and teaching: Testing policy hypotheses from a national commission report. *Educational Researcher* 27(1):5–15.

Davies, C. 1992. Listen to my song: A study of songs invented by children aged five to seven years. *British Journal of Music Education* 9(1):19–48.

Dewey, J. 1910. *Experience and education.* Chicago: University of Chicago Press.

Dowling, W. J. 1984. Development of musical schemata in children's spontaneous singing. In W. R. Crozier and A. J. Chapman, eds. *Cognitive processes in the perception of art,* 145–63. Amsterdam: Elsevier.

———. 1988. Tonal structure and children's early learning of music. In *Generative processes in music: The psychology of performance, improvisation, and composition,* ed. J.A. Sloboda, 113–28. Oxford: Clarendon Press.

Dowling, W. J., and D. L. Harwood. 1986. *Music cognition.* Orlando, Fla.: Academic Press.

Educational Leadership 51(5 February 1994). Themed issue devoted to "Teaching for Understanding."

Elliott, D. 1995. *Music matters: A new philosophy of music education.* New York: Oxford.

Espeland, M. 1987. Music in use: Responsive music listening in the primary school. *British Journal of Music Education* 4(3):283–97.

———. 1992. *Musikk i bruk (Music in use).* Norway: Stord Hangesund lærarhøgskule.

Gardner, H. 1983. *Frames of mind.* New York: Basic Books.

———. 1985. *The mind's new science*. New York: Basic Books.

———. 1991. *The unschooled mind*. New York: Basic Books.

———. 1993. *Frames of mind: The theory of multiple intelligence*. 2d ed. New York: Basic Books.

———. 1998. Is musical intelligence special? *Choral Journal* 38(8):23–34.

Gardner, H., and Boix-Mansilla, V. 1994a. Teaching for understanding in the disciplines—and beyond. *Teachers College Record* 96(2):198–217.

———. 1994b. Teaching for understanding—within and across the disciplines. *Educational Leadership* 51(5):14–18.

Glasser, W. 1986. *Control theory in the classroom*. New York: Perennial Library.

Goleman, D. 1995. *Emotional intelligence*. New York: Bantam Books.

Hargreaves, D. 1986. *The developmental psychology of music*. Cambridge: Cambridge University Press.

Hogg, N. 1993. *Identifying and resolving the dilemmas of music teaching: A study of junior secondary classrooms*. Ph.D. diss. Monash University, Australia.

———. 1994. Strategies to facilitate student composing. *Research Studies in Music Education* 2:15–24.

———. 1995. Identifying and resolving the dilemmas of music teaching. Paper presented at the American Educational Research Association Conference, San Francisco (April 22, 1995).

Hunter, M. 1976. *Rx improved instruction*. El Segundo, Calif.: T. I. P. Publications.

———. 1982. *Mastery teaching*. Thousand Oaks, Calif.: Corwin Press.

Kohn, A. 1996. *Beyond discipline: From compliance to community*. Alexandria, Va.: Association for Supervision and Curriculum Development.

Lewis, C. S. 1950. *The lion, the witch and the wardrobe: A story for children*. New York: Macmillan.

Meyer, L. B. 1956. *Emotion and meaning in music*. Chicago: University of Chicago Press.

Neisser, U. 1976. *Cognition and reality: Principles and implications of cognitive psychology*. San Francisco, Calif.: W. H. Freeman.

Ogonowski, C. 1998. *Quality time in the music classroom*. Master's thesis. Oakland University, Rochester, Michigan.

Perrone, Vito. 1994. How to engage students in learning. *Educational Leadership* 51(5):11–13.

Reimer, B. 1989. *A philosophy of music education*. Englewood Cliffs, N.J.: Prentice Hall.

Rist, R. 1970. Student social class and teacher expectations: The self-fulfilling prophecy in ghetto education. *Harvard Educational Review* 40:411–51.

Rogoff, B. 1990. *Apprenticeship in thinking: Cognitive development in social context*. New York: Oxford University Press.

Rogoff, B., and W. Gardner. 1984. Adult guidance of cognitive development. In *Everyday cognition: Its development in social context,* eds. B. Rogoff and J. Lave, 95–116. Cambridge: Harvard University Press.

Rogoff, B., and J. Lave, eds. 1984. *Everyday cognition: Its development in social context*. Cambridge: Harvard University Press.

Rosenthal, R., and L. Jacobson. 1968. *Pygmalion in the classroom: Teacher expectation and pupils' intellectual development*. New York: Holt, Rinehart and Winston.

Sadker, M., and D. Sadker. 1993. *Failing at fairness: How American schools cheat girls*. New York: Charles Scribner's Sons.

Seeman, H. 1994. *Preventing classroom discipline problems*. Lancaster, Pa.: Technomic.

Serafine, M. L. 1988. *Music as cognition: The development of thought in sound* (Part I). New York: Columbia University Press.

Sloboda, J. A. 1985. *The musical mind: The cognitive psychology of music*. Oxford: Clarendon Press.

———, ed. 1988. *Generative processes in music: The psychology of performance, improvisation, and composition*. Oxford: Clarendon Press.

Subotnick, M. 1995. The music and musicians of the future. In *Toward tomorrow: New visions for general music,* ed. S. L. Stauffer, 31–42.

Reston, Va.: MENC (Music Educators National Conference).

Sundin, B., G. E. McPherson, and G. Folkestad. 1998. *Children composing* (in English). Malmo, Sweden: Lund University, Malmo Academy of Music (Fax +46 (0)40-32 54 50).

Swanwick, K. 1988. *Music, mind and education.* London: Routledge.

———. 1999. *Teaching music musically.* London: Routledge.

Vosniadou, S., and W. Brewer. 1987. Theories of knowledge restructuring in development. *Review of Educational Research* 57(1):51–67.

Vygotsky, L. S. 1978. *Mind in society: The development of higher psychological processes,* eds. M. Cole, V. John-Steiner, S. Scribner, and E. Souberman. Cambridge: Harvard University Press.

Wertsch, J. V., ed. 1985. *Culture, communication and cognition: Vygotskian perspectives.* Cambridge: Cambridge University Press.

Wiggins, J. 1990. *Composition in the classroom: A tool for teaching.* Reston, Va.: MENC.

———. 1991. *Synthesizers in the general music classroom: An integrated approach.* Reston, Va.: MENC.

———. 1992. *The nature of children's musical learning in the context of a music classroom.* Doctoral diss. University of Illinois at Urbana-Champaign.

———. 1994. Children's strategies for solving compositional problems with peers. *Journal of Research in Music Education* 42(3):232–52.

———. 1995. Building structural understanding: Sam's story. *The Quarterly Journal of Music Teaching and Learning* 6(3):57–75.

———. 1998. Recurring themes: Same compositional strategies—different settings. Paper presented at the Southeastern Music Education Symposium, School of Music, University of Georgia (May 15, 1998).

———. 2000. The nature of shared musical understanding and its role in empowering independent musical thinking. *Bulletin* (Council for Research in Music Education) 143: 69–94.

Wiggins, J. H., and R. A. Wiggins. 1997. Integrating through conceptual connections. *Music Educators Journal* 83(4):38–41.

Wiggins, R. A. 1997. Integrating music *into* the curriculum is the wrong mind set: A response to Barry. *General Music Today* 10(1):5–9.

———. 2001. Interdisciplinary curriculum: Stakeholder concerns. *Music Educators Journal.* (In press).

Wolfgang, C. H., and C. D. Glickman. 1986. *Solving discipline problems: Strategies for classroom teachers.* 2d ed. Boston: Allyn and Bacon.

Wood, D., J. Bruner, and G. Ross. 1976. The role of tutoring in problem solving. *Journal of Child Psychology and Psychiatry* 17:89–100.

INDEX

harmonic structure, 227–241
meter, 224–226
on middle-level musical problems, 175–196
strategy for unit planning, 175–176
unit on monothematic works, 189–195
unit on texture, 176–188

V

Veblin, K. K., 291, 298
Voices
improvising with, 102
and singing by young children, 117–118
spontaneous singing, 28
Volume, 67
Vosniadou, S., 7–8, 300
Vygotsky, Lev S., 11–14, 274, 300

W

Walker, David, 159n., 246n.
Wertsch, John V., 12, 23, 300
Whole-class activity, 229–230
managing whole group, 262–265
classroom noise, 263–264, 267
discussion, 262–263
disruptive behavior, 264
meeting needs of all students, 264–265
scaffolding in, 257–258
Wiggins, G., 14, 36, 39, 83, 86, 109
Wiggins, Jackie H., 111, 111n., 233–234, 246, 268n., 269, 273, 291, 300
Wiggins, Robert A., 270–291, 273, 300

William Tell Overture (Rossini), 122–123
Wolfgang, C. H., 262, 269, 300
Wood, D., 14, 300

Y

Young students
entry-level musical problems for, 116–121, 123–130
lesson plans for
effects of tempo change, 163–168
entry-level, 123–130, 134–138
exploring contour and direction through listening, 134–138
iconic representation of beat, 124–127
identifying and representing duration and pitch, 127–130
using a song to develop a class performance, 138–142
musical experiences for, 117–121
creating, 119
listening, 119–120
moving, 118
notating, 120
playing, 118–119
singing, 117–118
technology, 120
nature of, 116

Z

Zone of proximal development, 13–14